AN INTRODUCTION TO
SOUTH ASIA

AN INTRODUCTION TO SOUTH ASIA

B. H. Farmer

METHUEN

London and New York

First published in 1983 by
Methuen & Co. Ltd
11 New Fetter Lane, London EC4P 4EE

Published in the USA by
Methuen & Co.
in association with Methuen, Inc.
733 Third Avenue, New York, NY 10017

Printed in Great Britain by
Richard Clay & Co. Ltd
The Chaucer Press,
Bungay, Suffolk

British Library Cataloguing in Publication Data

Farmer, B. H.
  An introduction to South Asia.
  1. South Asia—Description and travel
  I. Title
  915.4   DS337

  ISBN 0-416-72600-3
  ISBN 0-416-72610-0 Pbk (University paperback 841)

Library of Congress Cataloging in Publication Data

Farmer, B. H. (Bertram Hughes)
  An introduction to South Asia.

  Bibliography: p.
  Includes indexes.
  1. South Asia. I. Title.
  DS335.F37   1983   954   83-17402
  ISBN 0-416-72600-3
  ISBN 0-416-72610-0 (pbk.)

Contents

Preface

This book necessarily assumes that the reader will have access to an atlas or to other maps of South Asia; it being impossible to include in the book maps that would show all the places and areas mentioned, quite apart from the difficulty, given the Kashmir problem, of including maps acceptable both to India and Pakistan.

I am extremely indebted to those who have read and commented on parts of this book: Mr H. Brammer, Dr G. P. Chapman, Dr Pramit Chaudhuri, Dr Gordon Johnson, Professor W. H. Morris-Jones, Mr Steve Jones, and Dr Sudhir Wanmali. I have benefited greatly, as has the book, from their comments; but responsibility for errors and false emphases rests, of course, with me.

I am also very grateful to the ladies who have between them produced a fair typescript from my own untidy handiwork: Mrs C. Brown, Miss S. Dawson, Miss C. Houterman, Miss A. M. Mansfield, Mrs S. M. Pertwee, Mrs D. Pryer and Mrs F. Salmon; and to Miss E. Newbronner for assistance with the index.

Finally, my thanks are also for the kindness and forbearance shown to me and to my book by Mary Ann Kernan, Janice Price and Juliet Wight-Boycott of Methuen.

B. H. FARMER

St John's College,
Cambridge
18 December 1982

1 INTRODUCTION: THE IMPORTANCE AND INTEREST OF SOUTH ASIA

Of every five people in the world, one is a South Asian. That is, in terms of the definition adopted in this book, a resident in the vast subcontinent that covers 1,725,000 sq. miles (4,468,000 sq. kilometres) and that includes Bangladesh, Bhutan, India, the Maldives, Nepal, Pakistan and Sri Lanka: countries that differ enormously in area and population, but that together contain some 810 million people. On grounds of size and population alone, then, South Asia cannot fail to be of importance in the world scene; and the problems faced by its people, or created in the region for the rest of us, ought to be of the widest interest.

Perhaps the term 'South Asia' does, however, call for explanation. That it is unfamiliar is clear from the fact that the Centre of South Asian Studies in the University of Cambridge has become inured to the receipt of mail addressed to 'The Centre of Starvation Studies', or of 'Salvation Studies', and of enquiries about Indonesia or Vietnam. In Imperial days the region (plus Burma until 1935) could have been referred to as 'The Indian Empire', though that strictly would have been to leave Ceylon (now Sri Lanka) out in the cold (or heat). 'The Indian subcontinent' is a term that certainly recognizes the dominant position of India in both area and population (over three-quarters of South Asians live in India); but, since the partition of the Indian Empire, is apt to give offence to Pakistanis and (now) to Bangladeshis (I heard a speaker at a conference in Dhaka in 1976 refer to the 'Bangla–Pak subcontinent'). 'South Asia', then, may be unfamiliar and not unambiguous, but it is neutral and inoffensive.

The peoples of South Asia differ greatly between themselves. The reasons for this are rooted in the history of their origins and ancient civilizations (themselves of absorbing interest) and of external impact, especially by Europeans. The consequences of social differences, whether of religion or of caste or of some other source of division, are to be traced into recent and contemporary politics. The difficulties of achieving and preserving national unity and of maintaining stable international boundaries are, of course, all too familiar in the post-colonial world. But in South Asia, especially but not exclusively in its larger countries, these difficulties have had a particular cogency; and have from time to time excited the attention of the world at large — as when, for example, communal violence has erupted in India, or when India and Pakistan went to war over the emergence of an independent Bangladesh.

It is also pertinent to ask, again in the context of post-colonial politics more generally, why some countries in South Asia have managed to change their governments by 'democratic' means, or at any rate by the use of the ballot box; while others, notably Pakistan, have frequently found themselves under autocratic rule, usually by the military. What can be said, too, of stability, development and welfare under the two forms of government?

South Asia, I have said, has vast populations. In many parts of the subcontinent these are packed tightly into the countryside (though, for reasons to be explored, much more so in some areas than in others); and packed unbelievably tightly into some of the cities. The average density of population in this predominantly rural subcontinent is, for what it is worth in this varied terrain, over 470 per sq. mile (181 per sq. kilometre). This may be compared with some 26 per sq. mile (10 per sq. kilometre) for Africa and some 30 per sq. mile (12 per sq. kilometre) for South America. Populations, too, continue to rise in South Asia, though not at the same rate in all countries.

South Asia in fact provides instances of that kind of less-developed economy (China is another) with generally severe pressure of population and low standards of living. Since data on South Asia are both more available and more reliable than those for China (though not without their pitfalls), and since there is a relatively free interchange of research workers between South Asia and other parts of the world, they have proved highly attractive to students of development, both South Asian and foreign. Some of the latter have, rightly or wrongly, been especially interested in government policy and planning in South Asia in general and in India in particular as a 'democratic' alternative to the methods that have been pursued in China. One can also see foreign aid policies, with all their mixed motives, at work in South Asia.

Turning to international relations, the most spectacular and newsworthy events since independence have so far been internal to the subcontinent, in the shape of recurring conflict between the two main successors to the British Indian Empire, India and Pakistan. But India has also had a border dispute with, and suffered invasion from China; and has tended to be friendly to Russia; while Pakistan has built up links with the Islamic countries of the Middle East, with China, and at times (for the relationship has been a somewhat chequered one) with the United States. But action and interest have not solely depended on conflict or alliances against possible conflict: India, and at times Sri Lanka, have been prominent in the non-aligned movement, with its declared aim of steering clear of involvement with the superpowers. More specific has been the aim of converting the Indian Ocean into a lake of peace from which superpower rivalries would be excluded. Events in Iran and Afghanistan, to say nothing of the oil that lies on some of that ocean's shores, have increasingly made that pacific solution unlikely. South Asia, with its internal and external hostilities and its space relations, is bound to be drawn more and more into world affairs.

These, then are some of the main characteristics of South Asia and its people, and some of the principal issues that these peoples face: issues of national unity and types of government, of economic development and social change, of the reciprocal impact of South Asia and the wider world. This little book will try to provide its reader, in non-technical language, with ideas and information to enable him to reach sensible conclusions on these and other issues, many of which have been the subject of controversy. Its author's hope is that, while it cannot hope to be completely comprehensive, it will also succeed in conveying something of the fascination of the subcontinent, something of the character and humanity of its diverse peoples, something of their poverty and hardships, but also of their achievements; for all of these things have kept him in the spell of South Asia since he first set foot there over forty years ago.

2 THE ENVIRONMENTS OF SOUTH ASIA: NATURAL AND SOCIAL

The natural environment and its modification by human agency

The density of rural population in South Asia is largely, though by no means completely, explicable in terms of the variable fertility of the natural environment, as modified by human agency during the millennia of its occupance by human societies. There is a great arc of dense population (more than 500 persons per sq. mile, or 193 per sq. kilometre) stretching with but few interruptions all the way from the Punjab to West Bengal and on into Bangladesh: over considerable areas the density rises to 1000 or even to 1500 per sq. mile (390 or 590 per sq. kilometre), notably in north Bihar, West Bengal and Bangladesh. Patches of dense population (though not reaching these excessive densities except very locally) are to be found down the east coast of India, over most of the south Indian states of Tamil Nadu and Kerala, in south-western and central Sri Lanka, and between Bombay and Ahmedabad on the west coast of India. At the other extreme, there are sparse populations, down to as few as 50 persons per sq. mile (19 per sq. kilometre), or even less, in Baluchistan and elsewhere on the north-west frontiers of Pakistan, in the higher Himalaya, in the jungle-covered hills of the Indo–Burmese border, and in the driest parts of the Thar Desert (shared by India and Pakistan). Intermediate densities prevail elsewhere in the subcontinent.

The population map is not completely explicable in terms of varying fertility (as just defined) for two broad reasons. First, notwithstanding statements that are sometimes made to the contrary, the South Asia rural population is not, so to say, in equilibrium with its 'natural' environment, in spite of the long periods over which it has been adjusting itself to that environment — and in the process modifying it.[1] Some areas like northern Bihar and Bengal are manifestly overpopulated; others, like parts of the desert capable of more intensive cultivation under irrigation now being supplied, or the Dry Zone of Sri Lanka, or the eastern Deccan plateau area known as Dandakaranya, can receive and are receiving more cultivators yet. The second reason is, of course, that South Asia is not entirely agricultural, nor are all of its towns and cities 'country towns' which, like Thomas Hardy's Casterbridge, are 'but the pole, focus or nerve-knot of the surrounding country life', living by agriculture 'at one remove further from the fountain-head than the adjoining villages, no more': for then urban populations would bear some relation to rural population. Quite apart from ancient temple, craft and palace towns (urbanism in South Asia is very old), there are the great metropolitan cities like Bombay, Calcutta, Madras, Karachi and Colombo, grown (some would say overgrown) from ports established by the British, and each related, on the principle of 'metropolitan dominance', to a penumbra of denser population in its hinterland: the crowded populations of the plantation district of Sri Lanka, closely linked to Colombo port, are a case in point. The effect is magnified greatly in the hinterlands of the larger port-cities of the mainland. And there are also the newer industrial cities and administrative centres that have grown up, with relatively little dependence on local agricultural fertility or rural population, since independence. However, all this is largely to anticipate. Let us start with the 'natural' environment whose interrelated elements of physiography, soil and climate constitute natural fertility, conventional though this treatment may be; but admit at the outset that it has been heavily modified by man. Such an introduction to South Asia, especially for those unfamiliar with the subcontinent, will also provide a basis for the treatment of many other facets of South Asia today.

The physiography of South Asia is usually said to possess a basic simplicity, and to fall into three broad zones — plateau, plain and mountain. Indeed, so much seems evident from the 'glance at the map' which is all that most people take. One has, however, to be careful about the ascription of simplicity to landscapes that may be very differently perceived by those who live and work in them, necessarily in a restricted area. South Asians may turn out, on enquiry, to have as detailed a set of names for small regions, perceived as differing *inter se*, as the British have bestowed on, say, the parts of the Weald or the French on their *pays*. And the plains dweller may and does see the edge of a plateau as a local range of hills. Let us bear these possibilities in mind, then, in looking at the three broad zones of the small-scale map.

The plateau is certainly the dominant landform in peninsular India, the 'Deccan', which has much flat land at various levels, with step-like rises between them: over 600 feet (183 metres) in elevation in the Nagpur area, over 1600 feet (488 metres) in the Bombay Deccan, over 3000 feet (914 metres) in high Mysore and Chota Nagpur. There are also, however, coastal plains: narrow on the west, broadening out on the east into the great deltas that carry a very high population density. The principal rivers, moreover, have broad, plain-like valleys. But overall it is plateaux that dominate: plateaux cut, for the most part, in very ancient crystalline rocks — granites, gneisses, quartzites and the like. The crystalline rocks do not furnish very rich soil-forming material and tend not to bear such dense rural populations as more favourable bedrock.

The exceptions in the Deccan to the generalizations hazarded in the last sentence are of considerable human significance. They are:

1. The coastal, fluvial and deltaic plans aforesaid, with their alluvia: often rich soil-formers, though much depends on the precise material — for instance, coarse sands, not infrequent along coasts, spell soil poverty (it is an unscientific perception by economists, historians and others that all alluvium is fertile).
2. The area of some 200,000 sq. miles (over 500,000 sq. kilometres) in the hinterland of Bombay covered by outpourings of basalt, the so-called 'Deccan Trap'. This, in broad valley bottoms, weathers to give a deep, black soil, regur or 'black cotton soil', which is water-retentive and classed as 'good' or 'very good' but difficult because it flows under irrigation or heavy rainfall.
3. In down-faulted basins in the north-east Deccan are preserved remnants of Gondwana sediments which contain India's only really important coal-fields. Fortunately these are near deposits of iron ore.
4. (And this is a negative aspect for people.) The Aravalli Hills running out from the northern Deccan to Delhi are true ridges, not plateaux; they tend to have repelled settlement and forced traffic, military and civil, between the Indus plains and the Ganges plains round their northern extremity — hence the historical importance of the site of Delhi.

Outside the areas just enumerated, the natural resources of the crystalline plateaux of the Deccan and their outliers in Sri Lanka and Meghalaya are also best put in negative terms: not very fertile, generally speaking; limited coal; no hope of onshore oil (though certain very different geological conditions offshore are oil-yielding, as in the Bombay High); only sporadic opportunities for the deep tubewells that have proved so important in the Indo-gangetic plains, to which we now turn; intermediate densities of struggling peasants except when irrigated.

The Indo-gangetic Plain, one of the world's really great plains, rests on a great arc of alluvia all the way from Karachi to the Punjab and, past Delhi, down the Ganges and its tributaries to the Bengal delta. A narrower belt of alluvia runs up the Brahmaputra valley into Assam. Most of the alluvium in this vast area, and to a depth of several thousand feet, has been brought down through geological time and into the present by the erosion of the plateaux to the south and, to a greater extent, of the mountains to the north: a timely reminder to the conservation lobby that, much as men in general and South Asian men in particular have contributed to the erosion of hill areas, they are, on a geological timescale, but puny accelerators of a long-continuing process.

But the alluvia, physiography and soils of the great plain are by no means uniform. Quite apart from the transition from extreme aridity in the desert to extreme humidity in Bengal (of which more in a moment), and remembering the importance of the local scale to the cultivator in his fields, there are these contrasts:

1. The contrast of older and newer alluvium: the latter still being actively laid down in the floodplains of the rivers; the former at a somewhat higher level, and often terminating in a bluff overlooking the floodplains, this providing flood-free sites for settlements. The older alluvium tends to be more weathered and, other things being equal, less fertile; and is often dissected, sometimes into a fantastic network of gullies, like those that form the haunt of dacoits (robber bands) along the River Chambal not far from Agra.
2. The rather different contrast of the old and new deltas in Bengal: the former in the west moribund, not being actively built at the present time but pitted with ponds and swamps cut off from the rivers; the latter in the east (and covering much of Bangladesh) still being flooded from time to time or even annually, still accreting silt, still growing at its seaward margin. Many human phenomena, from land use to the distribution of endemic malaria, reflect the contrast of moribund and active deltas.

3. The contrast of coarse well-drained pebble fans at the foot of the mountain wall and the *tarai* and *duars* of the low-lying lands, formerly swampy and malarial, to plainward. The latter, with malaria controlled, has been the scene of very recent pioneer settlement in India (Uttar Pradesh) and in Nepal (whose southern frontier with India runs significantly through the former swamps).
4. The contrast between all of these and the deserts of both India and Pakistan, where the stark arid landforms of sand dune and alkali clay flat, take over from the gentle contours of the rest of the plains.

Turning to the mountains on the north-western, northern and north-eastern margins of the South Asian subcontinent, those to the north form a region of great geological and physiographic complexity. The mountains and hills are often shown as parallel or subparallel ranges with names like 'Siwalik Hills' or 'Inner' or 'Great Himalaya'. But here again there is a problem of scale. What appears as a range on a small-scale map is, at a larger scale and to the local inhabitants, a row of high peaks with radiating spurs, separated by deep valleys and by high passes at intervals. There are also broader interior valleys, of great human importance, like the Vale of Kashmir and the valley around Kathmandu (which is indeed Nepal to the Nepali). The closest approach to a continuous range, and even then cut at intervals by the rivers debouching on to the plains, is provided by the southernmost hills (locally called the Siwaliks). Northward, beyond the highest Himalaya (the 'abode of snow'), lie the great high plateaux of Tibet, part of which, in Ladakh, falls within the political boundaries of South Asian states (though part is disputed between India and China).

The north-western mountains and hills are very different: a series of ranges arranged like the loops of a theatre curtain gathered together by cords at intervals. Some ranges are geologically and physiographically relatively simple and built mainly of sandstones and limestones, others are more complex and volcanic. Between the ranges lie high plateaux, though these are more characteristic of Iran and Afghanistan than of South Asia as here defined; and across them are historic passes like the Khyber.

The north-eastern hills, on the borders between India and Bangladesh on the one hand and Burma on the other, are basically not dissimilar geologically from those of the west, and in plan there are similar parallel ranges, gathered in a great knot at the hairpin bend in the Brahmaputra. But whereas the western hills are largely arid or sub-arid, here in the east the monsoon rainfall is very heavy indeed, so that there has been much more dissection. This and the dense jungle cover make movement very difficult, as combatants in the Arakan and Burma campaigns in the Second World War will testify.

But difficult though these hills, and indeed most of the mountain belts outside the larger interior vales and passes may be, they form the homeland of a whole number of people, from the Pathans of the North-west Frontier through the Paharis of Himachal Pradesh and the Gurkhas of Nepal to the Nagas and Mizos of the eastern hills. Often these hill peoples straddle the frontiers, in some cases (as we shall see) disputed between South Asian countries and their neighbours. In some areas, notably in Nepal and in Himachal Pradesh and Uttar Pradesh, the habitable hills bear the sign of population pressure: deforestation, soil erosion, emigration and a remittance economy.

Moving to the climatic environment of South Asia, a number of points need to be emphasized. The first is the importance of seasonal rhythm: not that of summer and winter (though a hot season and a cold season can be recognized in the north) but that of a wet south-west and a dry north-east monsoon, or, in terms of the crop seasons, *kharif* and *rabi* respectively. Over much of South Asia 70, 80 or even as much as 90 per cent of the mean annual rainfall falls, on average, in the former season, roughly from June to September (inclusive); leaving the rest of the year as a dry season, or at any rate one of minor rains. The impact of this seasonal rhythm on the agricultural calendar and on communications (in the absence, and sometimes in the presence of railways or hard-top roads) need not be laboured. However, three variants of this simple pattern are worth a brief mention:

1. In the north-west of the subcontinent there is a tendency to some precipitation in 'winter' because of depressions. In Peshawar more rain falls between January and March than between June and September. Significant *rabi* rains are felt as far down the plains as western Uttar Pradesh, and are of great importance for crops, particularly wheat.

2. In Tamil Nadu and in the so-called 'Dry Zone' (the north and east) of Sri Lanka there is a rainfall maximum somewhere in the months October to January (when most of South Asia is dry); and a dry season, often *very* dry in the south-west monsoon. Here '*kharif*' and

'*rabi*' are irrelevant (which does not stop them being used) and replaced by local names. Thus *samba* in Tamil Nadu and *maha* in Sri Lanka are the main, wet season rice-growing periods. Here is, indeed, an anomaly rather than a variant.

3. In the Wet Zone (south-west) of Sri Lanka and in southern Kerala there is rain at all or most seasons, on average, with a dry season creeping in as one moves north up the west coast. Here is the film-maker's idea of a tropical paradise, in verdure clad all the year round and with romantic palm-fringed beaches. But they are not paradises for all who live in them. The climate, true, suits plantation crops like tea, rubber and coconut, but it is far from ideal for rice cultivation[2]; even if suitable high-yielding varieties were available, photosynthesis, other things being equal, is bound to be less effective under cloudy, rainy conditions than where hours of sunshine are longer.

Secondly, a perhaps obvious point must be made: that, whatever the rainy season (and the variants and anomalies together cover a relatively small proportion of the subcontinent), mean rainfall totals vary greatly from place to place, from the aridity or semi-aridity of Baluchistan and of the Thar Desert and its environs to the more than 200 inches (5080 mm) in parts of the Western Ghats (behind the west coast of the peninsula) and in the plateau of Meghalaya between the Brahmaputra valley and the delta of Bengal. The contrast between seasonally wet and always relatively dry areas has been a recurrent theme in Indian history and lies behind many regional variations in the contemporary economic map. There is, for instance, an axis of near-aridity running south from the Desert through the eastern Deccan to the 'burning sands of Ramnad' on the coasts of Coromandel opposite Sri Lanka (where, indeed, it can be recognized in the Tamil-occupied north). This axis, reflected as its low rainfall was in relatively light and open forest, has provided a zone for the north-south movement of peoples and armies, whereas the region of heavier rainfall and denser jungles to the east long remained relatively little penetrated, the homeland of relict tribal peoples. The axis of aridity was, moreover, a belt prone to famine when the exiguous rains failed: in 1918, parts of the Deccan behind Bombay harvested only 9 per cent of their crop area.

For variability of rainfall, linked to the vagaries of the south-west monsoon, is to be reckoned with by the cultivator in many parts of

South Asia, particularly in light rainfall areas where less-than-average rainfall is apt to mean that there is insufficient for crops or animals. Drought and crop failure are of concern to governments too: it is not surprising that an Indian Finance Minister once described his budget as 'a gamble in rain'.

It must also be remembered, especially by those used to the 'small rain' of temperate latitudes, that an inch of rain is usually far less effective in South Asia than in those latitudes or, in other words, a greater quantity of rain is necessary to achieve the same effect with vegetation or crops. This arises from high intensity. The mean amount of rain per rainy day over the subcontinent is over 0.8 inches (20 mm), more than six times the corresponding figure for Cambridge, England. And very high daily rainfalls and extremely high intensities for shorter periods are frequently recorded. The consequence is that much rain is lost by rapid run-off, which may be accelerated by deforestation and poor conservational practices in cultivated fields. Another consequence may be soil erosion.

A number of points have already been made about South Asian vegetation: one remains to be made. Very little 'natural' vegetation is left anywhere, if by this term is meant vegetation unaffected by man. Almost everywhere what passes for 'forest' or 'jungle' has been degraded by the action of people, or by their cattle and goats over the millennia. This applies even to much forest legally classified as 'reserved' or 'protected' (but not, of course, to deliberate plantations of trees: though these are un-'natural' in another sense).

Soils, too, have been mentioned *pari passu*; but in this case two further points must be mentioned. First, while Bangladesh, Sri Lanka and parts of Pakistan have good, modern soil surveys, these do not exist over large parts of India.[3] Secondly, the actual or potentially most fertile soils and densely-peopled rural areas are those developed on alluvia. But we have seen that the alluvia are highly variable, and that some (desert sands and alkali clay flats, coastal sands, leached or gullied older alluvium) are infertile and/or difficult. Moreover, over much of the great plains it is usually held that the alluvium has been degraded in fertility or structure, or both, by long cultivation with inadequate use of manure: Kipling called it the 'used-up, overhandled earth'.[4] (It is possible, however, that the tradition of ascribing loss of fertility to such South Asian alluvium derives from Englishmen's mistaken perceptions, with Fen peat and Romney marsh in mind, of a pristine fertility that these tropical and subtropical deposits never had.) We have also seen that 'good' or 'very good' marks may be awarded to black cotton soils.

The South Asian social environment approached through the caste system

To approach the South Asian social environment through the caste system is not to imply that to explain caste is to explain South Asian society. But caste is a phenomenon that many find fascinating, yet intensely puzzling, and some exploration of its nature and complexities, and of the controversies surrounding it, is necessary.

I shall proceed, at the risk of oversimplification and overgeneralization, by dissecting and commenting on a dictionary definition. The third edition of the *Concise Oxford Dictionary* defines caste thus:

> Indian hereditary class, with members socially equal, united in religion, and usually following the same trade, having no social intercourse with persons of other castes.

What, then, of the first word, 'Indian'? Is caste restricted to India, as at present defined or as bounded in imperial days? It is indeed often claimed that the caste system is peculiar to India, or at any rate to South Asia. Some would go further and see it as a cultural trait necessarily linked to Hinduism; others disagree. But the relationship of caste with both India and Hinduism will, I hope, become clearer as further parts of the dictionary definition are explored.

The words 'hereditary class' do convey something of the essence of caste, which is indeed inherited. A member of the relevant South Asian societies is inescapably a member of a caste, and this is, with few exceptions, that of his parents who, because of the endogamy which is also part of the essence of caste, are both of the same caste (or subcaste, or even segment of a subcaste). And caste endogamy tends to survive even when other caste restrictions drop away.

The word 'class' is, however, not without difficulty in its application to caste. Some sociologists argue that the caste system is not only more rigid, through the strict endogamy practised by relatively small groups, but that it is also more elaborately hierarchical than any class system. South Asians, they say, are more obsessed with status than anyone else; and status is defined by caste. Others would argue that such perceptions of caste contain an element of exaggeration, an ascription of oddity, of the kind often made by products of one civilization when confronted by another; and point to flexibility in the hierarchy as a result of caste mobility and sanskritization, of which more later. It is also often pointed out that caste and class in South Asia are, while often related, not identical.[5] The dominant landowners (and land spells wealth in rural South Asia) are generally of high caste. The landless are for the most part of low caste. But there is less correlation in the middle ranks of the caste and class hierarchies in the villages, and still less in the towns and among those with non-agricultural occupations, a point to which I shall return.

The point must also be made that, in spite of what will shortly be said about caste amongst Muslims, class stratification is a more adequate key than caste to social structure in Pakistan, at least so far as the Punjab and Sind are concerned. This is closely related to one of the most unequal land ownership patterns in South Asia. The Pakistan Planning Commission estimated that in 1959 3.3 million people (65 per cent of all landowners) held 15 per cent of the cultivated land in holdings of under 5 acres; while a mere 6000 people (0.1 per cent of landowners) also held 15 per cent of cultivated land in holdings of over 500 acres (in some cases very much in excess of that figure). Pakistan is indeed a landlord's country, in spite of measures of land reform to be reviewed in Chapter 6; and with political correlates to be considered in Chapter 4.

To return to India, the Marxist C. Meillassoux has a different view of the relation of caste to class. He sees caste as 'an attempt to maintain an evolving class relationship within the framework of a rigid status organization ... matched by a repressive religious ideology'.[6] In other words, class formation is hindered by caste and its related religious ideas.

That there are such religious ideas is generally recognized (even though their force and relevance is a matter for argument). One such idea is that of *karma*, often translated 'fate'. The belief is that a person's actions in one of his successive reincarnations and the extent to which he fulfils his *dharma* (right behaviour given his place in society, itself largely caste-related) will determine his circumstances, including his caste, in his next reincarnation.

The second religious idea, confined to Hindus, is that of pollution, or loss of ritual purity: this is a matter of much more moment the higher a caste's position in the hierarchy. Pollution may come about for a whole host of reasons: for a Brahmin, for example, by 'crossing the black water' to some overseas destination, or by eating meat, or by undertaking a whole range of jobs, from fishing (which takes life) through toddy-tapping (which produces alcohol) to washing clothes (which may be stained with excrement or other polluting exudations of the human body) and to handling animal carcasses or dead bodies or human excrement. The higher, 'clean' castes will not do polluting work. Most Brahmins will not even put a hand to the plough, though this, like distaste for manual work generally, is not entirely a matter of caste status; nor is such distaste confined to South Asian societies. A lower caste does some polluting work according to its ritual status; thus its members may catch fish, but not handle dead bodies. The lowest castes of all do the most polluting work, such as the handling of human excrement. Pollution also comes about through certain intercaste relations like accepting food from, or eating with members of a lower, polluting caste; or sexual relations with a person of such a caste; or through contact with someone of an 'untouchable' caste. If a Hindu of a 'clean' caste becomes polluted there may have to be rites of ritual purification or, in what are seen as more extreme cases (such as marriage out of caste), a sentence from a caste council of loss of caste status.

The precise operation of the concepts of ritual purity and ritual pollution varied, and still vary from place to place; they were, and are most strictly applied in South India. Some aspects of pollution and some of its consequences have diminished with 'modernization'. The reader may well recognize that the doctrines of *dharma* and *karma* and the notion of ritual pollution give caste a flavour quite different from that of class in a western society and this whether or not, with Meillassoux, he sees caste as resting on an anachronistic, irrational and repressive religious ideology, and obfuscasting for 'idealist' scholars the 'objective reality' of class formation. Louis Dumont, indeed, goes further and sees the opposition pure/impure as 'the very principle' of caste hierarchy.[7]

Returning to the dictionary definition, to what extent are members of a caste 'socially equal'? Here it is important to ask in what social framework and at what geographical scale one is operating. One can find apparent simplicity in a complex scene by thinking in terms of the four *varnas*, broad, apparently universal and supposedly original caste groups: Brahmins (priests) at the top; then Kshatriyas (warriors); then Vaishyas (cultivators, cowherds and others); and fourthly Sudras, manual workers serving the first three 'clean' *varnas*. This leaves the Untouchables outside the scheme altogether (Gandhi, who renamed them 'Harijan', 'sons of god', held that originally they were Sudras). Now the four *varnas* have some place in historical explanations or more recent rationalizations of the caste system. And there have been cases in which a caste claims the status of a particular *varna*, generally confining its aspirations to the two top strata, like those in Maharashtra who call themselves Saraswat Brahmins but are not recognized by other local Brahmins.

What does matter to a man in his daily life is not *varna*, or usually even caste in the sense of first-order subdivision of a *varna*, but a second- or lower-order subdivision, usually called *jāt* or *jāti*. This in British days often corresponded, especially for census purposes, to what was called a 'subcaste'. (A complication is that the group a man calls his *jāti* may vary according to the purpose for which he is relating himself to it.) It is at this level that, in some sense, 'social equality' in terms of status is to be found.

But social status (by caste) and economic status (by class) need not be identical, even in the village. Under some modern conditions, especially in towns and in the bureaucracy, the two may be wide apart. Thus I remember a government officer's *chaprassi* (messenger) in Madhya Pradesh who was a Brahmin. He carried his officer's files in the office and in the field. But at mealtimes in the field he ate first and apart.

Or there is the case of three coastal castes in Sri Lanka: Karāva, originally fishermen; Durāva, originally toddy-tappers; and Salāgama, originally weavers, later cinnamon-peelers.[8] Many, though by no means all members of these castes rose to affluence under western impact and with the coming of a plantation economy, especially in the nineteenth century, as carters, traders, and eventually plantation-owners and businessmen. But they were all three relatively low in the hierarchy as it was, and still is perceived by the dominant inland cultivating caste, the Goyigama, with whom they came into conflict particularly in the 1890s. It is significant that aspiring members of the newly affluent castes did not invoke western liberal ideas about the equality of man, still less Marxist principles of evolving class formation, but instead sought to establish themselves higher in the status hierarchy provided by caste. This applied especially to the Karāva, some of whom produced genealogies to support their claim to be of Kshatriya status, and thus superior to the Goyigama. But, whatever the caste status of the aspiring caste members, their rise in terms of economic status is clear; and that is the point here.

It may, then, be concluded that membership of a common *varna* or of a common caste will not guarantee social equality with other *varna* or caste members. Membership of a subcaste, or *jāti*, however perceived by the individual, may well do so in terms of ritual status, though not necessarily in economic or 'class' terms in the modern world (see also remarks on *gōtra* (lineage), pp. 19–20 below).

What of 'united in religion'? Since *karma*, *dharma* and ritual purity are Hindu concepts, is caste peculiar to Hindus? Some would indeed aver that, given the syncretic and variable nature of Hinduism, it is difficult or impossible to define a Hindu *except* as a person enmeshed in the caste system and bound by its ideology and sanctions.

But caste, or at any rate some of the features of caste, is not confined to Hindu society. In spite of the original professions of the Sikh *gurus* about the desirability of a caste-free society, there are endogamous groups among the Sikhs that are often described as castes.

Islam is, in theory, even more caste-free that pristine Sikhism; yet it was possible for a Muslim to edit a book on *Caste and Social Stratification among the Muslims* of India.[9] There are, it may be noted, Muslim Jāts as well as Sikh Jāts and Hindu Jāts: all cultivators, for the most part, in the plains of the two Punjabs and of UP, many forming the dominant caste in their villages, and credited by British civil servants with great industry and agricultural skill. Other Punjab castes are also represented among Muslims, Sikhs and Hindus.

The Buddhist majority in Sri Lanka have a caste system which is recognizable as such in spite of a number of peculiarities. There are no Brahmins or Kshatriyas (whatever may once have been the case). The Goyigama, inland at any rate, are both the majority and the dominant cultivating caste; but are divided into subcastes — there is a great social distance between the Rādalas, the village aristocrats (especially of the Kandyan areas) and the village cultivator with only a very little land, or none at all. There are also no Untouchables as understood by Hindus, for no Buddhist is unclean in the ritual sense; but there is a caste, the Rodiya, who are to a great extent outside the system and who traditionally lived by begging. As in India there is caste endogamy and a caste hierarchy, disputed though the order is and locally variant though it may be. And to some

Goyigama Christians marrying in caste is more important than marrying another Christian. For South Asian Christians too may preserve caste: in some places there is a high caste church and a low caste church.

Caste, then, is by no means an exclusively Hindu phenomenon; though many readers will suspect that it is peculiar to areas influenced by Hinduism in the past, perhaps in the case of Sri Lanka in the remote past so that the full Brahminical order was never established. Many contemporary Muslims, Sikhs and Christians are, of course, the descendants of converts from Hinduism who carried their caste with them into the new religious community.

A definition of caste in terms of adherence to a common religion, Hinduism, raises particular problems when one turns to the so-called 'tribal' population of India (and to some extent of the hill areas of Bangladesh). (The 'tribes' of the North-west Frontier of Pakistan are, of course, almost all Muslims.) Indeed, to use the terms 'tribe' or 'tribal' is also to run into problems of definition. The term usually carries the meaning primitive, or aboriginal, or jungle-dwelling, or hill-dwelling, and often too the implication of distinct language and animist religion, of being outside the mainstream of Hindu civilization. The term '*adivasi*', meaning literally original inhabitant, is now also often used with the same connotations and implications. But when one seeks to decide whether a given group of people are tribal, or alternatively a caste or groups of castes within Hindu society, difficulties arise. Thus the Nagas, Khasis and Mizos of north-east India are indubitably hill-dwellers, some of them jungle-dwellers, with strange languages unrelated to Indo–European tongues like Assamese or Bengali. But many of them are Christians, and some behave more like modern economic man than many an Assamese plains-dweller. Again, the large group in central India known as Gonds are often classed as tribal, for forest-dwellers many of them are; but they speak a Dravidian language related to the South Indian tongues, and are recognizably Hindu (they formerly had their own powerful kingdom, and were driven into the hills in historical times). It is clear, too, that many present castes represent former 'tribes' (in some at least of the senses just enumerated) who entered the Hindu fold by the process known, following M. N. Srinivas, as 'sanskritization'.[10] This is a process by means of which a group of people take on the rituals, customs and lifestyle of a caste in the Hindu hierarchy, including the absorption of the sacred literature in Sanskrit (hence the term), in order to claim higher ritual status (they may none the less retain some earlier practices). Some former tribes have succeeded in establishing themselves with relatively high status; but many Harijan castes are probably former tribals who were less successful. Some tribals are former castes who became cut off in the forest. Yet others, like some of the Khasis, became westernized and christianized before they could be sanskritized. When, then, with all these possibilities is a 'tribal' group a non-Hindu tribe and when is it a Hindu caste? F. G. Bailey has convincingly resolved the problem by postulating a spectrum with indubitable caste at one end and indubitable tribe at the other, other groups coming somewhere in between.[11] The Government of India has adopted another solution. Under the Constitution a list of peoples are designated Scheduled Tribes, and accorded certain privileges and benefits: the Scheduled Tribes numbered some 40 million, 7 per cent of the total population, in 1971. But a number of groups who appear to be towards the tribal end of Bailey's spectrum are excluded, and clamour to be included in order to share in the benefits. (There are also Scheduled Castes, Harijans, under the Constitution, whose inclusion is likewise subject to argument.)

The penultimate part of the dictionary definition is the phrase 'following the same trade'. One often sees lists ascribing specific occupations, sometimes very narrowly defined, to specific castes or subcastes: for example, to take a few beginning with 'B', Bhangi, sweepers; Bharbunja, grain-parchers (whatever they may be); Bhāts (of UP), hereditary genealogists and heralds. Indeed, a common western stereotype of caste depicts it as a system involving the rigid and incredibly finely-drawn division of labour. There is certainly in South Asia today a connection between caste and occupation. In the past, over parts of the subcontinent at any rate, and to some extent today, division of labour was expressed in the *jajmani* system, under which each caste in a village society fulfilled a specific ritual function and alone undertook specific jobs, under a higher caste patron, with the priestly Brahmin overall. In many ways, however, the patron–client connection involved in, or surviving from the *jajmani* system is a more important key to contemporary social relations than minute division of labour. For it must be remembered that the primary occupation in rural South Asia still is (as indeed it always was) the cultivation of the land: albeit subject to caste restrictions (e.g.

Brahmins not ploughing) and with very unequal access to the means of production — indeed, much landless and dependent, and formerly bonded or enslaved labour. And the occupational functions of the several castes and subcastes have been eroded and complicated by western impact: there was, after all, no hereditary caste of railway engine drivers, or of university dons. But pollution remains pollution: so, in the village as elsewhere, the Bhangis and other Harijan castes continue to sweep, the Chamars to work in leather, the Dhobis to wash clothes.

And so to 'no social intercourse with other people of other castes'. Here much depends on the meaning attached to 'social intercourse'. The *jajmani* system, like patron–client relationships more generally, involves a certain stylized system of social intercourse, with heavy emphasis on hierarchy, on ritual status and function, on dependence; superficially a system of co-operation, though sometimes today as in the past involving conflict between castes or between factions accreting about rival village bosses. We have also seen that concepts of pollution clearly imply a bar on some kinds of social intercourse, particularly on dining together and on receiving food or water from persons of certain castes: and these in many places remain in one form or another. But they tend to be weakening, especially because of the mobility brought by train and bus (not even a Brahmin wants to starve on a long train journey): so, even more, do complex rules about who may sit, or wear such-and-such clothes in whose presence. But, it must be emphasized, this does not mean that the caste hierarchy is any less marked in more fundamental ways (there are still upper caste patrons and low caste clients); or that deep-seated features like caste endogamy are weakening.

'No social intercourse with people of other castes' may be taken to imply that there is complete freedom of social intercourse *within* a *jāti* in a village, or even that such a *jāti* is an indivisible social unit. But this would be to ignore the importance of *gōtra* (lineage), those persons who trace their descent from a real or mythical common ancestor. For there is often great rivalry between lineages within a *jāti*, especially among dominant castes, who strive for village leadership. This is well brought out in M. N. Srinivas' masterpiece, *The Remembered Village*.[12] A desire to promote the interests of one's family or lineage is often construed in the West as nepotism; while factions are frequently based on rival lineages.

The reader will now, I hope, appreciate why the Indian villager (and not only the villager), enmeshed in *jāti* and *gōtra*, is sometimes said to live in a 'cellular society'.

There are, finally, a few important points about caste that fall outside the dictionary definition, or need to be drawn out of the foregoing discussion for separate treatment. The first is caste mobility. It is most important not to overemphasize the rigidity of the caste hierarchy, either historically or in contemporary South Asia. We have seen how tribes may become castes; with luck well off the bottom rungs of the ladder, all too often not even on a rung. And we have seen the rise in economic status, and in the claimed (but not generally acknowledged) caste status of some members of certain coastal castes in Sri Lanka. The more we come to know of South Asian social history, the more does it become clear that castes, or some caste members have climbed in the hierarchy by such means as sanskritization; or pioneer settlement in the course of which they left lowly status behind them; or by migration into the subcontinent and subsequent validation by the Brahmins as, say, a caste within the Kshatriyas; or, today, by moving to the cities and claiming a new caste status. Many examples of such upward mobility could be cited. By seeking to climb within the system, these groups affirm it. There can also be downward mobility. For example, there can be, or could be *de*sanskritization when a caste was dragged down in ritual status by the influence of a less sanskritized dominant caste; and Brahmins may fail to show their *gunas* or appropriate qualities by lack of learning and ritual purity, and so lose status relative to other local Brahmins.

For South Asian society was not, and is not without regard for moral and other qualities or for those qualities in action. It is not all a matter of status and of dominance by powerful groups, as anyone who has felt the force of South Indian (or Islamic) puritanism is aware; while *ahimsa* (non-violence) is very much a Buddhist and Hindu concept.

Clearly the occupational mobility and the urbanization of modern life, together with other of its features, can give a great fillip to caste mobility, just as it can weaken the joint family system.

Then, again the point has been made, but must be strongly stressed, that a particular caste hierarchy, with a number of *jātis* in a particular order, can be and often is, or was, a very local phenomenon. The same *jāti*, or at least a *jāti* with the same name, may be at different places in the hierarchy in two villages not very far apart; and may, in pre-British days, have had no contact except, perhaps, at great centres of pilgrimage. It may be that the three coastal castes in Sri Lanka formed, with others, their own local hierarchy; and that it was only with changing space relations brought about by the growth of trade, of communications and of commercial agriculture that some of them came into close and conflict-prone conflict with the Goyigama-dominated hierarchy inland.

With the British in their Indian Empire there came, not only modern transport, a new urbanization, and new space relations, but also the census, which sought to record each person's caste and subcaste. The inclusion in the same census subcaste of *jātis* formerly out of contact and at different places in local social and economic hierarchies sometimes meant that the unity of the group concerned was essentially a census construct. In visual terms, for the local caste pyramid (or, better, irregular tower-block) was substituted the horizontal stratum covering a wide area, and tending to be mapped by the unwary in, so to say, the same colour. Now, as political interactions developed between the Raj and its Indian subjects, the new identity and apparent validity given to region-wide caste by the census and officials who leant on it (e.g., in making caste-based concessions) reinforced the effects of new modes of transport and trade, and was seized on by a new social grouping, the caste association. There arose in UP, for example, associations of Kayasths (a 'writer' caste) who agitated in the interest of their newly identified caste fellows. At the same time, and for similar reasons, came a greater consciousness of *varna*.

André Béteille has emphasized that it is important not to make too much of the domination of South Asian society by an ideology of hierarchy, not to imagine that equality is a principle to be found only in other societies.[13] We have already seen that Sikhism was originally a revolt against the rigours of caste; and that, in theory at any rate, caste is repugnant to Islam. However caste-based Sinhalese Buddhist society may be, the Buddha himself disapproved of caste and sought escape from the domination of the Brahmins, replacing priests by monks. And a number of movements within Hinduism have, from time to time over the centuries, mounted attacks on at least some aspects of caste hierarchy and privilege.

British rule brought a new power situation that weakened some of the forces that had kept castes in their unequal places (though it also, as in attempts to unify Hindu law, in some cases ossified the hierarchy). The impact of the west also occasioned, as a reaction, not only Hindu and Buddhist revivalism but also movements, like the Brahmo Samaj founded by Ram Mohan Roy, whose aims included the removal of what were seen as the extremes of caste. The later Arya Samaj went further and envisaged a caste-free society. Later still, Mahatma Gandhi and his followers sought in particular to improve the lot of the Harijans, believing that untouchability was a late development, a pathological growth, on the caste system. The Indian Constitution contains provisions designed to improve the condition of backward classes; while an Indian Act of 1955 declares illegal the enforcement of disabilities on grounds of untouchability. And one may not infrequently meet good, sincere Gandhians engaged in welfare work for the benefit of Harijans or tribals. Indeed, it is not far-fetched to discern a strand of sincere egalitarianism running through South Asian social history, owing nothing originally and for long centuries to western liberalism, sometimes faint and hidden from view by the strong fabric of a status-ridden caste society, sometimes much clearer and more evident.

But on the other hand, there is also today a good deal of humbug and of political expediency about calls for greater equality. Some of the most strident advocates of equality are ambivalent or hypocritical where caste is concerned: and Harijans and tribals remain the most disadvantaged strata in South Asia's complex society, still refused temple entry and access to village wells, still (in the south at any rate) living in separate hamlets away from the villages of the 'clean' castes.

Now in those villages, and in most villages in South Asia, local power is still held, because the largest landholdings are still held, by members of whatever the locally dominant caste or castes may be. Power and dominance over others, though here enmeshed with caste status, are of as great significance in South Asia as in other 'traditional' agrarian societies. The relationships between dominant castes, dominant classes, landholding, agrarian change or lack of it, and politics and government action, will have to be explored later in this book.

It was at one time fashionable to see in these same South Asian villages, or in many of them at any rate, self-sufficient and self-governing 'village republics', each ruled by its *panchayat* or council, surviving as empires rose and fell and dynastic conflicts washed to and fro across the face of the subcontinent. This was the view of early nineteenth-century British writers like Sir Henry Maine, who made comparisons with a Europe that had lost the primitive communism and self-sufficiency that they thought they saw surviving in these 'republics'. Marx knew the work of some of these authors, and gave the picture a new colour with his writings on the unchanging village and its 'Asiatic mode of production', about which he wrote with something less than consistency.[14] The notion of primitive village communities was taken up with enthusiasm and idyllized by Indian nationalists, including Gandhi; and there were prescriptions for communal tenure (very rarely put into effect) and for a restoration of *Panchayati Raj*, rule by village councils (put into effect in India, as will be seen later). It may well be asked how all this squares with village caste hierarchies, their interaction with economic status, and the model of the dominant caste, even if the *jajmani* system may be seen as implying a functioning village community, albeit a very unequal one. It does seem clear, with hindsight, that the Englishmen who identified 'village republics' were smitten with a certain romanticism; and resurgent nationalism is often romantic; while Marx, so far as he relied on apparently empirical evidence, was misled by the British authors he read. It seems, too, that the operation of the British legal and revenue systems in the Indian Empire tended to give some preference to what had survived, or was seen as surviving, of corporate land tenures (though this is a thorny thicket not to be entered here). But there have not been lacking those who have stressed, not co-operation and idyllic harmony in the village community, but bipolarity between dominant and suppressed, exploiter and exploited. Notable among these was B. R. Ambedkar, himself an Untouchable and a doughty opponent of Gandhi, who saw village unity as a myth and the village itself as a cesspool of iniquity. The truth perhaps lies somewhere between harmonious co-operation and violent internal conflict, varying greatly with both time and place.

What of society in South Asian towns? First, the study of South Asian cities has not been free from echoes of the sociological controversy as to whether there is a sharp break, a dichotomy between urban and rural; or whether rural and urban settlements alike lie on a continuum. Weber contrasted 'traditional' rural society and 'rational' urban society (a distinction, false or not, that lingers on). Perhaps Marx was a dichotomist, with his strictures on 'the idiocy of rural life'. In the South Asian context, there have certainly been dichotomists among students of society. It is, however, possible to see in some of these the urban bias in urbanites' perceptions of the superiority or modernity of urban life, just as there may be rural bias in the minds of some who see rural life and society as idyllic.

On the other hand, a number of social theorists have envisaged a continuum, a gradual transition from village to city, so that it is hard to say where a specifically urban society begins. In many smaller towns and cities, and on or near the fringes of larger ones, are to be found 'urban villages', sometimes with their fields intact, sometimes without them, but still preserving the caste structure of village society. In some cities too, especially ancient ones, specific castes tend to cluster in specific *mohallas* (wards) or *thoks* (subdivisions of *mohallas*), as (on a smaller scale) in villages; sometimes there are caste *panchayats* undertaking administrative and judicial functions. But most larger towns and cities of South Asia consist of a mixture, in varying proportions, of 'traditional' social groupings on this basis, or a modification or erosion of it, and of what may be called loosely 'the new élites', the whole governed under western-style municipal institutions tending to supersede, in whole or in part, caste *panchayats* and other 'traditional' bodies.

By the 'new élites' one means those groups in society who, in contrast to the 'traditional élites' who held power and influence over wide areas in pre-British days, or who still dominate village or local society, have had a western-style education, can (and sometimes habitually do) speak English, and for the most part have adopted at least some of the insignia of the western middle classes.[15] These groups grew in numbers and influence in British days and after, while remaining a small proportion of the total population. In contemporary South Asia, they dominate, to a greater or lesser extent, the professions, the universities, the higher ranks of the public service (civil and military), and national politics. They tend to be recruited by open competition (apart from the politicians, of course, who have survived another kind of competition). Such open competition is irrespective of caste (though in India a number of places in the public service and in parliament are reserved for 'backward classes'). But for the most part, and to a greater extent in some spheres than others, they have a class base in the sense that many of them have not only received a western-style education but are the products of expensive local equivalents of the English public schools and of the more socially-esteemed universities. But there is also a caste base, for very few members of the lower castes, particularly tribals and Harijans, can aspire to or afford the requisite education. Caste is more obviously important in the business sectors of the 'new élites': members of *bania* (trader) castes, for example, are still prominent in industry and commerce in Bombay and surrounding areas; though the more modern sectors of industry would appear to have a wider base for recruitment. Cosmopolitanism is also a characteristic of at least some of the 'new élites' in India: that is, members of them in any one city will be drawn from all over the country, though not necessarily proportionally to population in the source areas, for a variety of reasons. Such city-dwellers seem a far cry, in location, in occupation, and in attitudes, from society in the villages or ancient towns from which their ancestors must have come; though perhaps not to such a great extent as in the case of the imitation Englishmen, the 'brown Sahibs', who passed into the Indian and Ceylon Civil Services towards the twilight of British Rule. And today one meets people who, wherever they may be serving, retain roots in their home regions and pride in its culture. Be that as it may, those in the 'new élites' who belong to Hindu or Hindu-influenced communities are still members of castes, for the most part marry in caste, and have not (for all their westernization) abandoned ancient rituals, customs and values.

In considering these élites we have, because of their cosmopolitanism and because some of their members, administrators and politicans at any rate, are operating and making decisions at national level (or state level in India or provincial level in Pakistan), moved far up the geographical scale from the village or from the locality-based *jāti*. I propose to end this introduction to contemporary South Asian society by mentioning briefly two other aspects of society that also have, or may have, far more than local significance: namely, religion and language. This will also enable a few threads trailed earlier to be tied together.

Hinduism is, of course, numerically the most important religion in South Asia. Over 80 per cent (453 million) of Indians are Hindus; there are important minorities in Sri Lanka and Bangladesh (far fewer now in Pakistan); and Hinduism, alone or in a syncretic amalgam with Buddhism, is significant in Nepal. It will be clear from the earlier discussion that it is not easy to define a Hindu, particularly amongst tribal peoples (where census figures anyway tend to be suspect). And what of the Harijans, as seen by 'clean' caste Hindus? It is also not easy (and this point has also already been made) to define Hinduism, which may to different individuals mean anything from animism to atheism, from polytheism to monotheism, from simple village cults to the higher flights of philosophy. Whatever Hinduism was originally it has over the centuries absorbed deities and ideas from the myriad peoples of the subcontinent and then, from time to time, seen attempts at purification by reformist sects, some of which survive within it. Absorptive syncretism and the schism of sects, together with the absence of a unifying creed, spell complexity and the proliferation of cults. Some have suggested that a Hindu is a man who in some way accepts the religious authority of the Brahmins; perhaps with, though not always with, acceptance of the caste system and of such observances as the prohibition on cow slaughter. Beyond this it is hard to go, for present purposes and with the present author's knowledge at any rate. What is clearer, however, is that Hinduism has been a potent force in creating some measure of national unity in India: through the process of sanskritization, and indeed through the existence of Sanskrit as a common sacred language which is the vehicle for the transmission of ancient literature, the common heritage all over India; through the great centres of pilgrimage, especially those of all-India significance; through the provision of a generally-understood Hindu idiom in which Indian nationalism could express itself (though this in turn tended to alienate the Muslims); perhaps through the conferment of legitimacy on a single all-India political power, the heir of the *chakravarti raj* of ancient tradition.

Islam contrasts strongly with Hinduism. It is, of course, not without its divisions (remember Omar Khayyam's two-and-seventy jarring sects). But its unyielding monotheism set it strongly apart from Hinduism and here made it generally quite incapable of compromise, still less absorption. Muslims look to Islamic countries of the Middle East: whereas there are but few Hindus outside India.

Muslims form all but 2 or 3 per cent of the population of Pakistan, and some 80 per cent of the population of Bangladesh. In India, in spite of partition in 1947 and the separation of Pakistan, they still number over 61 million, more than in most Muslim countries, and 11 per cent of the total population; but are very unevenly distributed. The strongest concentrations are in Kashmir (disputed with Pakistan), on the borders of Bangladesh, and locally in Kerala, with lesser concentrations spreading from Delhi down into UP and Bihar and in Hyderabad and its environs. In 1981 there were reports of Harijans converting to Islam in Tamil Nadu and elsewhere. The Maldives, like the Indian islands of Lakshadweep, are overwhelmingly Muslim.

Sikhs cluster most strongly around their sacred city, Amritsar, in

Punjab State of India, and spread out into adjacent states and areas (though there are now very few in Pakistan, since the migrations that followed partition). With a reputation for enterprise, they are to be found in relatively small numbers in towns all over India except the South. They total 10.4 million, 7.8 per cent of the Indian population. In their homeland in Punjab they are strongly assertive politically.

Buddhists were formerly only numerous in two areas: in Sri Lanka, where most of the majority Sinhala community are Buddhists of the Theravada or Hinayana persuasion and where resurgent Buddhism, intertwined with strong feelings about language and political identity, has been a major political force; and in Nepal, Sikkim and other northern hill areas, in the more syncretic Mahayana or lamaistic form. But after independence in India a large number of Harijan followers of Dr Ambedkar expressed their discontent with their lot by declaring themseves Buddhists. This movement was particularly strong in Maharashtra, Ambedkar's home State, where 3.3 million people were returned as Buddhists in 1971.

Jains, who arose as a Hindu reformist sect, are effectively confined to India and number 2.6 million, with highest concentrations in Maharashtra, Rajasthan, Gujarat and adjacent areas. They are mostly urban businessmen with a reputation for shrewdness.

Finally, Christians in India number 14.2 million, some 2.6 per cent of the total population; but with strong concentrations in the north-eastern hill States (where, it will be remembered, westernization came before sanskritization could take a hold), and in Kerala and adjacent parts of Tamil Nadu. Christian missionary activity has also made some headway amongst tribals and Harijans, who may be seen as having nothing to lose but their lowly status in the caste hierarchy; and, for all the tolerance of Hinduism, has from time to time provoked a reaction of some political importance.

It is not proposed to produce a wearisome catalogue of all the many South Asian languages. Suffice it to say that not everyone would agree on the list, in particular as to what in north India is a separate language or merely a regional dialect of Hindi; and that South Asian languages fall into well-marked major families and branches.[16] Thus languages of the Iranic branch of the Indo–European family, notably Pushtu and Baluchi, are spoken on the north-west frontier of Pakistan and in Baluchistan, straddling the frontiers with Iran and Afghanistan. A great swathe of tongues of the Indic branch of the same family occupy the Indo–gangetic plains and the northern and central Deccan:

Punjabi, Sindhi, Kashmiri, Hindi (*sensu lato*), Urdu, Nepali, Bengali, Assamese, Oriya, Gujarati and Marathi and, literally isolated, Sinhala. Sanskrit is an ancient member of the branch, the parent of at least some of the languages just enumerated. To the north and east are spoken a whole congeries of Tibeto–Burman languages, with outliers in Meghalaya. The southern Deccan is the homeland of the Dravidian languages, Tamil, Telugu, Kannada and Malayalam, with northern outliers in pockets of Gondi and, far away in Baluchistan, Brahui. Finally, some tribal peoples of the north-east Deccan and across into Meghalaya speak tongues unrelated to any of these.

Pakistan, as we shall see, has toyed with various internal political structures: but, in a broad way, the continued existence of Punjab and Sind as separate provinces recognizes the linguistic and cultural differences between them. Baluchistan only partially covers the territory in which Baluchi is spoken (and also includes Brahui speakers); while there has been intermittent pressure for the union of all Pushtu speakers in a Pakhtunistan. Here, especially with the Soviet intervention in Afghanistan, and the increased possibility of irredentist movements operating either way across the frontier, there are hostages to fortune indeed. Nepal and the north-east frontiers of India are a patchwork of languages just as they are a patchwork of peoples; but so far it is only in the latter region that language has been a factor in political fragmentation (yet to be discussed in more detail). Bangladesh is overwhelmingly Bengali speaking, except for the hill tracts and adjacent areas; but so are the people of India's West Bengal, so that language and culture could yet counter the religious factor that was the basis for partition. In Sri Lanka language is one factor in the communal division between Sinhala Buddhists and Tamil Hindus.

But in the Republic of India outside the border areas just singled out for special mention, language (see Table 2.1) has been a most potent factor in shaping and activating the political map since independence. India inherited from the Raj a patchwork quilt of British provinces and of princely states. By stages and not without hitches the latter were absorbed into a system of States federated to the Indian Union. But the resultant map bore little relationship to the linguistic pattern. Bombay State, for example, included Gujarati, Marathi and Kannada speakers, among the major tongues. Madras State included Tamil, Telugu, Kannada and Malayalam speakers as well as some peoples using Gondi and other tribal tongues. It was Telugu speakers who first successfully agitated against this state of affairs. In 1953 they succeeded, in spite of the initial opposition of Nehru, in securing the establishment of an over-whelmingly Telugu-speaking State, Andhra Pradesh, carved out of Madras and Hyderabad States (the latter had the boundaries of the old princely state). There followed in 1955 a States Reorganization Commission whose recommendations, or such as were accepted, formed the basis for redrawing the internal political map of India primarily on a linguistic basis. Madras State was limited, by and large, to Tamil-speakers (and later became Tamil Nadu). Kerala and Mysore (later Karnataka) were respectively dominated by Malayalam and Kannada speakers. Bombay State at this stage remained unified, but later (in 1960) split on a linguistic basis between Gujarat and Maharashtra (respectively speaking mainly Gujarati and Marathi). The Punjab of the Commission was also later split between a largely Punjabi-speaking Punjab and a Hindi-speaking Haryana — though here the assertiveness of the Sikhs in Punjab had much to do with partition. Orissa speaks Oriya (with a large number of tribal languages), West Bengal speaks Bengali, truncated Assam speaks Assamese. The rest of India is the 'Hindi belt' divided between Bihar, Uttar Pradesh, Madhya Pradesh (which also has many tribal languages), Himachal Pradesh, Rajasthan, the Union Territory of Delhi and, of course, Haryana. The boundaries between States in the Hindi belt did not basically arise from language differences though these do exist.

There are, of course, many modern Indian languages for which there is no corresponding State: notably Urdu, the *lingua franca* of the Mughal Empire, based on the local Hindi of the area north of Delhi with an admixture of Persian words, but also many tribal languages (although, with the partition of former Assam and the creation of the fragmented political pattern of north-eastern India some of these receive at least partial recognition). It is possible that there will in future be agitation for the political recognition of some of these, and indeed of some non-tribal languages (though, as we shall see, separatist movements in India are not all linguistically based). For linguistic separatism and regionalism in India have gathered some of the force that generated linguistic nationalism in Europe in the nineteenth and twentieth centuries, and led after much conflict to the political map as it is today. As W. H. Morris-Jones has said, 'language is perhaps the most important mark of group identification' because 'a means of communication is inescapably a delineator of group boundaries'.[17] Literature, newspapers, the understanding of the

Table 2.1 Languages in relation to States in India

Languages in schedule VIII	All-India total for languages (millions)	Number in state cited (millions)		Percentage of population
Assamese	8.96	Assam	8.91	59
Bengali	44.79	West Bengal	37.81	86
Gujarati	25.87	Gujarat	23.87	88
Hindi	208.51	Bihar	44.95	80
		Haryana	8.98	90
		Himachal P.	3.00	100
		Jammu and Kashmir	0.70	14
		Madhya P.	34.70	85
		Punjab	2.71	19
		Rajasthan	23.48	90
		Uttar Pradesh	78.21	89
		Delhi	3.10	78

Language	millions	State	millions	%
Kannada	21.71	Karnataka	19.33	67
Kashmiri	2.50	Jammu and Kashmir	2.45	49
Malayalam	21.94	Kerala	20.50	98
Marathi	41.77	Maharashtra	38.62	77
Oriya	19.86	Orissa	18.97	84
Punjabi	14.11	Punjab	10.77	77
Sanskrit	0.002	—	—	—
Sindhi	1.68	—	—	—
Tamil	37.69	Tamil Nadu	34.82	85
Telugu	44.76	Andhra P.	37.14	84
Urdu	28.62	—	—	—

Not in schedule VIII and mother tongue of more than 1 million

	millions		millions
Bhili	3.40	Konkani	1.51
Dogri	1.30	Kurukh/Oraon	1.24
Gondi	1.69	Santali	3.79
Gurkhali/Nepali	1.42	Tulu	1.16

Based on populations and mother tongues as recorded by *Census of India*, 1971
Schedule VIII of the Indian Constitution lists these fifteen 'Languages of India'

radio, political propaganda and in India some at any rate of the caste and other associations, necessarily stop at language boundaries. Not surprisingly regional politicians, skilled at working in the local language and sometimes knowing no other, cannot readily operate beyond the language frontier — and are in favour of including all who share their tongue in the same political unit, their State: they can rely on strong emotions. In Europe similar considerations have been associated with nationalism, with powerful movements for the identification of nation with language-group and for the political independence of that group. Yet in India, so far at any rate, politicians and others concerned have for the most part been content to work for Statehood within the Union, albeit with greater local autonomy and not without hostility to the Centre and its policies. Why is this so? The reader will be able to suggest some reasons already; others will follow.

Meanwhile, a point must be made in conclusion which brings us back to the local scale. As B. S. Cohn has made clear, the speech used by a man in any given village has an extremely local range (like a *jāti*) and changes gradually as one moves from village-group to village-group across country;[18] but our man will find the regional dialect comprehensible for most purposes across a wider area (though there may be turns of phrase confined to his caste). This is not peculiar to India, as any English fen-dweller knows (though with him class perhaps replaces caste). In the last two centuries or less there have developed standard regional languages over a wider area still — through the growth of literature, newspapers, education, communications and so on. It is these that we know by such names as Gujarati or Telugu, and these that form the vehicle for linguistic separatism. But many Indians, including some of the humblest, are able to speak in the standard regional language, or in some sort of Hindi (which can be understood over a far wider area than the 'Hindi' belt), while reverting to their very local dialect in their village or its environs.

The approach in the next chapter will be mainly historical. It will be concerned with the impact of Europe, and particularly Britain, on South Asia; with reactions to that impact; and with the coming of independence and partition and, in 1971, the separation of Bangladesh. Such a concentration on modern and, indeed, very recent history seems appropriate for this book.

But in taking such an approach one does not wish to ignore the importance to South Asians of their earlier history or of endogenous historical processes in the development of their economy, society and polity. That history stretches back a very long way, for the Indus civilization was flourishing some 4500 years ago; and those processes were at work, in spite of or in association with the dynastic changes that fill the duller sort of history books, over an equally long period, for all Karl Marx's 'unchanging' villages. The previous section of this chapter has shown what deep historical roots lie beneath, or are perceived as lying beneath the features and processes of contemporary society: for instance, the four *varnas*, the processes of sanskritization and caste mobility, the antiquity and caste-structured nature of urban life (and, of course, of the village), the absorptive syncretism of Hinduism, the coming of Islam and Sikhism. The student of South Asia who is not himself a South Asian must, indeed be constantly aware of the length of, and the continuities in the history of the subcontinent.[19]

If he is himself a South Asian, he will recognize the force of this long history, of perceived tradition, in his daily life, even if he rejects some of it. It is one of many paradoxes in at least Hindu society that this force is so strong in spite of the absence until very recently of the recording of history, of the chronology of events as these are understood in other societies. The Sinhala Buddhists have their monastic chronicles, the *Mahavansa* and *Culavansa*, recording (after the manner of the biblical books of Kings and Chronicles, perhaps) the acts of good kings, who were pillars of Buddhism, of bad kings who were not: and very potent influences these have been in the triple intertwining of language, religion and state in modern Sri Lanka. The Muslims of the subcontinent, particularly in the period of the Mughal emperors and their successors, have left rich historical sources: and these have assuredly had their influence on modern Muslims in the subcontinent. But it is not so with the Hindus. But they rely, with tremendous effect, on their ancient writings, the Vedas (hymns going back to 1000 BC and earlier, preserved first in oral tradition and written down in Sanskrit centuries later), with the associated Brahmanas, Upanishads and Sutras, all eventually held to be sacred; and the later Epics, (the Mahabharata and Ramayana). It is not easy for critical scholarship to disentangle myth from history in these writings, or in later genealogies and stories of heroes preserved in oral tradition. But something coming down from remote time forms part of the heritage of all contemporary Hindus, whatever their origin and whatever otherwise divides them. Let us not neglect, then, however contemporary our study, the sense of history and of tradition that is so alive to them as to other communities in South Asia.

References

1 Farmer, B.H. (1974) *Agricultural Colonization in India since Independence*, London, 36.
2 Farmer, B.H. (1979) 'The "Green Revolution" in South Asian ricefields: environment and production', *Journal of Development Studies*, 15, 311.
3 Farmer, B.H. (1974) op. cit., Chapter 8.
4 Kipling, R. (1964) 'The conversion of Aurelian McGoggin', in *Plain Tales from the Hills*, London, St Martin's Library Edition.
5 Béteille, A. (1977) *Inequality among Men*, Oxford, 130.
6 Meillassoux, C. (1973) 'Are there castes in India?', *Economy and Society*, 2, 90–111.
7 Dumont, L. (1970) *Homo Hierarchicus: The Caste System and its Implications*, London.
8 Roberts, M. (1981) *Caste Conflict and Élite Formation: the Rise of a Karáva Elite in Sri Lanka, 1500–1931*, Cambridge.
9 Imtiaz Ahmad (ed.) (1973) *Caste and Social Stratification among the Muslims*, New Delhi; Kaufmann, S. B. (1981) 'A Christian caste in Hindu society', *Modern Asian Studies*, 15, 203–34.
10 Srinivas, M.N. (1967) 'The cohesive role of Sanskritization' in Mason, P. (ed.), *India and Ceylon: Unity and Diversity*, London.
11 Bailey, F.G. (1961) '"Tribe" and "caste" in India', *Contributions to Indian Sociology*, 5, 7–19.
12 Srinivas, M.N. (1976) *The Remembered Village*, Berkeley, Cal.
13 Béteille, A. (1979) 'Homo hierarchicus, homo equalis', *Modern Asian Studies*, 13, 529–48. See also Parry, J. (1974) 'Egalitarian values in an hierarchical society', *South Asian Review*, 7, 95–121.
14 Thorner, D. (1966) 'Marx on India and the Asiatic mode of production', *Contributions to Indian Sociology*, 9, 33–66.
15 Béteille, A. (1967) 'Elites, status groups and caste in modern India', in Mason, P. (ed.), *India and Ceylon: Unity and Diversity*, London.
16 Schwartzberg, J. (ed.) (1978) *A Historical Atlas of South Asia*, Chicago and London, map X.B.1.
17 Morris-Jones, W.H. (1967) 'Language and region within the Indian Union', in Mason, P. (ed.), *India and Ceylon: Unity and Diversity*, London.
18 Cohn, B.S. (1971) *India: the Social Anthropology of a Civilization*, Englewood Cliffs, NJ, Chapter 4.
19 Spear, P. (1961) *India: a Modern History*, Ann Arbor.

3 THE BRITISH PERIOD, THE COMING OF INDEPENDENCE, AND PARTITION

**In the parts of this chapter concerned with the period before independence it is more convenient to use 'Ceylon' instead of 'Sri Lanka'; while 'India' means the whole area that became the British Indian Empire, unless the context requires otherwise.

The European impact was, of course, only the last in a long series of external influences on South Asia. By sea came, for example, voyagers from ancient Middle Eastern and Mediterranean civilizations. Later, Arab traders brought Islam to western and southern India, to Ceylon, and to the Maldive Islands; and, intermarrying with local women, founded communities that are Muslim still, but very different from north Indian Muslims. By land, over the great north-western passes, poured wave after wave of invaders, from the early Aryans who brought Indo–European languages to the ancestors of the Mughal emperors. By land, too, through the medium of Turki invaders Islam was brought to the northern parts of the subcontinent: here lie the historical roots of Pakistan and Bangladesh.

But South Asia was drawn into a new age with the arrival of European voyagers who had discovered the long sea route round the Cape of Good Hope and who sought the famed spices of the Orient. The first of these was the Portuguese Vasco da Gama, who found landfall at Calicut (modern Kozhikode, in Kerala) in 1498. In spite of conflict with local rulers and Arab traders, the Portuguese soon set up a chain of sea-linked fortresses in south India and Ceylon ('Colombo' is a Portuguese name), made converts to Christianity, and intermarried with local people. In course of time they also brought a number of crops from the New World; for example, tobacco, maize, potatoes, manioc and chillies. Goa, their headquarters, remained a Portuguese possession until annexed by independent India in 1962; and, with several smaller former Portuguese colonies, is still a Union Territory, ruled directly from New Delhi. On the heels of the Portuguese came the Dutch, who ruled the Low Country of Ceylon for 137 years;

continued the process begun by the Portuguese whereby that area was differentiated from the Up-country, Kandyan area; and had a lasting effect on law. But India they quickly left for a richer source of spices in the islands of the East Indies.

The British East India Company established itself at Surat in 1608, at Madras (mainly to buy textiles) in 1641, and at Calcutta in 1691 (Bombay grew to importance later); and rapidly dominated the Portuguese at sea.

The French Compagnie des Indes Orientales founded Pondicherry in 1674, but was relatively inactive till the 1720s. By 1740 it had a number of additional posts on the east coast of India, and one at Chandernagore north of Calcutta, and was the only serious rival to the British. The clash of the two companies in India was brought about not so much by rivalry in trade as by the wars between Britain and France in Europe. Ultimately the French were defeated by Clive at Plassey in Bengal in 1757, and in south India at Wandiwash (Vandivasi) in 1760; while the Dutch were ousted from Ceylon in 1795–6, basically in order to deny the splendid natural harbour at Trincomalee to the French during the wars. From the 1760s onwards in India, and from 1795–6 in Ceylon, the British were the only European force to be reckoned with in South Asia, at least until the Russians began to peer over the northern mountains in the 1860s; though the French continued to hold Pondicherry, Chandernagore and other small establishments until they were amicably ceded to independent India. Pondicherry, a fascinating fossil town, still shows a French influence and like Goa remains a Union Territory.

Thus far in the narrative the British agent in South Asia was not the government in London but the East India Company; though the newly-won territories in Ceylon, at first administered by the Company, in 1802 became a Crown Colony. Colonial rule was extended to the whole island in 1815. A number of points about Company rule must be stressed. First, the Company's main motive was profit through trade, which was also the private motive of its servants. Political activities by the Company were occasioned by, or sought justification in the protection of trade. Interest lay not so much in spices as in indigo, sugar and, above all, textiles, the silk and cotton products of longstanding and high-quality handloom industries. Some of the textiles were exchanged for spices in South-east Asia. Local agents were essential to this trade: so arose, slowly at first, an element in a 'new élite'.

Secondly, trade was at first carried on through posts, often fortified, built on land held from local rulers. Most of the posts were for obvious reasons coastal. There was, in the earliest phase, no question of wide territorial conquest or of sovereignty; though the Company, like its French rivals, made alliances with local rulers.

In time, the Company's servants went further and sponsored rulers of their choice, as when Clive after his victory at Plassey installed Mir Jafar as the Mughal Emperor's Governor of Bengal. But Mir Jafar did not survive long; and soon the Company's servants had made themselves the rulers of Bengal and Bihar. I say 'the Company's servants' deliberately, for modern historians see these servants as 'the real founders of empire', like the conquistadors.[1] Private profit led them afield. The acquiescence of the Company back in London was purchased by promise of rich land revenue. By 1805 rule had been extended to the Sutlej, to much of what was to become the Madras Presidency, and to patches north of Surat. So did trading posts become territory and so was British influence extended to ever widening areas of India. So, too, did higher administration pass into the hands of the Company's officials.

However, the British Government had already stepped in to curb and control the powers of the Company and its servants. Parliament was in particular alarmed by the near-bankruptcy that resulted from political adventure in Bengal; for much of the promised revenue had run into private pockets, and expansion was costly. A Regulating Act was passed in 1773; while the India Act of 1784 made the Company responsible to Parliament and declared 'that to pursue schemes of conquest and extension of dominion in India are measures repugnant to the ... policy of this nation'. Nevertheless, as is indeed implicit in what has just been said, further acquisitions were made in the remaining years of Company rule: that is, until the Rebellion of 1857. Notably, the rest of Punjab and Sind were added.

In 1858 the British Crown assumed the government of the Company's territories and suzerainty over the princely rulers. By 1914, the Indian Empire had grown to its territorial full extent.

Let us now discuss some of the more important economic and social consequences of British rule, especially as they affect, or help to explain patterns and processes in contemporary South Asia, our prime concern: while recognizing that many of the effects of imperialism are the subjects of controversy, and that some will remain for examination in later chapters.

The economic impact

Some of the concrete economic effects of British rule are obvious enough. Thus by independence undivided India had some 45,000 miles of railways: 29 miles per thousand sq. miles of area, 132 miles per million population — both high figures for an underdeveloped colonial territory.[2] The corresponding figures for Ceylon are 898 miles; 36 miles per thousand sq. miles; and 135 miles per million population. There were however, substantial gaps in the Indian network: notably in the north-eastern Deccan, Rajasthan, Baluchistan and the Frontier Province.

Roads existed in India long before British days. But the British extended the network (at first largely for strategic reasons) until at independence there were 130,000 miles of surfaced roads in India and nearly 11,000 miles in Ceylon. The density of the network was relatively high in some areas, especially in the Madras Presidency and the Wet Zone and hills of Ceylon, but was low in many others; and villages innumerable remained without all-weather roads.

Irrigation, again, is by no means a British invention; though evolving technology under the Raj was able to achieve engineering feats beyond the ken of ancient constructors, skilled though they were. The British were responsible for a series of major canal works, concentrated principally in the Punjab and in Sind (turning deserts into granaries) and in the Doab between the Ganges and Yamuna (Jumna). Canals were also constructed to take off from the lower reaches of the east coast rivers, and in the Bombay Deccan. In Ceylon restoration of ancient tanks and of their dependent channel systems began in the 1850s; and there was some new construction.

The railways had much to do with the spreading of a money economy and with increasing the output of cash crops (though these, in the shape for example of cotton, oil seeds and spices, were no strangers to the Indian scene in pre-British days). They also made it possible to switch food grains from surplus to deficit or famine areas (though of course not enabling the poor to purchase). Irrigation works brought new lands into cultivation and gave at least the potential for surpluses both on them and on lands already cultivated. There has been much argument as to whether the British achieved the right mix of railways and irrigation works. Indian 'nationalist' historians — and others — are apt to argue that judged by economic criteria too much was invested in railways because of their strategic significance, and that the cost to the Indian economy was high. For a long time, too, irrigation works were not initiated unless they were expected to be commercially viable as judged by rather narrow criteria.

In aggregate and during the British period as a whole, the Indian cultivated area increased. Though in some areas and at some periods the waste appears to have crept back, 'there came, at a different date in different regions, a critical point in time beyond which rural settlement advanced strongly into the waste, no longer to relapse into major phases of retreat'.[3] In most places this advance was a matter of piecemeal encroachment, but there were government-organized colonization schemes, most notably in Punjab; and in Assam and Kerala tea and other plantations were established, serving an export market. What is much more controversial is the trend in agricultural production and productivity. Morris D. Morris started with the assumption, far from generally accepted, that 'traditional' Indian agriculture was of low productivity, for environmental reasons.[4] He pointed out that the population only grew between 1872 and 1921 at 0.4 per cent per annum (the 'population explosion' in most of India coming after the latter date), and presumably at a no higher rate earlier in the nineteenth century. (Though the population of Madras Presidency is thought to have increased by 300 per cent in the nineteenth century.) He concluded that production from the newly opened and newly irrigated land might well have led to a rise in productivity per acre and per man. Others disagree, often leaning on the work of G. Blyn, who concluded after patient analysis of elusive data that over the period 1891–1947 at any rate *per capita* agricultural output declined.[5] There were, however, substantial differences between crops (wheat doing better than rice) and between regions, Bengal tending to drag down the all-India averages. More recent work by M. M. Islam has reached conclusions for the period 1920–46 less adverse to Bengal than Blyn's, and suggested that trend rates for Bengal proper were in turn dragged down by Bihar and Orissa, included in Bengal in early statistics. As we shall see, wheat outshines rice in the modern 'Green Revolution' too; and Bihar continues to be an agriculturally depressed state. A moral for our own times is that aggregate statistics often conceal great regional and other disparities; while temporal trends mask violent fluctuations due to the vagaries of the monsoon.

Even more controversial is the question of the extent to which the complex systems of land tenure and land revenue that the successor states inherited from the Raj reflect the changes (some would say the distortions, accidental or deliberate) introduced by the British. On this whole subject there is a vast jungle of literature. All that can be said here is, first, that the British inherited a situation already of great complexity, though behind the complexity lay adaptation to the local situation, and two relatively simple principles: that hereditary land tenure was based on occupation rather than ownership in the sense familiar in England; and that revenue was due to the ruler, 'a wage for a protector' according to Hardy.[6] The revenue might be collected by an intermediary *zamindar*, a tax-farmer not a 'landlord' (except on land in his own occupance that he let to tenants). Behind both lay a hierarchical society (as we have seen) reflected in a pyramid of rights to the produce of land; so much so that André Béteille doubts whether the Indian village of the past can sensibly be described as a peasant community.[7]

Secondly, the British reaction to this unfamiliar state of affairs in the Bengal of the 1790s (which included Bihar) was to make a Permanent Settlement with the *zamindars* for the revenue, and to empower them to transfer their rights by sale or otherwise. The *zamindars* in fact became landlords, though not the improving sort as the British had hoped. The status of the actual cultivators tended to be depressed: *zamindars* encroached on customary rights and made various exactions. Matters worsened as population increased and tenants became cheap. Permanent Settlements were not made in other areas. But revenue settlements with *zamindars* of varied provenance were widespread in the plains west of Bihar, in the Central Provinces, and in parts of the South; and led to a growing market in revenue-collecting rights and to sales of land by revenue defaulters. In the 1890s Congress began to agitate against *zamindars*, seen as lackeys of the Raj; and, in power after independence, abolished them.

Thirdly, in Bombay and Madras Presidencies and in the plains of Assam the dominant form of revenue settlement eventually made by the British was *raiyatwari* (*ryotwari*): that is, the government collected the periodically-adjusted revenue itself, theoretically from the actual cultivator. In most *raiyatwari* areas, however, there was once again a pyramid of holders of rights, varying from area to area in nomenclature and character, and including Brahmins who only cultivated through tenants and labourers, together with other kinds of 'landlord'. As Dharma Kumar has said, 'the village was not always and everywhere a simple community of peasant proprietors; often it was far more differentiated and complex'; as, indeed, the visitor to a contemporary South India finds when invited 'to meet the *raiyats*'. When a land market developed and land came to be pledged as a security for loans, the registered *raiyat* was often a landlord, not the actual cultivator. And evictions meant a high turnover, especially of small men. The network of village-level officials required to keep records and to collect *raiyatwari* revenue not only gave ample scope for corruption but provided readymade *dramatis personae* in politics.

Fourthly, there is no doubt that the weight of the revenue assessment, under whatever system, often fell heavily on the actual cultivator. Where, as under *raiyatwari* at any rate, it was usually collected in cash, the burden tended to be felt more heavily still. After 1900, however, political pressure saw to it that land revenue was of decreasing relative importance to the Raj. From about the same time, too, government-organized research in plant-breeding and agronomy have to be set against the depressing effects of the revenue system.

Fifthly, it is an important part of the 'nationalist' charge that in destroying the ancient village the British vastly increased, if they did not bring into being, the class of landless labourers whose plight is now so prominent a part of the Indian village scene. Dharma Kumar has, however, convincingly shown that for the Madras Presidency at any rate such labourers (and, indeed, agrestic servitude confined to specific castes) antedate the British agrarian impact; and estimated that they formed some 10 to 15 per cent of the population in the early nineteenth century and 15 to 20 per cent in the period 1871–1901, hardly a catastrophic increase. This is, of course, not to say that particular villages and families did not suffer a more marked increase in landlessness.

Sixthly, the princely states lay outside the British administration and were in theory at any rate free to levy land revenues as their rulers pleased. Sometimes, however, the British leant on the ruler, as when Gwalior was induced to give up its old system of revenue-farming.

Finally, agrarian revolt, at any rate partly arising from grievances about land tenure and revenue, is no new phenomenon in the Indian countryside; and some Districts were always difficult to govern.

In Ceylon, as early as 1802 *rajakariya* tenures involving labour service to the government were abolished and 'peasant proprietorship' instituted, coupled with a tax on paddy land (abolished in 1892, whereafter there was no land revenue in the colony). More controversially, an enactment of 1840 declared waste land to be Crown property, enabling plantations Up-country to be established with great rapidity but depriving villages of land they had customarily used for shifting cultivation, pasture and other purposes (the economic effects of this measure have, however, probably been exaggerated).[8] For this and other reasons it may well be that landlessness increased during the British period; but figures are not easy to interpret.

Argument over the effects of British rule waxes even warmer as one turns from agriculture to industry. Morris D. Morris, in his provocative reinterpretation of nineteenth-century Indian economic history, contests the familiar view that the British found a society ready for an industrial revolution and prevented its development.[9] He sees 'traditional' society as beset by political instability, low productivity in manufactures as in agriculture, low incomes, and undeveloped internal trade. He envisages the *pax britannica*, with British commerce and infrastructural provision, as the environment in which, far from textile handicrafts being exterminated (as Marx and others predicted), these industries survived and may even have grown as cheap imported yarn benefited the handloom weavers (though what of the spinners?). Taken with his views on agricultural growth, there emerges a picture, albeit shadowy and tentatively sketched, of a rise in real *per capita* incomes during the British period, a picture that contrasts strongly with that drawn by other authors, notably Jawaharlal Nehru, who held that foreign political domination led to a rapid destruction of the economy that India had built up, the result being 'poverty and degradation beyond measure'. Indian economic historians and others have indeed not been slow to challenge Morris' views on a number of scores. Thus it is held (with reason) that in some respects, notably in terms of pre-industrial textile technology India was in advance of most other countries; while recent research shows that inland trade is of long standing (though limited and local in its effects). Indeed, marked interregional disparities characterized the 'traditional' economy, and survive today.

It is, again, argued that even if the handicrafts survived the flood of cheap Lancashire cotton (as undoubtedly they did, in some areas at any rate), then the weavers must have become much worse off as prices tumbled. Much contemporary evidence indeed forces one to this conclusion.

But the gravamen of the charge against the Raj does not concern the handloom weavers, or even agriculture and food supply: it concerns the failure of India to generate an Industrial Revolution at a time when modern factory production was spreading in many countries of Europe and North America. India was, of course, not without factories set up in the British period: jute mills at Calcutta, cotton mills along the Bombay–Ahmedabad axis, at Nagpur, and in the South (especially Madras and Coimbatore). The earliest of these textile ventures date from 1854, but the fastest growth was in the 1870s (except in the South, whose boom period came between the two world wars). Meanwhile, coal and iron ore mining were becoming firmly established; and in 1911 the great Tata iron and steel plant at Jamshedpur, in south-eastern Bihar, began production. By 1941 India was producing annually a million tons of steel, three-quarters of its requirement. There also grew during the days of the Raj many sugar, some cement factories, and a number of minor consumer-goods industries. At independence 50 per cent of India's exports were of manufactures.

However, throughout the British period India remained heavily dependent on imports of manufactures, mainly from Britain, where the government bought most of its stores. Factory industry never played more than a small part in the economy; never employed more than 2 per cent of the workforce; made but few machines; and failed utterly to penetrate most regions. In fact, the industries mentioned were, with few exception, located in or near the three great company ports, or within their penumbras. One exception was the textile industry of Kanpur, (UP); another was the sugar industry with its dependence on fresh cane supplies.

Indian historians, whatever their parent school of thought, indeed stress the quantitative and regional insignificance of industrialization in the British period. Explanations vary from the simplistics of the rapacious-colonialism school to the apologetics of those who see *laissez faire* as the basic ideology of the nineteenth-century British, and official inaction compounded by deference to Lancashire interests as the explanation for slow overall industrial growth. Selective protection, however, came after 1917, and is held responsible for considerable growth between the wars in steel, sugar, cotton and match production.

The legacy of the British to independent India, Pakistan and Bangladesh is, then, clear in terms of concrete construction like railways, roads and irrigation works (and also, one must emphasize in terms of a modern commercial infrastructure and a framework of law and administration lacking in many other developing countries).

These countries entered independence with rapid increases of population, with agriculture barely able to keep pace, or unable to keep pace with those increases; with a complex and inequitable agrarian structure; and with sizeable, but relatively insignificant and regionally non-existent factory industries. What is controversial, but well beyond the scope of this book, is the extent to which agriculture and industry might have been more developed if British policy had been different, or if imperialism had never penetrated the subcontinent.

In many ways the imprint of Britain on Ceylon is clearer and heavier.[10] The economy of an island which was sixth-sevenths forested towards the end of the eighteenth century, but producing rice to feed itself as well as spices, was transformed into an export economy producing tea, rubber and coconut products for an overseas market from foreign and locally owned plantations and from smallholdings; and importing great quantities of rice. Population trebled between 1872 and independence. Industries were largely confined to the making and mending of machinery for the plantations. Economic activity centred on the Wet Zone and the Hills; the Dry Zone, apart from surviving rice-growing villages and a few modern irrigation and colonization schemes, slept under a heavy pall of malaria.

As for Nepal, the main direct impact of the British period was not so much economic as demographic (see p. 49).

The social impact

Deliberate efforts by the British to change the nature of South Asian society tended to be confined to the abolition of customs repugnant to them, such as *satti* ('suttee'), the burning of the living Hindu widow with the corpse of her husband, declared illegal in 1829; or *rajakariya*. But the motive for the latter reform was partly the hindrance that *rajakariya* offered to the mobility of labour, judged necessary for the burgeoning plantation economy. Indeed, the most important changes in society brought about in both India and Ceylon by the British were the result of measures instituted with other purposes in mind. Some of these have already been discussed. Others were the largely uncovenanted effects of the concept of equality before the law, and of educational activity; though it is important not to exaggerate these effects.

As early as 1835 it had been 'declared that the content of higher education [in India] should be Western learning, including science, and that the language of instruction should be English'.[11] But action was another matter. Slowly, a number of government schools were started, and Christian missions took educational initiatives. But it was not till 1857 that the first three universities, significantly those in Calcutta, Bombay and Madras, were founded; and a grant-in-aid system for private schools and colleges was introduced. Not surprisingly, early effects of the new education were largely concentrated in the three Presidencies (of which Bengal led) and especially in the Presidency cities; though Poona provided a secondary centre in the Bombay Presidency.[12] British territories elsewhere, and even more the princely states, lagged behind, in most cases till well after the end of the nineteenth century; though the Anglo-Oriental College at Aligarh (UP), later to become Aligarh Muslim University, was founded in 1875; and Allahabad University and Punjab University, Lahore in 1887.

In Ceylon western-style education made relatively little headway before 1870.[13] Thereafter there was a rapid development with a strong concentration in two areas: around Colombo (on the Indian port-city pattern) and in the Ceylon Tamil-settled Jaffna Peninsula.

In nineteenth-century India those in the Presidencies who benefited from the new education came from highly restricted social groups: in Bengal from upper Hindu castes such as Brahmins, Kayasthas (writers) and Baidyas (traditionally physicians) — leaving the Muslims well behind; in Bombay from Brahmins, Gujarati trading castes, Prabhus (writers) and Parsis (again, Muslims were less well represented, especially in Sind); in Madras, Tamil areas were ahead of Telugu areas, and Brahmins at first held a position of overwhelming strength, though towards the end of the nineteenth century the share of Vaisya and Sudra castes in the secondary schools was increasing (it also increased later in the universities). Data are lacking for nineteenth-century Sri Lanka: but one may safely guess that members of the Low Country Goyigama, the three coastal castes (see Chapter 2), and upper caste Jaffna Tamils, benefited most.

In the twentieth century western-style education gathered momentum in India, here through official action, there through missions, but increasingly through institutions set up by local people, often as a Hindu or Buddhist reaction to Christian missionaries. Only four more universities were, however, founded between 1900 and 1920; though nine appeared between 1920 and independence (including Dacca – now Dhaka – University in 1922 in predominately Muslim East Bengal). On the eve of independence there were still great blanks in

Rajasthan and Gujarat, and in central and south-central India. In the future West and East Pakistan Punjab University (Lahore) and Dacca University respectively stood alone, as did the University of Ceylon, founded as University College, Colombo in 1921. Some of the blanks on the map of India were at least partially filled by colleges affiliated to universities in other areas, or by various technical institutions. And schools of many kinds were creeping steadily over the map, though very unevenly. In fact, literacy grew steadily in both India and Ceylon from the 1880s until independence;[14] but at independence still tended in India to be highest in coastal areas of the three Presidencies and in Travancore-Cochin (now Kerala) — though even there it touched only some 10 per cent of the population. Literacy remained very low (under 5 per cent) in much of Rajasthan, in Hyderabad, and in the east central Deccan; and was almost non-existent in Nepal.

Many nineteenth-century writers of widely differing persuasions, from Karl Marx to James Mill and to British administrators, were in broad agreement that Indian society had been historically resistant to change, particularly structural change, because of what Marx called 'the dissolution of society into stereotyped and disconnected atoms', but that the British conquest was bringing about rapid alteration in society. Not surprisingly these authors differed sharply between themselves in a number of ways. To Marx the British impact was destructive of what, as we saw in Chapter 2, he envisaged as 'village republics' yet he saw colonialism as a modernizing force which would lay 'the material foundations of Western society in Asia'. James Mill also envisaged abrupt transformation, while criticizing the British administrators.

We have seen that a great deal of controversy surrounds economic and tenurial change during the British period. Not surprisingly controversy also surrounds the nature of the accompanying social changes. Stokes has, however, made a convincing case, in opposition to the nineteenth-century writers just mentioned and their latter-day counterparts, for the view that for most of India social stagnation rather than revolution was the hallmark of the British period.[15] He is primarily concerned with the century ending in 1857, but also looks ahead to later phases of British rule.

In the decades that immediately followed Plassey the social and cultural impact was indeed small. The East India Company, though it introduced English-style high-level administrative and judicial institutions, still behaved like an Indian ruler in other respects, and upheld Hindu and Muslim law and religious practice. But after the turn of the century came a period when ideology at any rate was couched in the language of Evangelicalism, Utilitarianism and 'improvement', and was accordingly censorious about local society and culture, especially religion. However, recent research has shown what a gulf there was between ideology and pronouncement on the one hand and practice and achievement on the other (this is a gulf not unknown in contemporary South Asia). This was especially true in the days before railways and telegraphs began to increase the effectiveness of administration and of 'improvement'. For all the precocious rise of the new intelligentsias of the port-cities, fluent in English and reacting in their various ways to western learning, vernacular languages and indigenous cultures prevailed in 'the interior' and still more so in the princely states. Indeed, the work of some recent historians lays bare the British officer in the countryside, not as the fountainhead from which change flowed, but 'as a prisoner if not a puppet of local social forces': of hereditary administrators (Brahmins, Kayasths or Muslims), of equally hereditary and caste-determined village officers who came from the same group whatever paper reforms might be made in land revenue systems (a state of affairs not unknown today). This is a far cry from Mill's notion that he who shapes the land revenue shapes society; or from the view of Indian nationalist historians who see the British revenue system as a source of gross social distortion.

Again, 'although rural society must have undergone a profound change by the suppression of open violence and the turning of individual and group struggle into a battle for land rights through the courts, there was no complete structural change'. Careful local research often shows that old élite castes hold their own on the land or appear in new guise; or that changes thought to have been brought about by the Company and the Raj had already been seeping their way through the social fabric in earlier times; or that the decay of old élites was relatively slow, as in the case of minor Rajput rajas in north and central India (some of whom adjusted and held their own).

In short, in the countryside neither Marx' prognostications of decay and resurrection into westernization, nor the hopes of some British officials and writers that 'progress' would bring 'improved' capitalist agriculture, were fulfilled. However, the grip of the traditional administrative castes and groups on government offices was to some extent weakened by the institution in 1860 of open competition based on educational qualifications, and the associated rise of a western-educated middle class of administrators, of a kind that is lacking or attenuated in many developing countries.

If the relatively slow and temporally and spatially uneven process of change in Indian society is accepted, there still remains argument about the reasons for it. Some western historians stress the general weakness of colonialism as a force making for economic and social change. Some Indian scholars (and people who have recently undergone the colonial experience tend not to think of it as a mere brush-past in the corridors of history) fall back on the theory of the dual economy, of an enforced growth of commercial sectors that suit the ends of the colonizing power, while the 'subsistence' sector stagnates socially as well as economically. Latter-day Marxists, unlike their founding father, indeed think in terms of the stagnating rather than the revolutionary effects of colonialism; for example, through its alliances with the landlords and through the supposed comprador-like quality of the bourgeoisie.

Although, clearly, there are many areas of controversy, and although much empirical research remains to be done, it seems fair to conclude that the British period saw, so far as most of the Indian Empire was concerned, much less drastic social change than had been predicted for it. Social change there was, but it was very unevenly distributed over the country and affected different castes and communities very differentially. It was least of all in some of the princely states. It was a matter of adaptive change (of a sort that still goes on) rather than of revolution.

Another way of looking at the problem is that used by L.I. and S.H. Rudolph.[16] They rebel against the assumption that modernity is opposed to tradition, that modernization means the destruction of tradition: an assumption that is of course implicit in the views of the nineteenth-century authors already reviewed, and, indeed, in those of some modern exponents of 'development'. In particular, they see the caste associations already mentioned in Chapter 2 as a political response in a traditional mode to conditions associated with British rule.

Milton Singer also is disenchanted with the modern/traditional dichotomy.[17] Indeed, from his own observations in Madras he envisages a process of 'traditionalization' whereby innovations are given legitimacy and meaning within the Hindu value system;

whereby, indeed, India's traditionalism, far from being an obstacle to change, is 'rather a built-in adaptive mechanism for making changes'. He concludes that this mechanism is not unique to India, with its prominent syncretic tendencies, though the Indian rate and style may well be distinctive.

What of social change in Ceylon and Nepal during the British period? Ceylon saw more rapid transformation than many parts of India, because of the rapid establishment of a plantation economy contrasting with a subsistence-oriented peasant system (though the boundary between the two was less distinct than that required by the classic theory of dualism). With the plantation economy came an influx of Indian Tamil labour and a new dimension to the Sinhala/Tamil plurality that was such a longstanding feature of the island society and polity.[18] With the new economy, too, came a rapid commercialization and a great deal of economic individualism, with social effects working through land tenure and the rise of a new urban and English-speaking élite, including in prominent positions the members of the three coastal castes that have already attracted our attention in Chapter 2. That these castes fought the Goyigama within a caste framework may be seen as a further example of the modernity of tradition. But the Dry Zone of northern and eastern Ceylon saw much slower change.

Nepal is a very different case, at the opposite end of the spectrum in terms of the pace of westernization. Cut down to size by the British after the Gurkha War of 1814–15, its buffer-state function and almost complete isolation in the days of the Raj preserved its fossil status, an exaggeration of that of some princely states within the Indian Empire. However, in the nineteenth century the Ranas succeeded in establishing themselves as hereditary prime ministers and effectively the rulers under a figure-head king. And peace after a long period of wars resulted in relatively rapid population change, with pressure on land resources, the transmutation of pastoral peoples into settled agriculturalists, increasing concentration of land in the hands of upper castes, and the growth of landlessness;[19] while Gurkhas serving in the Indian Army and Nepalis more generally migrating to work in India began to generate a 'remittance economy'.

The political impact and political change

If one turns from social to political change during the British period, one finds that the story has been told in a number of different ways.

First, it has been told in terms of datable events and concentration on the performance of the Indian National Congress as the premier 'nationalist' institution. Congress was founded in 1885 as an all-India body. Its roots were, however, in the three Presidency cities and in Poona. Its early members came principally from the English-educated élites. In its early years it had no permanent organization; it met annually in various cities, passed resolutions, and tried to impress its policies on the Government of India and an opinion in Britain. While it grew in prestige and subsumed other associations, it remained relatively weak up to the end of the nineteenth century. In the twentieth century the pace of political change in British India quickened markedly. In 1905 Curzon, the Viceroy, announced the partition of the Bengal Presidency into a new Province of Eastern Bengal and Assam (which had a Muslim majority), and Western Bengal (comprising the rest of Bengal with Bihar and Orissa). This inflamed Bengali opinion and led to the appearance of terrorist movements, not only in Bengal, but also in the Bombay Presidency and Punjab; while Congress split into moderate and extremist wings. In 1906 the All-India Muslim League was founded. Then came the First World War and the Russian Revolution which respectively shook faith in the whole structure of western superiority,[20] and raised hopes that, if one despotism could fall, so could another, the British. There followed the arrival of Gandhi, and the launching of a great movement of protest and, in the Punjab, the Jallianwallah Bagh massacre when troops fired on a prohibited meeting: this led to a mood of deep anger and resentment. Soon Gandhi rose to dominance in the Congress, and established links with the masses, later in somewhat uneasy partnership with Nehru. And so events moved on until Britain eventually conceded independence after the Second World War; and partition became inevitable given the intransigence of Jinnah and the Muslim League.

But the tale can also, and not inconsistently, be told in terms of successive British reactions to an ever-strengthening national movement and of successive constitutional devices to give Indians more power (some would say so that, with Indians as co-operators rather than combatants, the Raj might be preserved). Such historiography emphasizes, not only British reactions to Indian nationalism, but the differing policies of Conservative, Liberal and (later) Labour governments at Westminster. Thus, in 1905 and following the advent of a Liberal government, there came the Morley–Minto reforms and the India Act of 1909: Indians were admitted to executive offices; and the Imperial Legislative Council was enlarged to sixty members, twenty-seven of them indirectly elected, and its powers broadened. Six of the new constituencies were for Muslim landholders. In 1917 the Montagu declaration proclaimed that 'the policy of H.M. government ... is that of the increasing association of Indians in every branch of the administration, and the gradual development of self-governing institutions, with a view to the progressive realisation of responsible government in India as an integral part of the Empire'. This was followed by the India Act 1919 and the Montagu–Chelmsford reforms which, *inter alia*, enlarged the central legislature and introduced 'dyarchy' and ministerial responsibility in the provinces. Dyarchy (which operated from 1921 to 1937) is seen by Percival Spear as a first step towards the federation that is independent India, and has been very clearly explained by him.[21] It involved dual responsibility: in each province the governor's executive consisted of councillors, responsible to him only, and ministers, responsible both to him and to the enlarged and largely elected provincial legislature. Certain subjects were reserved to the former, others transferred to the latter. The principle of communal electorates was extended. This cumbrous and unloved system was boycotted by Congress; worked by other political parties in Punjab and Madras (where the Unionist and Justice parties, the latter a development of the anti-Brahmin movement, respectively took office); and elsewhere depended on shifting coalitions of elected members. In 1930 came the proposal for a Round Table Conference to consider further constitutional advance; such a conference had long been demanded by Congress, which, however, imposed conditions unacceptable to the (Labour) government in Britain. The 1935 India Act further extended the features of the 1919 Act, especially in terms of popular representation. Dyarchy was abolished in the provinces and ministers given responsibility for all fields; but retained at the centre. The federal principle was also extended: notably, the princes were given an opportunity to adhere (which in the event they declined). Congress decided to take part in elections; won clear majorities in five out of eleven provinces; and became the largest party at the centre. Then came the Second World War, the resignation of Congress ministries (because the Viceroy declared war on behalf of India), and the complex of events leading to partition and independence on 15 August 1947.

The Ceylon story can be told similarly, though it demands gentler tones and a slower pace. As early as 1835 a Sinhala member and a Tamil member were nominated to the Legislative Council, which underwent reforms in 1912 and again in 1921. On both occasions officials remained in a majority; on both occasions there was communal representation; on the earlier occasion the franchise was restricted, so far as Ceylonese were concerned, to the English educated. It was, however, not until 1919, in the wake of an outbreak of communal rioting in 1915, that the Ceylon National Congress was formed: it emulated, and was in close touch with the Indian Congress. A constitutional commission reported in 1931, and was followed by the introduction of universal suffrage, territorial (not communal) electorates, and limited ministerial responsibility. Hard on the heels of a further commission (1944–5) and of Indian independence came Ceylon Independence Day, 4 February 1948.

Both of the modes of narration just followed have value as partial unearthings of the roots of politics in contemporary South Asia. This is especially true if they embody some account of the ideas and ideals of the prominent characters. Thus Gandhi may be seen as a shrewd politician with enormous mass appeal because of his thoroughly Indian framework of reference (the 'modernity of tradition' again) and because of his concern, not unmixed with political calculation, for the poor generally and for the Harijans in particular; and with the strong desire that India should avoid what he saw as the social miseries that had attended the industrial revolution in the west — hence his emphasis on decentralized cottage industries. And Nehru may be seen as a thoroughly westernized figure, but filled with a fervent love of his country that he was able to convey to mass audiences; but — and here lay the tension with the Gandhian view — an ardent modernizer, deeply impressed with the industrialization that had been achieved in the Soviet Union. Again, study of the composition of prominent supporters of Congress show what a diverse group they were. Congress, it may be said, was a movement, even a bandwagon heading for independence, not a political party with a single ideology; and this, with the Nehru–Gandhi tension, had much to do with oscillations of economic policy and contradictions in politics after independence. Jinnah, likewise, and the composition of the Muslim League leadership deserve study.

But to tell the story of pre-independence political change in these ways is to place undue emphasis on the role of Congress and the

Muslim League and of the English-educated élite; an élite that was wafer-thin even in the Presidency cities, and even more attenuated, or absent altogether, elsewhere in the subcontinent, even though it had a near-monopoly of the new legislative bodies. It is also to place too much emphasis on Indian nationalism, as though one were speaking of, say, Czech nationalism in nineteenth-century Europe and not of whatever emotions and motives activated the vast population of South Asia, divided by language, culture and caste, to say nothing of the Muslims and their claim that they were a separate nation altogether. And it is to think of ideals rather than interests, of personalities rather than pressure-groups. In other words, in some lights it is to be thoroughly old-fashioned.

Questions have in fact been asked like these. What of political moment was happening in Indian society at large under the Raj? Were there links between the politics of Congress, the Muslim League and other 'national' bodies and those of lower, regional and local, levels? Were caste and other associations a means of exerting pressure upwards from these levels or was nothing happening, was the countryside inert and inactive, except for acts of occasional though spectacular rebellion like those of 1857? These and similar questions have been asked, and answers sought for some parts of British India, particularly but not exclusively by the so-called 'Cambridge School' of historians which Stokes sees as having its intellectual roots in neo-Machiavellianism and its doctrines of self-interested élites and 'the end of ideology'.[22]

One answer to the first question just posed is, of course, that apart from the princely states, or most of them (where British rule preserved and fossilized dynasties that might otherwise have gone the way of Nineveh and Tyre) the establishment of the Raj meant the extinction of the old rulers, the old 'first-line élite' politically speaking: gone were the Sikh lords of the Punjab, the Nawabs of Oudh in the north and of Arcot in the south, and many another ruler in between. In some areas they were followed into limbo by what Stokes has called 'the second line of the political élite', the former rural magnates who could not successfully transmute themselves into the revenue-collecting *zamindars* required by the British.[23] But under the old rulers there had also been an élite literate in the local languages, or in Persian, derived from Brahmin, writer and other upper castes. Some of these adapted by becoming early members of the new English-educated élite. On the neo-Machiavellian view of Indian political history, Indian 'nationalism' was a matter of the pressure exerted on the British by these English-educated élites which were divided among themselves, self-interested and intensely competitive; and which drew their power from their ability to understand and to utilize the pressures coming from other elements in rural and urban society and to convert them into pressures on the Raj. Thus some of the Chitpavan Brahmins of Poona, prominent in the period of Mahratta rule, moved into English education and on into the public service, the professions and eventually politics, especially when these warmed up after the turn of the century. They played a crucial part in Congress and its splits and protests; and Congress had intricate links in Maharashtra that were parochial, provincial and 'national', and so over the years became known more widely to a highly disparate constituency.

Across India in the United Provinces, by the late 1880s threads went back from the local Congress to wealthy city notables thoroughly embedded in 'traditional' society, who (contrary to contemporary British views that Congress was no more than a set of disaffected *déracinés*) used it to publicize their interests and grievances. These same notables were prominent in acts of conspicuous piety, especially the financing of Hindu religious institutions. Hence Congress rhetoric had itself to be conveyed in Hindu terms and this contributed to the alienation from it of local Muslim leaders.

But it is for the Madras Presidency that the work of David Washbrook and Christopher Baker has given us the most vivid picture yet to emerge of politics at local and provincial levels under the Raj: though some of their colouring remains controversial. They hold that the Madras Presidency, far from being the most lethargic of the provinces during the nineteenth century, untouched as it was by the Rebellion of 1857, was alive with evolving political activity of a kind that came to foreshadow a number of developments characterizing the South in independent India. In Madras the British had destroyed the old warrior élite of that highly varied territory; and early relied for *raiyatwari* revenue collection and local administration through village headmen on members of locally dominant castes whom Washbrook has called 'rural-local bosses'. Politics at that time were very much a matter of the locality, of the means by which those who, through dominance in landholding, held economic, and thus political power in the villages though there were regional differences. But from the 1870s onwards the provincial government began to interfere much more in local affairs, forcing the 'rural-local bosses' to take it more seriously when planning their political strategies. And, with the introduction in the 1880s of local boards and committees for various purposes, and with the improvement of communications, the increased commercialization of agriculture and other economic changes, the 'bosses' began to operate in a wider arena. From the same period dates the proliferation of new horizontal organizations, including caste associations of the sort mentioned in Chapter 2, and communal (including Muslim) organizations, some of them at any rate reflecting categories invented or used by the British. By 1920 some of the 'bosses' were dominating new official district-level bodies and had begun even to enter the Legislative Council.

Meanwhile, some of the Tamil Brahmins (and, slowly, other castes) became English-educated, and set themselves up as intermediaries between the provincial government and both 'rural-local bosses' and city magnates. For various reasons the English-educated élite was in Madras less hostile to the Raj than its counterparts in Bengal and Bombay; and this may have something to do with the Presidency's reputation for quietude and torpor. Members of the new élite worked (on the Washbrook thesis, predominantly for reasons of self-interest) not only through the Legislative Council but also through the University and the High Court; and were prone to nepotism, factionalism and shifting alliances. In time they appear as members of various nascent political parties, including the Congress (which gave them a link with national politics) and the Justice Party, which links backward to the anti-Brahmin movement and forward through various transmutations and vicissitudes to the important regional party, the DMK (Dravida Munnetra Kazhagam) of recent politics.

The Justice Party was indeed the only political party willing to work the new Montagu–Chelmsford constitution of 1920, and it did so for a decade. But Congress in the 1920s and early 1930s was rebuilt, and became the channel for all kinds of dissidence in the new political climate; and in the later 1930s grew in importance. Like the Raj itself, it came, not without travail, to link locality to province and province to nation: in the 1920s and 1930s it spread markedly into localities. This structural aspect of Congress is something to be returned to in discussion of post-independence politics.

Ceylon has so far not received the ministrations of the neo-Machiavellians; and is too small to exhibit all levels of political activity from locality to province and nation. However, recent studies have enlivened the plain tale of constitutional advance to representative government and independence, and towards institutions of local government, by relating political change to movements in local societies.[24] Superficially there are parallels with India, especially the South. Thus the colonial government used local notables as village headmen and middle-level administrators, and indeed threw its weight on their side in their conflict with the *parvenus* of the coastal castes. And Ceylon developed its own English-educated élite which became prominent in many associations and movements, particularly Buddhist revivalism, and pressures for more representative government. But this élite was more varied in composition, by caste, community and religion, than that in most parts of India; rather than acting as brokers for local notables, absorbed many of them, first in the Low Country and Jaffna, later in the Kandyan hills, last of all in the Dry Zone; held a monopoly of politics at the national level; and often scorned, rather than cultivated links with the villages, till Bandaranaike forged his crucial relationship with frustrated vernacular-educated rural leaders.

Ceylon had, on the face of it, a far easier journey to independence, so much so that the country and students of it hardly noticed the difference on 4 February 1948. But there had been Sinhala–Tamil wrangles over constitutional reform; and the discontents of the Sinhala village leaders lay only just beneath the calm surface to erupt in communal violence in the years after 1956.

Looking back at the subcontinent as a whole, much work remains to be done before the whole complex of changing political relationships between Raj and society has been evaluated everywhere, within whatever framework of ideas; and before the historical *fons et origo* of political traits in post-independence South Asia can be uncovered. Nowhere outside the Madras Presidency has work so detailed as that of Washbrook and Baker been done. We know something of the other two Presidencies and of the United Provinces. But there remain sketchy outlines or isolated shafts of light elsewhere; and we know little of politics in the princely states, yet there must have been politics, however traditional and fossilized under some rulers. Where we do know something of political evolution under the Raj, we must be struck by the variety of responses to colonial rule, itself far from uniformly applied. This variety is not surprising given the rich social and economic diversity of the subcontinent and the variable rates and directions of social and educational change. Enough is known too, though puzzles remain for solution, to enable one to hazard explanations of such phenomena as the package of mixed, if not mutually contradictory ideologies with which the Congress Party entered independence; the competitive faction-fighting and frequent regrouping, the possession of massive vote banks that have dismayed starry-eyed western liberals and socialists who thought that the lofty ideals of Nehru and the ordered processes of Westminster would characterize 'the world's greatest democracy'; the rise of regional parties like the DMK in what is now Tamil Nadu, yet within an overall Indian political system; the recurrent communal tensions in Sri Lanka; and the anachronisms of Nepal.

Enough has been said, moreover, to raise the question of the nature of Indian nationalism. Is India one nation, or two, or many? Are Muslims a separate nation? If so, in what sense? Some of the threads in Muslim separatism have already entered the fabric of our story. But others deserve separate treatment.

Muslim separatism

It is, in my view, a simplistic distortion of history during the British period to trace an ever-widening gap between Muslims and other Indians, or a continuously gathering momentum in the desire of Muslims for separate political treatment, culminating inevitably in partition. Muslim separatism has a history of a century or more, in the course of which, under such influences as changing British perceptions and policies, and shifting relations between government, Muslim leaders and organizations, and other political bodies (notably Congress) the issue appeared in one form or another, then receded for a while, until it reached what many Muslims (and others) would until quite near the end of the story have seen as a surprising dénouement: partition and the emergence of Pakistan.[25]

First, however, it is important to ask, in elaboration of what has been said in Chapter 2, 'Who were these Indian Muslims?' The answer is that throughout the British period, though with some changes over time, they were highly varied, not only in terms of origin and sectarian allegiance, but also in terms of social and economic status. At one extreme was the old élite of areas like UP, stripped of the power that they or their ancestors had held under the Mughals and their successors; but in many cases retaining land and influence in the villages, and, in some cases, subordinate offices under the Raj. At the other extreme, and most notably in Bengal, were poor tenant cultivators, mostly holding land from Hindus. In between came a wide range of people, varying from area to area, but including cultivators, traders, and weavers, as well as *ulamas* (men learned in Islamic religious knowledge, who were at a great intellectual distance from illiterate Muslims of village and town, whom some see as practising a 'folk' Islam with accretions from Hinduism). The British came by the last decades of the nineteenth century, however, to see these highly varied Indian Muslims as a 'community', as an entity contrasting strongly and simply with Hindus because of such factors as their monotheism; their supposed social equality under Islam; and their presumed memory of their days as rulers of all (or most) of India, which was apt to make the British anxious. It was to a considerable extent this British perception of a monolithic Muslim bloc that helped to make Indian Muslims feel that they *were* an entity. The self-image of at least the new, small group of western-educated Muslims came to match that perception. And it was the felt need of the Raj to 'divide and rule' (as some see it) or at any rate to 'balance and rule' (as others, including Peter Hardy see it) that further strengthened a Muslim sense of identity.

But the Muslim self-image was complicated, and Muslim aspirations and actions confused because of controversy about the nature of an Islamic polity; especially when the *ulama* came to be involved in politics. Was India under the Raj *dar-ul-Islam*, 'the abode of Islam', where Islamic law (the *sharia*) was in force? Or was it *dar-ul-harb*, 'the abode of war', not under Islamic law and government based thereon, and to be made so, if necessary by force? If the former, where did the Raj fit into the classical scheme of things, which envisaged *dar-ul-Islam* under a pious Muslim ruler — if not the universal *khalifa* (caliph) of early times, then a sultan acting as his deputy in a specific territory? And at a later stage there was the confusing effect on the Muslim conception of Islamic polity of essentially western ideas of nationhood. (We shall see that controversy over the Islamic polity, particularly about the nature of an Islamic republic, still continues in and about Pakistan.)

Now when the 1857 Rebellion and its aftermath were over and done with, there eventually came about something of a Muslim–British reconciliation: partly, no doubt, because of 'balance and rule' policies, partly because of the ideas and work of Muslims like Sir Syed Ahmed Khan, the founder of what was to become Aligarh Muslim

University, for he and his like had no doubts about the legitimacy and benefits of British rule. Muslims, especially the western-educated from Aligarh, grew in community-consciousness, which was recognized and enhanced by the British in the 1880s by the nomination of Muslims to local boards and, twenty years later, by the creation of separate Muslim electorates; and further enhanced by competition for jobs with educated Hindus, and by communal friction and disturbances. Some Muslims joined Congress; others, Muslim associations. By this time several different categories of Indian Muslims (with those from UP usually in the lead) had drawn closer together politically: but there was no unanimity about strategy or tactics; the politically active were still largely the English-educated; there was (as in so many political arenas) suspicion of 'smart-alecs' from Bengal; and the Muslim League was for some years after its foundation in 1906 'a feeble and under-weight suckling', to quote Hardy.

Violent Hindu reaction to Curzon's partition of Bengal (seen as favourable to some Muslim claims) further exacerbated communal differences. And educated Muslims began to be affected by the pan-Islamic movement, itself a reaction to European imperialism and its treatment of Muslims in the Middle East and North Africa. New political linkages were forged when younger Muslims, impatient with the pro-British stance of their seniors, allied with the *ulama*, who had ties with the Muslim masses notwithstanding their intellectual distance from them. In 1911 Muhammad Iqbal, the notable Urdu poet–philosopher and already a force in the Punjab, proclaimed that the Muslims were a 'nation', albeit with a peculiar uniting bond. But in 1916 there came the 'Lucknow Pact' under which Congress accepted the idea of separate communal electorates in the provinces. In the next few years Muslims and Congress were further brought together by the assiduous work of Gandhi and by joint agitation over the allied conquest of Turkey and hence of its ruler, seen as the *khalifa*. At this time, though there were many currents of opinion, one prominent view was that of Maulana Kalam Azad (who went on to become Minister of Education in independent India) that, while Hindus and Muslims should work together against the British, free India should be a federation of religious communities: Muslims were 'not to form a separate state'.

Post-war developments (p. 50) strengthened calls for a combined movement against the British. However, with the collapse of the joint agitation following the abolition of the caliphate by the revolutionary

Turkish National Assembly, and given also a number of developments within India, communal antagonisms were once more
sharpened (though Gandhi at all times preached communal harmony). Jinnah finally parted company with Congress in 1920. For
several years Muslim politics were in a state of division, even
confusion. There was some drawing away from separatism in 1927,
when Congress agreed to a package deal put forward by Muslim
members of legislatures under which, *inter alia*, joint electorates were
conceded in return for the attainment of other Muslim objectives; and
the Muslim League itself split over the attitudes to be taken to the
statutory (Simon) commission then in India. In 1929 Jinnah, on
behalf of the then reunited League, proposed his 'Fourteen Points',
under which there was to be *inter alia* a federal constitution with
guaranteed power for Muslims in majority, and safeguards in
minority, provinces. These were rejected by Congress. Then came the
events leading up to the India Act of 1935, with the British plan for a
federation. But Muslim fears of Hindu domination in a new India
were not calmed. There still continued a certain confusion among
educated Muslims about political ideology and goals. Amid the
confusion, however, a number of movements gave linkages, which
Jinnah was to utilize, to wider constituencies.

The name Pakistan had been invented in 1933 by a Punjabi student
in Cambridge, Chaudhuri Rahmat Ali, for a fully independent
Muslim territory, to include Punjab, the Frontier Province, Baluchistan and Kashmir, which he regarded as the home of a separate nation
and 'no part of India'. It was not until 1937 that he advanced a similar
claim for the Muslim majority areas of Bengal. After 1937, too, Jinnah
set about reviving the Muslim League, astutely exploiting linkages
and capitalizing on a variety of grievances and of Congress activities
which might be construed as foreshadowing a Hindu Raj; and
endeavouring to overcome opposition among Muslims, particularly in
Punjab (still dominated by the Unionist Party) and in Bengal, where,
as in other Muslim-majority Provinces, his League fared badly, even
disastrously in the 1937 elections. Jinnah's real base was in the
Muslim-*minority* United Provinces. Then, on 23 March 1940, Jinnah
having declared that the Muslims of India were a nation needing a
homeland, the League passed what became known as 'the Pakistan
resolution', declaring *inter alia* that '... the areas in which the Muslims
are numerically in a majority should be grouped to constitute
"independent states" ...'. The wording of the whole resolution is not

without vagueness and ambiguity; though the underlying principle —
partition — is clear enough. But some see the resolution as an overbid
and, to change the metaphor, ultimate partition as Jinnah hoist with
his own petard.

Be that as it may, Congress reactions were not completely hostile,
much as its leaders subscribed to the one-nation theory. Gandhi said
that although he would oppose partition non-violently, he 'could not
forcibly resist the proposed partition if the Muslims really insisted
upon it'. Jinnah and the League meanwhile gained strength (though
still not dominant in Punjab till 1946). The League forged links with
many new groups of Muslims, and did well in elections held in 1946.
Congress, however, still sought to inherit an independent and
undivided India; while the British government, though by this time
sensing the need for concessions to League demands, hankered after
some sort of federation of Muslim and other areas, linked at the
summit. After tortuous negotiations with the British, Jinnah and the
League withdrew and decided on 'direct action'. This released
pent-up communal emotions in Calcutta and elsewhere, and wild
violence ensued. Further negotiations brought only deadlock.
Mountbatten arrived as Viceroy and, finally but swiftly, came the plan
for the transfer of power to two separate Dominions, India and
Pakistan (in two wings, West and East), with conditional provision for
the partition of Punjab and Bengal, the actual boundary to be settled
by commissions. This gave Jinnah less than he had apparently been
playing for; but he, and Congress, agreed to the plan, both with
reluctance (though for different reasons).

Thus did independence and partition come on 15 August 1947. To
some citizens of Pakistan and pro-Pakistan scholars, partition was the
inevitable result of history. To others, it appears as a solution
ultimately difficult, if not impossible to avoid; yet it is not easy to say
when it became so. But it is clear that to have included the Muslim
majority areas in an undivided independent India would have left
great tensions to be resolved in the new state, to say nothing of the
problems surrounding the notion (or notions) of a Muslim polity. Yet
the tensions were not completely solved by partition, because of the
large number of Muslims left as a minority in India. It is particularly
ironical that the Muslims of UP, some of whom played such a
dominant part in the evolution of separatism, are left outside
Pakistan, to say nothing of the sizeable communities in West Bengal,
old Hyderabad State, Kerala and elsewhere; while parts of Punjab and

Bengal, whose Muslim politicians long resisted the League, fell to Pakistan and suffered partition from India.

But the narrative of separatism and partition is not yet quite told. Two days after the inauguration of independence, there came the award of the Boundary Commissions for Punjab and Bengal. Although accepted by the two new states, it increased communal tension and infuriated the Sikhs, who found their historic homeland bisected. Many Hindus and Sikhs attempted to leave West Pakistan for India, and Muslims to move from India to West Pakistan. In the highly-charged communal atmosphere of the time, large numbers of those who tried to move were massacred, Sikhs and Hindus by Muslims, Muslims by Hindus and Sikhs. The Punjab was the worse affected area, but there were parallel movements to and from East Pakistan. The two new countries were thus faced with an extremely difficult situation at the outset of their independence.

Something like 7.4 million people, however, succeeded in moving from Pakistan to India, and 7.2 million from India to Pakistan.[26] Migrations of Hindus from East Pakistan continued in waves long after partition. The rehabilitation and resettlement of these vast numbers of peoples put a severe strain on the newly independent governments.

The Boundary Commission for Punjab under Sir Cyril (later Lord) Radcliffe were given these terms of reference: 'To demarcate the boundaries of the two parts of the Punjab, on the basis of ascertaining the contiguous majority areas of Muslims and non-Muslims. In doing so it will also take into account other factors.' The Commission for Bengal, also under Sir Cyril, had similar terms of reference. The Commissions in fact drew boundaries that cut across lines of communication, and, in some cases in Punjab, separated the headworks of irrigation canals from the irrigated areas. But the economic and other consequences of partition in general and of the new boundaries in particular; the eruption of the Kashmir dispute and of other problems associated with the accession of princely states to India or to Pakistan; the whole difficult course of relations between India and Pakistan; and the severance of Bangladesh, the former East Pakistan, from the western wing — all of these matters belong properly to ensuing chapters.

References

1 Stokes, E. (1978) *The Peasant and the Raj: Studies in Agrarian Society and Peasant Rebellion in India*, Cambridge, Chapter I, especially p. 26;

Marshall, P. J. (1981) '"A free though conquering people": Britain and Asia in the eighteenth century', an Inaugural Lecture, London; Kumar, D. (ed.) (1982) *The Cambridge Economic History of India*, Vol. 2, Cambridge.

2 Schwartzberg, J. E. (ed.) (1978) *A Historical Atlas of South Asia*, Chicago and London, 125–6, 247–8; Murphey, R. (1977) *The Outsiders: The Western Experience in India and China*, Ann Arbor, 109–11.

3 Farmer, B. H. (1974) *Agricultural Colonization in India since Independence*, London, 10–15.

4 Morris, M. D. *et al.* (1969) *Indian Economy in the Nineteenth Century: A Symposium*, Delhi; Kumar, D. (ed.) (1982) *The Cambridge Economic History of India*, Vol. 2, Cambridge.

5 Blyn, G. (1966) *Agricultural Trends in India, 1891–1947: Output, Availability and Productivity*, Philadelphia and London; Islam, M. M. (1978) *Bengal Agriculture, 1920–1946: a Quantitative Study*, Cambridge; Baker, C. J. (1980) 'Review of Islam (1978)', *Modern Asian Studies*, 14, 513–18.

6 Hardy, P. (1972) *The Muslims of British India*, Cambridge, 42–50; Stokes, E. (1978) op. cit.; Kumar, Dharma (1965) *Land and Caste in South India: Agricultural Labour in Madras Presidency in the Nineteenth Century*, Cambridge.

7 Béteille, A. (1980) 'The Indian village: past and present', in Hobsbawm, E. J. *et al.* (eds), *Peasants in History: Essays in Honour of Daniel Thorner*, Calcutta.

8 Farmer, B. H. (1957) *Pioneer Peasant Colonization in Ceylon*, London, 81–2, 109–12.

9 Morris, M. D. *et al.* (1969) op. cit.; Macpherson, W. J. (1972) 'Economic development in India under the British Crown, 1858–1947', in Youngson, A. J. (ed.), *Economic Development in the Long Run*, London, 126–91; Morris, M. D. (1974) 'Private industrial investment on the Indian subcontinent, 1900–1939', *Modern Asian Studies*, 8, 535–55.

10 Farmer, B. H. (1957) op. cit., Chapter 4; Snodgrass, D. R. (1966) *Ceylon: an Export Economy in Transition*, Homewood, Ill.

11 Spear, P. (1972) *India: A Modern History*, 2nd edn, Ann Arbor.

12 Seal, A. (1968) *The Emergence of Indian Nationalism: Competition and Collaboration in the Later Nineteenth Century*, Cambridge, Chapter 2.

13 De Silva, C. R. (1977) in De Silva, K. M. (ed.), *Sri Lanka: A Survey*, London, 405.

14 Schwartzberg, J. E. (ed.) (1978) op. cit., p. 104.

15 Stokes, E. (1978) op. cit., Chapter 1.

16 Rudolph, L. I. and Rudolph, S. H. (1967) *The Modernity of Tradition: Political Development in India*, Chicago and London.

17 Singer, M. (1971) 'Beyond tradition and modernity in Madras', *Comparative Studies in Society and History*, 13, 160–95.

18 Farmer, B. H. (1963) *Ceylon: A Divided Nation*, London.

19 Macfarlane, A. (1976) *Resources and Population: A Study of the Gurungs of Nepal*, Cambridge.
20 Spear, P. (1961) *India: A Modern History*, Ann Arbor, 341.
21 Spear, P. (1961) op. cit., pp. 353–6.
22 Stokes, E. (1978) op. cit., pp. 269–70; Seal, A. (1968) op. cit.; Johnson, G. (1973) *Provincial Politics and Indian Nationalism: Bombay and the Indian National Congress 1880–1915*, Cambridge; Bayly, C. A. (1973) 'Patrons and politics in northern India', *Modern Asian Studies*, 7, 349–88; Baker, C. J. (1976) *The Politics of South India 1920–1937*, Cambridge; Washbrook, D. A. (1976) *The Emergence of Provincial Politics: The Madras Presidency 1870–1920*, Cambridge; Baker, C. J. *et al.* (eds) (1981) *Power, Profit and Politics*, ten papers in *Modern Asian Studies*, 15, 355–721.
23 Stokes, E. (1978) op. cit., p. 63.
24 De Silva, K. M. (1977) in De Silva, K. M. (ed.), *Sri Lanka: A Survey*, London; Roberts, M. (1981) *Caste Conflict and Elite Information: The Rise of a Karava Elite in Sri Lanka, 1500–1931*, Cambridge.
25 Hardy, P. (1972) *The Muslims of British India*, Cambridge; is an excellent general work, from which the account given here of the evolution of Muslim politics is largely derived. See also: Robinson, F. (1974) *Separatism among Indian Muslims: The Politics of the United Provinces Muslims, 1860–1923*, Cambridge; Jalal, A. and Seal, A. (1981) 'Alternative to partition: Muslim politics between the wars', 415–54 in Baker, C. J. *et al.* op. cit. For a more pro-Pakistan (and especially pro-Jinnah) account see: Rushbrook Williams, L. F. (1966) *The State of Pakistan*, London.
26 Spate, O. H. K. and Learmonth, A. T. A. (1967) *India and Pakistan*, 3rd edn, London, 129–30.

4 POLITICAL DEVELOPMENTS WITHIN SOUTH ASIA SINCE INDEPENDENCE

This chapter will be concerned, first, with problems of internal political geography; that is, of the organization of territory within South Asia, beginning with one that was solved with relative ease and with stable results, namely, the absorption of the princely states into India and Pakistan; and moving on to an exception to this generalization — Kashmir, a bone of contention between the two countries to this day. There follows a discussion of another dispute between the two neighbours, over water rather than land, that concerning the Indus waters.

We then turn to the internal territorial problems of Pakistan: tensions between East and West wings, leading to the secession of the former, to become Bangladesh; and to other problems of potential secession or at any rate of separatism or increased local autonomy. (By secession I mean formal withdrawal from a country's political system; by separatism I mean a movement in favour of separate existence within such a system; by increased local autonomy I mean a higher degree of self-government within such a system; and by irredentism I mean the advocacy of political union with groups held to be similar on linguistic or other grounds but presently within a different country.) Similar problems will then be taken up for India and (briefly) Sri Lanka and Nepal.

Discussion then moves on to an examination of the contrasting political histories and political systems of independent India, Sri Lanka, Pakistan and Bangladesh, and of modern Nepal and Bhutan (in that order).

The absorption of the princely states

The Indian Empire came to include, in addition to its British-administered provinces, over 600 princely states, covering a quarter of the area and accounting for more than a fifth of the population, and varying from giants like Hyderabad and Mysore, as big as a

European country, to tiny principalities covering a few square miles only. Each of them had some kind of treaty relationship with the British, and each recognized British suzerainty. From this suzerainty they were released at independence, leaving them theoretically free to decide their future allegiance. The twelve states falling within the borders of Pakistan (including Bahawalpur, Khairpur and the states of Baluchistan) had Muslim rulers and largely Muslim peoples; they readily joined Pakistan. The situation facing India was a much more difficult one for a number of reasons: the size and tradition of quasi-independence of the larger states; the range of internal economic and social conditions, from relatively progressive and advanced states like Mysore to those with overwhelmingly tribal populations owing allegiance to rulers whom they invested with divine qualities (as in the case of Bastar, north-east of the Godavari in the eastern Deccan); and states where the ruler was of a different religious persuasion from the mass of his subjects.

However, through the vigorous and not particularly kid-gloved activities of the Congress politician, Sirdar Vallabhbhai Patel, ably assisted by a remarkable Civil Servant, V.P. Menon, most of the rulers were persuaded to accede to the Indian Union.[1] In return they were guaranteed their privy purses and personal privileges, later abolished by Mrs Gandhi. Thus ended what many Indians had come to regard as an anachronism and what was certainly the result of the arresting, by the British, of a kaleidoscopic political map made up of very many fragments which had only fallen into a static pattern for relatively short periods when some great ruler had given a higher degree of internal unity. Certainly too, the simplification of the internal political map in the early months of independence was a great achievement; and provided the base from which further change was to proceed. Some princely territories were simply absorbed into surrounding States (I shall use a capital initial letter for the units that made up, or make up the Indian Union). Some were grouped with neighbouring princely territories to form new units that were to prove no more than transient: for example 'Pepsu' (Punjab and East Punjab States Union), Madhya Bharat (mainly in the Malwa Plateau) and Vindhya Pradesh (in hill areas south of eastern UP). Except for Hyderabad, Jammu and Kashmir (to receive special treatment in a moment), only Mysore retained its identity when Patel had completed his activities in 1947 and 1948.

Difficulties arose, however, over Hyderabad, the small state of Junagadh (Junagarh) in the Kathiawar peninsula, and Jammu and

Kashmir. The Nizam of Hyderabad was a Muslim supported by a Muslim governing élite and ruling over a mainly Hindu population, and conscious both of his membership of an ancient dynasty and of the special relationship he had always had with the British. He understood that, landlocked as his state was, he could not ignore developments in India, but nevertheless he vacillated, hankering after independence. Initial negotiations ended in a standstill agreement to run for a year, during the course of which the Congress organized agitation; some of the Muslims of Hyderabad formed an armed body called the Razakars; and amid the mounting disorder the Communists got control of two districts. Before the year was over further negotiations broke down and Indian troops marched in to take over the state in what was officially described as a 'police action'. Pakistan was not surprisingly incensed by this action against a Muslim ruler and his supporters.

Perhaps one should also recall here the annexation by India of Goa and other Portuguese territories after military action taken in December 1961, contrasting with the cession by France of its Indian territories after peaceful negotiations; and add that the little Himalayan state of Sikkim, which previously had a 'special protected relationship' with India (as it had earlier with the Indian Empire) became a State of the Indian Union in May 1975.

Junagadh, like Hyderabad, had a Hindu population and a Muslim prince who, though his state was set entirely in Indian territory, acceded to Pakistan. India marched in and held a plebiscite which resulted in a vote for union with India, which then ensued. Pakistan protested without effect. The Kashmir situation was much more complicated and long-lasting, and deserves a separate section.

The Kashmir problem

The state of Jammu and Kashmir covered over 80,000 sq. miles of highly varied population and terrain. It had been put together by Maharajara Gulab Singh, a Dogra Rajput (and a Hindu), during the Sikh Wars of the mid-nineteenth century. It included Jammu, the rulers' home base in Dogra territory; Kashmir proper, around Srinagar, with mainly Muslim population but an important Brahmin community (to which the Nehrus originally belonged); Ladakh, a high plateau area bordering Tibet, with a sparse, Mahayana Budhist population; and the Frontier Districts of the north-west, including Baltistan and Gilgit, with mainly Muslim peoples. Before independence both the Muslim League and allies of Nehru and the Congress (in the shape of Sheikh Abdullah and his followers) were active in the state: as partition drew near, the former favoured accession to Pakistan, the latter to India. Faced with the same choice as his brother princes, the Maharaja vacillated, and seems to have thought, like the Nizam, of independence. Meanwhile a revolt broke out, first in Gilgit, then in Baltistan; its leaders declared independence from the Maharaja and allegiance to Pakistan (which was accepted). Soon there was rebellion also in south-western Kashmir proper, where Muslims declared 'Azad Kashmir' (Free Kashmir) and established links, which India accused Pakistan of encouraging, with tribesmen in the North-west Frontier areas of Pakistan who proceeded to invade Kashmir proper. At last, by now thoroughly beleaguered and with invaders very near Srinagar, the Maharaja acceded to India (on 26 October 1947). Indian troops were sent in and the tribal incursion halted; and Sheikh Abdullah set up an interim administration. The Indian Army was deployed against Azad Kashmir as well as against the tribesmen, and soon Pakistani regular forces were brought in. So, lamentably soon after independence and partition, the two new countries, both members of the Commonwealth, were engaged in hostilities, which in fact continued until after protracted and complex negotiations a ceasefire was agreed on 30 December 1948. The ceasefire line, dating originally from 29 July 1949 but later modified, has become a *de facto* international frontier, separating the Indian State of Jammu and Kashmir from the Pakistan-held territory of Azad Kashmir. To this day neither country recognizes the jurisdiction of the other over the former territories of the Maharaja. A plebiscite, agreed to in principle by India, has never been held; and when, in 1953, Sheikh Abdullah revived the proposal and claimed special status for Kashmir, he (though he had been Chief Minister for six years) was imprisoned. The Kashmir Assembly did, however, in 1957 declare the state to be an integral part of India, without prejudice to India's claim to the whole former princely state, though anti-Indian movements in Kashmir are by no means dead. The whole Kashmir imbroglio has poisoned relations between India and Pakistan, who in fact fought their second war (that of 1965) largely as a result of new tensions in Kashmir, though there had been a separate dispute over boundaries in the Rann of Kutch, involving armed clashes, in the winter of 1964–5.

Barrels of ink have been spilt in controversy over the Kashmir dispute. But the dispute is basically a clash between two principles: that of self-determination in the shape of the right of Muslim majority areas contiguous to Pakistan to accede to it; and that of the right of a recognized ruler, in this case the Maharaja of Jammu and Kashmir, to accede to a territorial union, that of India. In invoking the second principle India would appear to have the law on its side (though it did not recognize that principle in the cases of Hyderabad and Junagadh). It is sometimes said that Nehru's Kashmiri descent made him particularly unbending over Kashmir; but this is probably not a serious factor. What *is* serious still is the strategic importance of Kashmir vis-à-vis both Russia and China (as we shall see in the next chapter). What *was* serious in the earlier years of the imbroglio, and might become serious again, is the position of Kashmir in relation to the headwaters of the Indus river system, to the dispute over which we now turn.

The Indus waters dispute[2]

The construction of major irrigation canals dependent on the tributaries of the Indus (Jhelum, Chenab, Ravi, Sutlej and Beas) and the establishment of colonization schemes in the Punjab, the land of those five rivers, was one of the great achievemenets of the British period. The Indo–Pakistan frontier was so drawn (with an eye primarily to contiguous Muslim majority districts) as to leave the headworks of certain canals vital to Pakistan in Indian territory: notably the Madhopur works on the Ravi and the Ferozepur works on the Sutlej. The threat to Pakistan became greater with developments in Kashmir, for the Indus, Jhelum and Chenab pass through Indian-held territory there. Following the hostilities in Kashmir, the supply of water from Madhopur and Ferozepore was indeed cut off, though it remains a matter of dispute on whose orders and at what level. As a consequence, it is said, cultivation failed on a million acres of land in Pakistan. Nehru in fact intervened to settle this particular incident; but the general question of water-ownership and water-use that lay behind it became a matter of bitter controversy between India and Pakistan. In the event, and after protracted negotiation, the dispute was settled following an initiative taken by the World Bank. The result was the Indus Waters Treaty signed on 19 September 1960, and a permanent Indus Waters Commission. Under the Treaty, and in broad terms, Pakistan is assigned the waters of the Indus, Jhelum and Chenab for use in its Punjab plains and India the waters of the remaining three rivers. To make Pakistan's canals independent of these three rivers, massive works have been constructed within Pakistan to take Indus and Jhelum water boldly across country — at great capital expense. India, with Ravi, Sutlej and Beas water no longer needed in Pakistan, has been able to construct new works designed to irrigate large areas including the colonization schemes in Haryana and Rajasthan.[3] All this is often held up as a positive measure of co-operation between India and Pakistan, who have quarrelled so violently over so much else; and indeed it is. It is also held up as a shining example of international helpfulness, for finance for new works came from the World Bank and from a number of western industrialized countries as well as from India and Pakistan. But there is also no gainsaying the fact that an economically optimum solution to the problem of utilizing the Indus waters would have arrived at a very different pattern, without the expensive interriver works in Pakistan (notwithstanding that these were to some extent foreshadowed by the British Triple Canals Project (1905–17), with its bold transfer of water from the Jhelum to the Chenab and on to the Ravi to feed the Lower Bari Doab Canal). The simple fact is that an expensive solution was forced by the layout of the new political boundaries in relation to the rivers and their dependent canals. Moreover, India's new Rajasthan Canal, made possible by the allocation to it of Sutlej and Beas waters, is itself a doubtful proposition in economic terms;[4] though significantly, it will (if and when completed) provide along the border with Pakistan a belt of irrigated and settled country to replace desert and semidesert, ideal tank country.

East Pakistan becomes Bangladesh

Ian Stephens, a great friend of Pakistan, wrote in 1968:

> Regarded simply as land ... Pakistan seems about the craziest political structure that mankind could have devised. ... For though she is a unitary national state ... she nevertheless consists of two entirely separate blocks of territory placed about 1,000 miles apart — and with another, bigger and stronger, and more often than not unfriendly block, India, sandwiched between.[5]

Was, then, the secession of East Pakistan in 1972 merely a matter of strain occasioned by physical separation, in spite of the distance-reducing effects of radio and the aeroplane? Even if one accepts that the strain was increased by the existence of geographical contrast without the complementarity that may go with it (of the sort that classical French geographers never ceased to emphasize in the case of their country); and was compounded too by the cultural and linguistic differences between Bengalis and West Pakistanis (the latter by no means uniform, as we shall have occasion to stress): even if one accepts all this, then one still would have rather too simple a view of the forces at work.

There has, indeed, been considerable controversy on this matter. Some Pakistanis, and some of their staunch western friends like L.F. Rushbrook Williams, see the separation as basically the result of discontent fostered and fed by an India never reconciled to partition, which went on to arm guerilla bands of Bengalis, and, on 20 November 1971, to mount a full-scale invasion.[6] Rushbrook Williams sees India's hands freed to take military action by the Indo–Soviet Treaty of August 1971; and Russia, indeed, as lurking only just off-stage. He further sees western liberal opinion, for the most part firmly behind Bangladesh and its 'liberation', as deluded by clever Indian propaganda, particularly about Pal バングラデッシュ a 中 9 (@) eastern wing, and about the magnitude of th 気軍 (パキスタン) by India.

One writes near to the events. But the truth seems to involve a number of factors over and above those already enumerated and dismissed as simplistic: factors resulting from insensitivity, incapacity and other failings on the part of successive governments of Pakistan. Some of these are, indeed, admitted by certain western writers favourable to Pakistan; though they usually failed, if writing in the 1960s, to see secession as likely (perhaps, they would say, because they reckoned without massive India intervention). Ian Stephens did, however, write in 1968 that 'Permanent disgruntlement of the East Wing would be Pakistan's death-blow.[7]

And disgruntlement there was a-plenty, and with reason. Because of the relatively low number of Bengali Muslim public servants at partition, many officials were brought from West Pakistan, and some of these despised Bengalis and were insensitive to their feelings. Industrialists and businessmen too, came in from the West wing, replacing Hindus who went to India on partition, and became dominant. Again, Bengalis are strongly attached to their language, and proud of the very considerable literature in it. Jinnah's wish that

Urdu should be the national language of the whole of Pakistan was interpreted over-zealously, and the language question became a burning issue. A government decision in 1954 to recognize Bengali also as a national language came too late. The original capital was Karachi; and the idea of declaring Dacca as a 'second capital' also came too late — and the associated symbolic buildings remained uncompleted at secession. East Pakistanis, too, came to believe that it was *their* wing that earned foreign exchange and massive government revenue, from both of which the West wing, with its evident industrialization, benefitted more than they did. Some Dacca economists went so far as to proclaim that their wing was being exploited by the west as if it were a colonial possession.

Discontent grew when military rule came to Pakistan in October, 1958; and broke out in student unrest and political violence; and an underground movement became ever stronger (with what degree and kind of encouragement from India remaining, as we have seen, a matter of controversy). Matters came to a head when, in November 1970, the relief of distress and loss caused by a devastating cyclone in the Bengal delta was directed with many inadequacies from far away Islamabad, the new capital near Rawalpindi; and even more when in the following month a general election at last took place and resulted in a landslide victory for the Awami ('People's') League, Sheikh Mujibur Rahman's party, in the East and Mr Zulfigar Ali Bhutto's Pakistan People's Party (PPP) in the West. Thus were politics polarized between the two wings when at last they surfaced from under military rule. The part played by various political and military leaders in the ensuing crisis are also still a matter for argument. What is clear however is that the President and Chief Martial Law Administrator, General Yahya Khan, announced on 1 March 1971 that the National Assembly would not meet two days later as previously announced; that this precipitated violent demonstrations in East Pakistan; that the military regime then harshly clamped down there amid cries of 'Punjabi imperialism', proscribing the Awami League and arresting Sheikh Mujib; that millions of refugees fled to India and that a combination of guerilla activity and India intervention led eventually to the surrender of the Pakistani forces in the East, the release of Mujib, and the independence of Bangladesh early in 1972 (not recognized by Bhutto, who had taken over the Presidency from Yahya Khan, till 1974).

East Bengal, then, in which the Muslim League had its original home in 1906, became Bangladesh and seceded from Pakistan. It is, some may believe, representative of West Pakistani attitudes to Bengali Muslims, if not prophetic, that East Bengal was excluded from Iqbal's 'Northwestern Muslim State' and from Chaudhuri Rahmat Ali's original definition of Pakistan (though he envisaged most of Bengal and Assam as a separate 'Muslim fatherland' under the title 'Bang-i-Islam', and Hyderabad as a third, 'Usmanistan').[8]

Now Hafeez Malik, having cited these facts, goes on to say that 'the nationalisms of East and West Pakistan were destined to differ because the ideological conceptions and symbols in the divided state failed to generate mutual appeal';[9] while L. Ziring goes further and asserts that 'To many Pakistanis, the sense of nationalism remains rudimentary', provincialism being a stronger force, and leaders proving incapable of engendering national purpose.[10] He sees all too much of Pakistani 'nationalism' as negative: fear of Hindus in the subcontinent as a whole; fear of fellow-Pakistanis, Bengalis or Punjabis or Pathans, within the state. Leaders, he says, have provoked subnational controversy rather than promoting ideas of national interdependence which 'might well have avoided the agony of Bangladesh'. To secessionist and separatist tensions remaining in Pakistan after the severance of Bangladesh we shall return shortly. Meanwhile, what of these tensions within Bangladesh itself?

Superficially at any rate, Bangladesh is fortunate in having an overwhelmingly Bengali population with a strong sense of identity; though, in spite of waves of migration to India since partition, there are still substantial Hindu minorities (especially on the borders of West Bengal); and the so-called 'Biharis', Urdu-speaking Muslims who came over from India, by no means all from Bihar, presented a difficult problem because of their language and because, at the time of secession at any rate, they were thought to have pro-Pakistani sympathies and were shabbily treated. And some tribal minorities, especially in the Chittagong Hill Tracts east of the delta, have been restive and have been influenced by turbulence amongst tribal confrères across the frontier in north-eastern India. There is also the question of the nature of Bangladeshi 'nationalism'. Is it primarily Bengali, and secular as Sheikh Mujib proclaimed (some would say under Indian influence)? Or is it Muslim, while remaining distinctly Bengali? If the former, why does it not seek to unite all Bengalis, Hindus and Muslim, from West Bengal as well as Bangladesh? An 'Amra Bangali' movement was in fact formed in 1962 with the aim of uniting all Bengalis in Assam and Tripura as well as in West Bengal, Bangladesh, Bihar and Orissa. The movement has gone through various vicissitudes. Though it received an initial fillip from the independence of Bangladesh, it later declined; but in 1980 was said to be gaining strength again because of reaction to anti-Bengali feeling in Assam (yet to be discussed) and of West Bengal grievances against the Indian government. It remains, however, of a fringe, chauvinist nature.

Potential secession and separatism in Pakistan

It has already been hinted that the people of post-1972 Pakistan are 'by no means uniform', and that sub-national tensions remain in areas peripheral to the politically and demographically dominant Punjab. Such tensions may in fact be considered under three heads: Pushtu speakers and the Pakthunistan movement; the Baluchis (not entirely separable from the first); and the Sindhis.

It will be remembered that Pushtu speakers are to be found mainly along the North-west Frontier, including parts of Baluchistan, and straddle the boundary with Afghanistan. They include most of the turbulent Pathan tribesmen who caused so much trouble to the Raj as it pushed up into the hills and, in 1893, drew the Durand Line as a frontier with the buffer-state of Afghanistan, dividing the Pushtu-speakers (Pakhtuns) so that approximately two-thirds were on the British side of the line and one-third on the Afghan. Idiosyncratic political behaviour merging into separatism has long been characteristic of the area. Thus, in the years before independence, the 'Frontier Gandhi', Abdul Ghaffar Khan, was a close ally of the Congress Party and no friend of the Pakistan movement. In 1947, however, a referendum in the North-west Frontier Province resulted in an overwhelming vote in favour of joining Pakistan; but Abdul Ghaffar Khan's party boycotted the referendum. With the aid of his son, Abdul Wali Khan, he persistently proclaimed that the Pakhtuns are a nation deserving a territory of its own, Pakhtunistan (whose precise area varies between successive formulations, sometimes even including Baluchistan). He consistently agitated against Pakistan's rule, for long years from exile in Afghanistan, at other times from within Pakistan (where, for example, he formed the National Awami Party (NAP), not to be confused with Mujib's Awami League, in conjunction with certain Bengali leaders in Dacca in 1957). The attitude of the government of Afghanistan has wavered from time to time, but it has often supported the idea of Pakhtunistan; and drew fresh courage from the weakening of Pakistan by the secession of Bangladesh. There are those, too, who see the hand of India in the Pakhtunistan movement; while Russian influence in Afghanistan is clearly another dangerously complicating factor. Successive régimes in Pakistan over the years have done much to woo the tribesmen, not least by generous measures of economic and educational development. They appear to have acted more tactfully than in Bangladesh. But it is clear that their successors for the foreseeable future will have to deal not only with the age-old turbulence and lawlessness of the frontier, so familiar to the servants of the Raj, but also with the possibility of a secessionist-irredentist movement fomented from outside the boundaries of Pakistan, whatever the degree of internal support; or at any rate with attempts to extract the maximum degree of local autonomy.

Baluchistan, we have noted, has sometimes been included in the claims of the advocates of Pakhtunistan. But Baluchi separatism and secessionism deserve a paragraph to themselves because the Baluchis are a distinct group, to say nothing of the Brahui and other minorities; though, like the Pakhtuns, Baluchis also live across the Pakistan frontier — in their case in Iran as well as in Afghanistan. Britain ruled its part of Baluchi territory through tribal chiefs, who at the time of partition acceded to Pakistan, but have presented problems of control to that country, as they did to the Raj before it. In large areas of sparsely-peopled territory the writ of the government rarely runs, and then not for long; and here it appears that secessionist movements are most easily fomented from abroad; though some believe that Baluchi nationalism is spontaneously emerging. In this case the main (but perhaps not the only) culprit is Iraq, whose longstanding feud with Iran makes it ready to support a 'Greater Baluchistan' including substantial parts of that country as well as of Afghanistan and, of course, of Pakistani Baluchistan.[11] Successive governments of Pakistan have tried various methods of attempting to control Baluchistan (where, as in NWFP, the National Awami Party (NAP) was at one time active and held the reins of government); and have instituted a number of developmental and educational measures. But our conclusion must at present be similar to that reached for the Pushtu areas at the end of the previous paragraph; adding that the revolution in Iran and Russian intervention in Afghanistan clearly do nothing to stabilize the situation.

The problem of the Sindhis, the distinct linguistic group formerly dominant in the province of Sind, is different. Here fears of Punjabi domination by the indigenous inhabitants has been compounded by the immigration, after partition, of large numbers of Urdu speakers formerly resident in India, who have come to occupy positions of economic dominance in the cities formerly held by Hindu Sindhis who fled to India. (Only 9 per cent of the population of Karachi is Sindhi speaking.) Here there is no question of irredentism, hardly any question of secession; but there is marked separatist regionalism of the kind shortly to be encountered in India; and there have been language riots and other disturbances.

For most of its independent existence Pakistan has been divided into four Provinces: Punjab, Sind, North-west Frontier Province and Baluchistan, which tend to perpetuate the British pattern but may also be seen as some reflection of linguistic distributions and regional sentiment; though not, of course, to the same extent as in the India of the last two decades. The Constitution of 1973 faced the issue of provincial autonomy; but has been overtaken by military rule.

Separatism and regional autonomy in India

Chapter 2 of this book has sufficiently stressed the importance of language in reshaping the political map of India since independence. A word must, however, be said about: (1) the forces that revolutionized the map of north-east India and, in spite of the concessions made to them, continue to generate tensions and disturbances, especially but not exclusively among tribal people; (2) territorial problems of 'tribals' elsewhere, especially in connection with the Jharkand movement; (3) moves to dissect linguistic states on non-linguistic grounds, notably in relation to the Telangana region of Andhra Pradesh; and (4) cases where political feeling in linguistic states involves a desire for increased autonomy for the state as a whole, as in Tamil Nadu.

The political fragmentation of Assam has been one of the most remarkable features of post-independence India.[12] The State of Assam at independence consisted of the former British province of the same name, with its princely states and 'excluded districts' in tribal territories; but less Sylhet District, which became part of East Pakistan. But by 1977 Assam State proper had become little more than a strip along the Brahmaputra; around it in a horseshoe runs

Arunachal Pradesh, the former NEFA (North-east Frontier Agency), with its congeries of tribes, ruled as a Union Territory direct from New Delhi; Nagaland, a separate state since 1963; Manipur and Tripura, old princely states which, in spite of their small size, graduated from Union Territories to full statehood in 1972; and Meghalaya, 'the abode of the clouds', in the Khasi, Garo and Jaintia Hills which, after much agitation, became an autonomous state within Assam in 1970 and a full State in 1972. Finally, running south between Manipur and Tripura is Mizoram ('hillmen's country') also now a Union Territory. All of the States and territories apart from Assam State are dominated by 'tribal' populations, though there has been substantial Bengali immigration into Manipur and Tripura, as into Assam State. Now, as Chapter 2 has shown, other parts of India, especially the hilly belts running east–west across the central Deccan, also have large tribal populations: some of them have agitated for autonomy, but so far none have succeeded. Why, then, have such substantial concessions been made to tribal feeling in north-east India, leading to the extraordinary fragmentation of the political map and to the recognition of mini-states? (And perhaps the process is not at an end: there are irredentist calls for a Greater Nagaland (there are Nagas in Assam State and in Burma) and for autonomy for several tribal groups left in Assam State.)

First, let us note the extreme strategic vulnerability of north-east India, especially given tensions between India and China. The whole region is joined to the rest of India by an absurdly narrow corridor, only some twenty miles wide at one point, running from West Bengal round the north-western extremity of Bangladesh. A broad gauge railway and national highway had to be specially constructed through this corridor after independence. Not surprisingly, then, India is extremely sensitive to agitation and revolt within its north-eastern region; this was especially so following the Chinese incursions through NEFA (whose northern boundary China does not recognize) in 1962.

Secondly, though some of the tribal peoples in the hills almost surrounding the plain of Assam became Hinduized (particularly in Tripura and Manipur), most of them resisted the process and retained their own religions till western impact: animist in most areas, Mahayana Buddhist in NEFA. Social distances between plainsmen and hillmen are therefore greater here than in many other, more Hinduized parts of India. The north-eastern tribesmen, moreover, far from weakly retreating, often raided the Assamese plainsmen, whom they tended to despise; British control of the hills, where it existed, was introduced in an effort to prevent marauding. However, one of the most important effects of British intervention in the hills was the entry of Christian missionaries of several different sects, so that the proportion of Christians is high among many tribal groups (though not in Arunachal Pradesh): nearly 100 per cent among the Mizos, 50–60 per cent among most Naga groups. (It is said that Christian tribals who speak English do so with the accent of their original missionaries; so that English-speaking Khasis have a Welsh accent and believe Aberystwyth to be the centre of the universe.) With the missions came literacy, in many hill areas higher than in Assam proper, and the growth of an educated middle class with western ideas who spearheaded movements for rebellion, or autonomy and statehood (or even secession) in independent India, sometimes in conflict with more conservative traditional leaders; and who tended, where old imperial frontiers ran clean through tribal homelands (as among Nagas and Mizos) to harbour irredentism. Altogether, then, one can see why tribal peoples in the north-east do not feel particularly drawn to India, and why separatism or even rebellion can flourish.

Given, then, the exposed but vital frontier position of the Indian north-east, it is not surprising that the Government in New Delhi, though repressive in some times and places, has also sought to appease rebellious tribal feeling by conceding autonomy or statehood to small areas whose people are, in any case, for the most part less 'Indian' than tribal people in other parts of the country. That it has not altogether succeeded is shown by continuing unrest, complex in detail but fundamentally separatist in essence, that agitates some elements in most states of the north-east and that is compounded by border disputes (especially between Nagaland and Assam) and by resentment of settlement by outsiders, particularly Bengalis (who form 63 per cent of the population of Tripura). Some Bengalis react by showing anti-tribal hostility; others by supporting Amra Bangali as already mentioned. Mid-1979 saw a period of renewed ferment throughout the north-east, felt even in remote and previously immune Arunachal, while severe disturbances (including massacres) were reported in 1983.

What of the Assamese in their rump of a Valley State? Historically their land was regarded as *mlechcha* (foreign); and their name comes, in fact, from that of a Thai people — though they have been

Indianized, Brahminized and Sanskritized over the centuries, and now speak an Indo–European language. Contemporary Assamese look to India for protection, particularly against Bengali immigration, in 1980 the cause of agitation and rioting in the course of which oil was prevented from flowing from Assam through the pipeline to India (once again through the corridor). The plains and hill slopes of Assam were very sparsely peopled in the early nineteenth century;[13] and so provided ample scope for tea plantations, which brought in immigrant labourers, some of them Bengali, who stayed to settle as peasant cultivators, and were joined later — and are joined still — by numerous Muslims from East Bengal who tended to cultivate more intensively than the easy-going Assamese, to become more wealthy, and to arouse great jealousy. In Assam State, indeed, something of a siege mentality has developed.

Of tribal movements in India outside the north-east, as yet unsuccessful in securing autonomy, one of the most notable is the Jharkhand movement. Founded and sustained by a colourful educated Munda, Jaipal Singh, its objective is the formation of a new State in tribal areas in south Bihar, extending also into West Bengal and Orissa.[14] These areas have a tribal population of over six million. Various concessions have been wrung from the Bihar Government; and the Jharkhand Party has at times been quite successful in the polls (it was the second biggest party in the Bihar Assembly in 1952) though at other times it merged with Congress. Similar but so far less notable tribal movements and parties, led almost invariably by educated men of tribal origin who have acquired middle-class status, have sprung up in other parts of India, and made even less successful demands for statehood. And more may arise in future as a new generation of educated tribal leaders is able to capitalize on grievances against intrusive plainsmen in such areas as that known as Dandakaranya on the borders of Madhya Pradesh, Orissa and Andhra Pradesh.[15]

Of a quite different character is the Telangana movement. When in 1953 the State of Andhra Pradesh was formed to unite Telugu-speakers in the old Madras Presidency and in Hyderabad State, it was feared by leaders in Telengana, the dry, poor and backward Telugu-speaking part of Hyderabad, that their region would be disadvantaged compared with coastal Andhra, the Krishna-Godavari delta region, with its more sophisticated people.[16] Accordingly, Congress politicians from the two regions reached a 'gentleman's agreement' before merger which contained safeguards for the people of Telengana: particularly in respect of the use in Telengana of revenues collected there; reserved educational facilities; and, above all, the reservation of jobs in government service. But later there were bitter complaints that the agreement was not being honoured; a long, tangled dispute that broke out into violence (notably in 1969); and demands for a separate Telengana State (which had, in fact, been conditionally recommended by the States Reorganization Commission). The dispute provoked a violent reaction from coastal Andhra and from its people resident in Telengana (a parallel with Amra Bangali here) and to calls for a separate (coastal) Andhra State. The whole dispute has involved many complicated political manoeuvres, in the state, at the centre, and between the two; but so far has not issued in the partition of Andhra Pradesh.

It has been pointed out that there is a fundamental clash here between political regionalism, with its claim for special treatment for local people, and the 'homeland principle', that an Indian has a right to live and work anywhere in India; and that pressure for reserved education and employment is related to the enormous growth since 1960 of educational facilities and, in consequence, of the numbers of those clamouring for jobs, particularly jobs in the government service.[17]

Not surprisingly, other parts of India have also had their regional discontents and separatist movements: notably Vidarbha, in eastern Maharashtra (whose claim was indeed also recognized by the States Reorganization Commission); the Saurashtra (peninsular) area of Gujarat; and the poverty-stricken east of UP. None of these have yet been conceded. But India has clearly not done with separatism, or perhaps even secessionism and irredentism in the troubled north-east; but we must also bear in mind, and shall shortly turn to, forces making for the containment of such movements within the Indian political system.

Again, there is the phenomenon of the pre-existing linguistic State, or of dominant groups within it, working for a much higher degree of autonomy: in particular, there is the case of DMK (Dravida Munnetra Kazhagam) in Tamil Nadu. This important political party has its historical roots in the anti-Brahmin movement and the Justice Party mentioned in Chapter 3. It has fed on the strong emotions generated in Tamil Nadu by the Tamil language and its defence against what is seen as 'Hindi imperialism': the alleged attempt by the north to impose its language on the south. Hindi is, indeed, recognized by the Constitution as the Indian national language, though English is retained with associate status for an indefinite transitional period (and tends to be strongly supported in the south). In the early 1960s, the DMK was frankly secessionist. But since 1963 demands for secession have been illegal. The DMK has also split, and now comprises a strong group of parties confined to Tamil Nadu (in spite of the wider 'Dravida' in its title); dedicated to securing the maximum degree of state autonomy; and with a populist programme having a wide appeal in the State. But 1983 saw another regional party (Telugu Desam) returned to power in Andhra Pradesh, and the formation of a council of southern States not ruled by Mrs Gandhi's Congress (I) Party (see below, p. 89). Mrs Gandhi reacted by announcing the appointment of a commission to enquire into relations between central government and the States.

Akali Dal in Punjab is also a strong party confined to one State which presses for more autonomy. It is a party of a single community, the Sikhs, and has become more extreme in the 1980s, though not as extreme as some other Sikh movements. The Communist Party of India (Marxist) in West Bengal, and some groupings in Kerala, are also strong on State autonomy, for ideological reasons.

Finally, the point should be made that, if one looks at the political units in north-western India as a whole, then Punjab, Haryana, Himachal Pradesh, and Jammu and Kashmir together form a region of small States, some formed by the partition of earlier larger States, in a strategically sensitive area. Superficially, there is a parallel with north-eastern India and, in the case of the first three States named, an apparent willingness in such an area to concede statehood. But the ethnic basis of the States is clearly very different from those of the north-eastern 'mini-States'.

Secession and separatism in Sri Lanka and Nepal

As already hinted, Sri Lanka has been the scene of bitter wrangling, and worse, between its Sinhala and Tamil communities. More must be said about these problems shortly. Let us just note here that some Tamil political movements are in favour of secession to form an independent country, Tamil Eelam, which would include the Northern and Eastern Provinces whose majority populations are Tamils. The viability of such a miniature state as Tamil Eelam must be gravely in doubt.

Nepal, we have noted, is a patchwork of peoples. Conceivably, it may in future witness separatist, secessionist or irredentist movements as some of its people gain in education and expectations, and experience unemployment and frustration.

The Indian political system

We must turn now from issues of separatism in South Asia, which some have perhaps tended to overstress in what Rajni Kothari, with reference to India, has called 'an almost paranoid concern with stability'.[18] India has always attracted prophets of doom, and, almost equally, those who have set it on a pedestal as 'the world's greatest (or, at any rate, 'biggest') democracy'.

The Indian political system is relatively simple in its constitutional arrangements, with which we begin; almost overwhelmingly complex and confusing in its party politics and political behaviour at its various levels.[19] Let us ask in what ways, and to what extent it copes with demands and stresses that might otherwise endanger national unity and the constitution. Let us also ask whether, and if so how, it is achieving political development, as at least some political scientists see that ambiguous process — as a means of achieving the politicization of society, the highly complex and fragmented society of India; or, as Morris-Jones puts it, 'the containment in peaceful interpenetration' of the 'diverse and in principle competitive languages of politics': the modern westernized language of constitution, of higher administration and judiciary, of the upper levels of political parties; the 'traditional' language of caste and community in 'a host of tiny worlds'; the 'saintly' language of Gandhi (or some of Gandhi) and of his disciples like Vinoba Bhave and Jayaprakash Narayan.[20]

India, we have seen, has a federal constitution. At the Centre, in New Delhi, are the President, the two houses of Parliament, the Lok Sabha, 'House of the People', directly elected from constituencies all over India by universal adult suffrage, and the Rajya Sabha, 'Council of the States', which has twelve members nominated by the President and other members elected by elected members of State legislatures; the Prime Minister and Union Cabinet; and the great ministries and departments. These arrangements clearly derive more from Westminster than from Washington. In each State capital there is a Governor (appointed by the President); an elected assembly (in some States an Upper House too); a Chief Minister and a Council of Ministers; and the State bureaucracy. (We have seen that Union Territories are administered direct from New Delhi.)

Some subjects are reserved to the Centre, some to the States; some are concurrent, that is, the concern of both, though central laws override State enactments. Central subjects include foreign affairs and defence, communications, banking, and customs. State subjects include agriculture (though there is a central Department of Agriculture), land revenue, law, order and local government and education (though there are departments at the Centre for some of these subjects). The concurrent list includes trade, industry and economic planning. In terms of finance, the Centre has a source of strength in being allotted the fruit of 'growth' taxes like income tax, corporation tax, and customs and excise; though some of these do not grow as much as they might because of widespread evasion by the so-called 'black economy'. The States collect land revenue, sales taxes and a number of other imposts. Land revenue in particular has come to contribute a diminishing proportion of the national budget, taking Centre and States together; while repeated proposals for an agricultural income tax, which would be a State matter, have broken on vested agricultural interests. The Centre, then, tends to be more financially powerful than the States; and makes grants to them for purposes which give it a substantial leverage not perhaps altogether foreseen by those who formulated the constitution.

Under the constitution the President (who is elected by members of both Union Houses and of State legislatures, sitting together) has considerable powers, including the declaration of a State of emergency under threat of external attack or internal disturbance; and the institution of 'Presidential Rule', under which a state government can be suspended if the President is satisfied that its rule cannot be maintained in accordance with the constitution; its powers are then exercised by the President, those of the State legislature being 'exercisable by or under the authority' of the Parliament in New Delhi. The use of these powers, nearly always exercised on the advice of the Prime Minister, have occasioned considerable controversy. 'Presidential Rule' has so far, however, always eventually issued in elections and the restoration of parliamentary government in the States concerned.

A federal constitution is, of course, *prima facie* a means of containing regionalism, even separatism, though not, of course, secession unless those pressing for secession can be persuaded to accept separate treatment within a federation as a solution. But for a federal structure effectively to contain strong separatist tensions demands a certain flexibility and a bargaining capacity. It is certainly possible to maintain that India (some would say unlike Pakistan) has shown these qualities: for example in conceding linguistic States and in fragmenting Assam (though protagonists of Telangana and Vidarbha would invoke inflexibility, even repression; so would some of the Nagas and their friends).

The constitution provides for an independent higher judiciary which has played an important role, not least in larger constitutional questions.

Under the constitution, general elections to the Lok Sabha must take place every five years, unless the House is dissolved within a shorter period. General elections duly took place in 1952, 1957, 1962, 1967 and 1971. In 1975 the President on the advice of the Prime Minister, Mrs Indira Gandhi, declared a state of internal emergency (hereafter 'The Emergency'). So no general election took place when it fell due in 1976. Mrs Gandhi in due course announced a general election for mid-March 1977, at which her Congress Party was defeated. Morarji Desai, at the head of the Janata coalition (of which more in a moment) was asked to form a government, which survived only till August 1979. The ensuing general election then once more returned Mrs Gandhi to power. So far, then, elections in India have followed the pattern prescribed by the constitution, a situation not unlike that in Sri Lanka but very different from that in Pakistan and Bangladesh, to say nothing of the host of 'new' states outside South Asia which have started out with Westminster-style constitutions but fallen under autocratic rule of one sort or another. Many Indians who speak the language of 'modern' politics take pride in this, even if they stand abashed by The Emergency. Their liberal friends in the west (or some of them) take it as a feather in India's cap. Why, then, has India been able to maintain general elections? The answer to this question may emerge more fully by the end of this section. For the moment, it is worth quoting some of the views of Anthony Low, who invokes such factors as the long history of electoral procedures in India; the dominant role of the Congress Party (shortly to be explored), with its 'modern' ideology, initially at any rate; forces working against military rule (more of which later); and the constitutional means, just outlined, for dealing with 'emergencies' but for which, Low maintains, 'democracy' in India might well have collapsed.[21] Low's emphasis on the last factor would, of course, not win universal approval, especially from the left, who see the whole constitutional-cum-Congress apparatus as a means of repression by the national bourgeoisie and its allies; nor by those who still cannot reconcile themselves to The Emergency, seeing Mrs Gandhi's call for elections in 1977 as a merely tactical move designed to maintain power, which went wrong; or by those who have cried after each recent general election that it will be India's last.

State legislative assemblies (Vidhan Sabha) are directly elected for five-year periods, the constituencies being of course much smaller than those for the Lok Sabha. State upper houses, where they exist, are called Legislative Councils (Vidhan Parishad) and filled by a combination of election and nomination. State elections have, like general elections, also taken place when constitutionally due, though necessarily the pattern has been somewhat distorted by periods of President's Rule. Thus elections were held in most States in 1952, 1957, 1962, 1967, and 1972, 1977–8 and 1980; but there were elections in Andhra in 1955, in Orissa in 1961 and in Kerala in 1960.

Turning to the principal political parties that have contended in the several general and State elections, the scene was not surprisingly dominated in the early years of independence by the Congress Party that had grown out of the Indian National Congress and whose history under the Raj was sketched in Chapter 3. Congress suffered growing pains in developing from a movement into a party. But in the days of Nehru its sway was so generally undisputed that India was often described as a one-party state. Moreover, it could rely on the loyalty of the vast bureaucracy, the 'steel frame' that the Raj had built (albeit on earlier foundations) and on the armed forces and police; and Nehru is one of those figures in history to whom the overworked word 'charismatic' is aptly attached. In the first four elections it held successively 74, 75, 73 and 55 per cent of the seats in the Lok Sabha; and 45, 48, 45 and 41 per cent of the votes.[22] In State assemblies the corresponding figures are 68, 65, 61 and 48 per cent of seats; and 42, 45, 44 and 40 per cent of votes. In neither case did Congress, for all its commanding position, ever secure a majority of votes cast. It is thus possible to exaggerate the dominance of Congress, even in the earlier years of independence. But the opposition to it was diverse and fragmented; and it remains true that an assessment of the Indian political system up to the early 1970s is largely, though not completely, an assessment of the functioning of Congress.

The point has already been made that Congress[23] before independence was 'not a political party with a single ideology'. In becoming a political party after independence it continued to shelter a wide spectrum of opinion under its spreading umbrella, from Nehru-style socialists, hasty for economic changes such as industrialization, to Gandhian idealists, looking back to a supposedly idyllic Indian past that should be a model for the future; from wealthy businessmen and rural 'big men' to ardent champions of the nationalization of the commanding heights of the economy, if not the collectivization of agriculture. Not surprisingly there were oscillations and contradictions in economic policy, as we shall see in Chapter 6.

But until his death in 1964 the dominating figure of Jawaharlal Nehru held Congress together as a single party; and Nehru saw to it that many potentially divergent factions were kept under the Congress umbrella. True, there were splinterings-off: a group left to become the Socialist Party in 1948, and the radical Gandhian socialist, Kripalani, departed in 1951, having failed in a closely fought battle to gain the Congress Presidency, and set up his Kisan Mazdoor Praja Party (KMPP). But Congress then sailed into smoother waters; Nehru's command of it became complete and unchallenged; and, so far as there was a consensus, it was left of centre like Nehru himself. Even when Nehru died in 1964, the succession passed smoothly to Lal Bahadur Shastri, who, however, died in 1966 (in Tashkent, in connection with a Soviet attempt to mediate between India and Pakistan).

But faction and divergence within the party surfaced in the two succession crises that followed Shastri's death. Now, towards the end of the Nehru era new leaders were becoming powerful and important in the States, more 'traditional' than 'modern' in 'political language'. The most notable was K. Kamaraj Nadar, of Tamil Nadu, whose name is associated with the Kamaraj Plan under which a number of Central Ministers and Chief Ministers of States relinquished office to take up organizational work for the party, and in consequence of which a number of the new leaders, including Kamaraj himself (as Congress President) became powerful at the Centre. They were known as the Syndicate. Some aspects of these developments will be taken up when we are considering linkages within the Indian political system. For the moment, the important point is that Kamaraj had much to do with the smooth succession of Shastri, by something like a consensus, and after Morarji Desai, an obvious contender, was persuaded to second Shastri's nomination. But by the time of Shastri's death Kamaraj's position was weaker, the Syndicate had lost cohesion (as all bodies in India now do sooner or later), factional division had become evident, and there was a contest between Indira Gandhi and Morarji Desai (won by the former) rather than a carefully contrived consensus. Dissension and open defection increased after Congress' relatively poor showing in the 1967 elections (Kamaraj himself lost his seat). The crisis deepened, and the split came, as a result of infighting over the election of a President of India in 1969. It would be wearisome to recount all the details. Suffice it to say that Mrs Gandhi was a key figure; that in the course of the campaign she relieved Morarji Desai of his Cabinet office as Minister of Finance, he then resigning as Deputy Prime Minister; that Mrs Gandhi then nation-alized certain banks (this is often seen as a dramatic vote-catching move, a lurch to the left that was more apparent than real; but it served to isolate the more conservative Morarji and the Syndicate). The Congress then split, Morarji and the Syndicate heading what became known as Congress (O) ('O' for 'organization'), and Mrs Gandhi and her supporters Congress (R) ('R' for 'ruling'). Some two years later, in March 1971 Mrs Gandhi called for a general election and her Congress secured something like two-thirds of the Lok Sabha seats, the Congress (O) being routed and reduced to a rump. Mrs Gandhi's great slogan was *'gharibi hatao'* ('out with poverty'), consistent with a lurch to the left but in some eyes more populist rhetoric than ideology or intention. Then, on the crest of the wave following the defeat of Pakistan in the Bangladesh war, came the State Assembly elections of March 1972, in which a slightly higher proportion still of the seats went to the 'new' Indira Congress (though only 48 per cent of the vote).

But to a considerable extent Mrs Gandhi's new-found dominance was an illusion; it was certainly not based on the same firm foundations as her father's had been. R. L. Hardgrave has said that 'Indira Gandhi destroyed the boss-structure of the old Congress, but she did not replace it with an effective structure linking the Centre with the local party units'.[24] He may well be right, for we have seen the importance of such linkages in the political movements of the period before independence; and shall return to the subject later in this chapter. By 1974 six Chief Ministers had been 'eased out of office' and six States were under President's Rule; an exercise of centralized power which, in retrospect, has been seen as removing the former responsiveness of the Centre to pressures from below. In 1974, it was becoming clear that Mrs Gandhi's government could not dispel poverty as promised. While many factors in the situation were well beyond the control of any government, Congress under Mrs Gandhi was still an umbrella organization, with many factions and individuals hostile to radical economic and social change. Inflation, the oil crisis and crop failures all added fuel to mounting discontent, especially among urban people in low income groups.[25] Jayaprakash Narayan, already mentioned as an outstanding disciple of Mahatma Gandhi, provided the leadership for a campaign which was, however, limited in both its class and its regional appeal. Then, in 1975, Mrs Gandhi was convicted in the Allahabad High Court of offences in the previous general election. There soon followed, on 26 June 1975, ostensibly because of a gathering threat to internal security, some think more because of the Allahabad judgement, the declaration of The Emergency (a state of internal emergency had been in evidence since the Bangladesh war of 1971).

The Emergency deserves at least a paragraph to itself, novel event that it then was in Indian political life. Under The Emergency many leaders, major and minor, of opposition parties were imprisoned (including Morarji Desai); civil liberties were suspended and the press muzzled by censorship (though that did not stop people from talking freely to those whom they trusted, as was evident in Delhi in December 1976); and there seem to have been many abuses of police powers. It has become notorious that, in pursuance of a no doubt desirable family planning campaign, there were enforced sterilizations. And, under the energetic if misguided leadership of Mrs Gandhi's late son, Sanjay, slums were cleared in Delhi and elsewhere at a great cost in human suffering. Undoubtedly The Emergency alienated many members of the urban élite, particularly intellectuals previously sympathetic to the 'new' Congress, imbued as many of them were with liberal notions of representative government, and rigidly authoritarian as the government of India had overnight become. How far alienation spread to other classes will probably, however, be a matter of contention for some time to come.[26]

What is clear, however, is the more recent parliamentary and electoral history of the Congress Party. In January 1977, to the surprise of many observers, a general election was announced, and The Emergency was relaxed; freedom of speech, publication and assembly were restored. Soon afterwards, Jagjivan Ram, the Harijan leader from Bihar and Defence Minister in Mrs Gandhi's Cabinet, resigned and left the Congress (R) to found his own party, 'Congress for Democracy'. In the March 1977 election Mrs Gandhi's party won only 28 per cent of the Lok Sabha seats: the mighty Congress that had dominated the political scene for so long was at a low ebb. The new government was in fact formed by the Janata coalition and was headed by Morarji Desai. To complete the history of Congress, following its defeat in the 1977 election there came a period of recrimination between factions within it and a further split in January 1978. Mrs Gandhi and her supporters, 'Congress (I)', claimed to be the 'real' Congress, and broke away from an apparently larger group (Congress (S)) then headed by Y. B. Chavan (who later rejoined her). In doing so she once again proclaimed a populist slogan over the heads of the squabbling politicians; this time it was 'forward to socialism'. In state elections in Karnataka, Andhra and Maharashtra Congress (I) did well, largely at the expense of the rival 'Congress (U)' (formerly (S): Congress has now almost run out of postscript initials). With the break-up in August 1979 of the Janata coalition and the fall of the government that it had formed, there ensued a general election that resulted in an overwhelming victory for Congress (I) and its allies: a two-thirds majority, in fact, in the Lok Sabha (but only 42 per cent of those voting in a 55 per cent turnout). In elections for nine State Assemblies held in May 1980 Congress (I) captured power in eight, with absolute majorities in all of these and two-thirds majorities in six. The ninth was Tamil Nadu, won by the All India Anna DMK which had split from the 'old' DMK some years before and had previously been in power under its filmstar Chief Minister, M. G. Ramachandran: the 'old' DMK in alliance with Congress (I) came far behind, so that Tamil Nadu maintained its idiosyncratic regionalism.

So once more the Congress, or *a* Congress came back to power at the centre and in a significant number of States, confounding the commentators who thought that The Emergency had bitten so deeply into popular consciousness that Mrs Gandhi and her Congress, whatever it was called and whatever its rhetoric, was lost for ever. Once again, there was controversy over the reasons for Mrs Gandhi's comeback; those most frequently cited were the poor performance of the Janata government and the blatant divisions within it.

So much, then, for narrative. Before proceeding to comment, it will be as well to look at other principal political parties and their record (omitting minor parties, which are legion and often ephemeral).

First, we can dismiss quickly those splinters from the Congress that, whatever their claims to legitimacy and to the inheritance of the legacy of Mahatma Gandhi and Nehru, have failed in electoral competition with the remarkable Indira Gandhi. Congress (O) and the Syndicate behind it, Congress (U), Jagjivan Ram's Congress for Democracy, all have fallen by the wayside or become mere rumps. For the time being, Congress once again means Indira Gandhi. But he would be both bold and foolish who would predict that there will not be further schisms; and one of these may yet leave Mrs Gandhi in a minority splinter group, for reasons to be mentioned when we consider linkages in the Indian political system.

Secondly, there are parties with an almost exclusively regional bases. Of the chief of these (Jharkhand, the DMK and its derivatives, Akali Dal in Punjab) enough has already been said. More may yet arise as the arrangement and rearrangement of political parties in the regions of India begins to rival in kaleidoscropic variety the shifting pattern of princely states in pre-British India (cf. p. 81).

Thirdly, there have been and are parties to which the label 'right-wing' has been applied. Thus the Swatantra Party (the name means 'freedom') was founded in 1959 as a party of 'free enterprise' just after the Congress Party had taken one of its apparent lurches to the left and declared itself in favour of co-operative joint farming.[27] Swatantra has contained some strange bedfellows: from former princes, landlords and urban businessmen to distinguished liberals like the former Congress leaders C. Rajagopalachari and N. G. Ranga. In the 1967 elections it was, with 44 seats, the largest party in the Lok Sabha but has since, in spite of a number of alliances (some of them apparently contradictory in ideological terms), suffered eclipse; it merged in the Lok Dal in 1974 and no longer fits readily into the 'right-wing' category. Swatantra has never deserved the label of 'Hindu communalist party', but this is not true of the Jan (or Jana) Sangh ('People's Party'), in spite of its protestations to the contrary; for its parent body, the RSS (Rashtriya Swayamsevak Sangh) was certainly strongly communalist. Jan Sangh has, for example, stood for cow protection and hostility to Pakistan. Its economic policy was not very different from Swatantra's, though more vague. Jan Sangh's fortunes and alliances have varied over the years. It was a component of the Janata coalition and so shared power at the Centre from 1977 to 1979. It had also been a component in various State coalition governments and in Delhi city administrations. The Lok Dal was formed in 1974 by Charan Singh (caretaker Prime Minister between the fall of the Janata government in 1979 and the formation of Mrs Gandhi's new administration in 1980) and embodied, in addition to Swatantra and a number of regional parties (some with a strong dominant-caste tinge), the Samyukta Socialist Party (SSP). It is therefore very doubtfully dubbed a right- *or* left-wing party. Indeed, Charan Singh's own power base lies among UP Jat farmers — particularly 'middle peasants'. In 1980 Lok Dal was the second strongest party in the Lok Sabha, with 41 seats; its leader was George Fernandes, labour leader and Socialist. So much for simplistic ideological ascriptions! Earlier, the Janata Party was an even broader, and as it proved unstable coalition of the Jan Sangh, Lok Dal, Congress (O) and Fernandes' Socialist Party, joined also by Jagjivan Ram and his Congress for Democracy.

But, thirdly, ideological ascriptions have a truer ring when applied to the Communist Parties, of which the chief are the Communist Party of India (CPI), the Communist Party (Marxist) (CPI(M) or CPM) and the Communist Party (Marxist–Leninist) (CPI(ML)). The CPI dates back to 1928, and has generally been seen as pro-Moscow, and willing to cooperate with the 'national bourgeoisie' to 'complete the anti-imperialist, anti-feudal, democratic revolution'. It formed that rare species, an elected Communist government, in Kerala in 1958. It supported Mrs Gandhi at the time of the Congress split of 1969, but its relationship with Congress has not been an easy one, and has varied from State to State. In the 1980 Lok Sabha it held only 11 seats. The CPI(M) split from the CPI in 1964, holding an ideological position further to the left and claiming to be the true Communist Party. It has been viewed as pro-Peking. It derives its greatest strength in Kerala and West Bengal, and to a lesser extent in Andhra. The two Communist parties came together in coalition governments in Kerala and West Bengal in 1967; but more usually have engaged in bitter dissent, the CPI(M) generally proving the stronger in elections. It formed a coalition government with Janata in West Bengal in 1977. In the Lok Sabha of 1980 the CPI(M) had 35 seats (it was the third strongest party) to the CPI's 11 seats; though in the subsequent State Assembly elections in Bihar the CPI outshone its rival. The third Communist party, the CPI(ML) was formed in 1969 and is openly Maoist and revolutionary, supporting terrorist and guerilla movements of the sort that have come to be called 'Naxalite' after an uprising in the Naxalbari area of West Bengal. (As I write there are reports of Naxalite activity in Tamil Nadu and counter-reports that the trouble is really police repression of agrarian revolt by disadvantaged groups, whose leaders are merely labelled 'Naxalite'.)

There have also been a number of parties that have embodied the word 'socialist' in their titles. Most have sprung from movements originally within Congress. Here we need only to be concerned with the Samyukta Socialist Party (SSP), which emerged in 1964, suffered a great deal of factional conflict, and then formed the Socialist Party and merged with the Praja Socialist Party (PSP), a mixed but largely Gandhian group in which Jayaprakash Narayan was a leading light till he withdrew from politics in 1954. One faction then entered the Lok Dal, which in turn became a member of the Janata coalition. Another, George Fernandes' Socialist Party, entered Janata direct, as we have seen.

Now one observation that may be made, albeit at a rather superficial level, on this incomplete catalogue of parties is that the Indian party political system is clearly very different from that of most, if not all, western democracies. Not only is there the phenomenon of single-party dominance in the heyday of Congress (which some may feel returned with Mrs Gandhi's successes in 1980); but there is also the enormous array of parties; and the prevalence of factional splits and of the recombination of factions, sometimes apparently diametrically opposed in ideology, in a constantly shifting pattern of coalitions. One politician in Haryana is said to have changed parties four times in a single day.

Faction in Indian politics is something that has for many years attracted the attention of western researchers, sometimes to the annoyance of Indians.[28] Faction is indeed a characteristic of, though not unique to Indian politics at all levels, central, State and regional; and it merges, through the linkages shortly to be discussed, with the highly local factions, often cutting vertically across caste strata, that are such a characteristic feature of the Indian village. Are shifting political factions, at higher levels, then, but an upward reflection of an age-old village phenomenon, a translation into the language of 'modern' politics of 'traditional' modes? Some factional splitting is undoubtedly ideological and completely 'modern': for example, the schisms to which the Marxist left the world over is prone; and some at any rate of the socialist splinterings have been apparently ideological, as when individuals and followers left the Congress at various stages to found new parties. But some socialists, it will be remembered, have entered into apparently unholy combinations to try and secure electoral advantage — as, for that matter, have communists. Faction often seems, indeed, to be a matter of a leader carrying 'his men' with him out of one party and into independence, or into another party, for no reasons of ideology or principle, but for what is calculated to be short-term advantage. One does not claim, obviously, that this is a practice exclusively Indian; but it does seem in India to be a matter of a 'traditional' mode being used in a 'modern' constitutional frame.

This leads on naturally to the question of linkages. How does the 'big man', whatever his party, acquire his following? We have met in Chapter 3 recent work suggesting that in pre-independence India local bosses and magnates mediated between the Raj and rural and urban society, playing their part in larger and larger arenas with the passage of time; and that Congress over the years stretched down from the new élite in the port and other cities to lower and lower levels, to join hands with 'big men' of various kinds and at various levels. We have further seen that this research, in common with other work of the 'neo-Machiavellians', sees self-interest, or at least the interest of caste, or family, or faction (or some combination of these) as the dominant if not the only motive in this development. Chapter 2, further, has shown the importance of patron–client relationships extending vertically across the caste hierarchy. It is possible to suggest, then, that here lies the clue to the self-interested factionalism and contradictory recombinations of recent Indian politics; and that 'traditional' modes have grown more prevalent as vernacular-speaking politicians, hailing from the linguistic States (Kamaraj is a case in point) become of greater importance to those operating in central politics because of the following they command lower down the political system. Higher level politicians need this following electorally; and are able to bargain with lower level politicians because they can offer them the fruits of office (power, influence, and affluence, often by corrupt means) and the patronage that goes with office: jobs for relatives and followers, contracts, preferential access to credit or fertilizer or other goods and services at government disposal. In this game the bureaucrat holds an uneasy position but, at the lower levels at any rate, tends to find himself in the pocket of the local 'big man'.

How does the local 'big man', whoever he may be, translate his influence into the votes required by those at higher levels with whom he has bargained? And to what extent can the rhetoric and spectacular actions of national leaders appeal over the heads of such a man to the actual voter — or how far can there be a wave of spontaneous repugnance amongst the actual electors at, say, The Emergency or the ineffectiveness of the national Janata government? And there are related questions: to what extent are Harijans, or Muslims, or other groups feeling themselves disadvantaged, able freely to exercise a protest vote? And to what extent is there substance in claims that India is 'developing' politically, that genuine participation has spread to an even wider populace, particularly but not exclusively with the institution of Panchayati Raj (the system of elected local government at district and subdistrict ('block') levels now responsible for much official development expenditure)? Here one comes up against a dearth of sufficient objective information. It is not enough to write about Indian elections from a desk in the city. It is somewhat better to canvass voters on their expectations from elections (whether Panch-ayat, or State, or national) and on the way they voted, as has indeed been done;[29] but still unsatisfactory because the method may not, and one suspects does not elicit how voters have in fact behaved, especially if they were subject to intimidation or even exclusion from the polling booths. The truth is only likely to emerge from participant observation as understood by anthropologists. Yet in the nature of things (especially of things about to be mentioned) it is a rare dispassionate but participant observer who is able to report on actual election behaviour in villages, or most urban areas for that matter; if he does so report, there is the vexing question of the honest anthropologist, 'How typical is my village'? Enough is known, however, to make it clear that in many places 'vote banks' are an established feature: caste leaders or leaders of factions (perhaps cross-caste) may be able, or say they are able to deliver a block of votes to a candidate or his lower level agent. In such cases the genuine wishes and frustration of, say, Harijans are unlikely to be gratified, unless (and this is obviously rare) the disadvantaged group is able to find an effective leader with sufficient upward linkages. Such a leader will tend to be very, very local in his impact; so that, trapped in the cellular structure of caste and village, the frustrations of the really disadvantaged Indians tend not to find expression at national, or even state level (except, perhaps, through social workers and sympathetic newspapers). For, in spite of (or even because of) Panchayati Raj, the dominant castes still dominate, by and large, though because of caste mobility new castes may aspire to and secure dominance. Hence there are severe limitations to the extent to which national leaders (Mrs Gandhi in particular) can mount a populist appeal over the heads of politicians and 'big men', particularly to disadvantaged rural groups. And doubt must be cast on claims that this party or that attracts '*the* Harijan' or '*the* Muslim' vote.

And that is not all. There are reports of electoral malpractices, particularly in UP and Bihar, that effectively disenfranchise some at any rate of the village poor; and also react adversely on the role of women in elections.[30] These malpractices are alleged to include the falsification of electoral rolls; the suborning of officials, some at quite a high level, so that they turn a blind eye, or even actively assist particular interests; the location of polling booths in places to which Harijans would fear to come; the 'capturing' of polling booths and the stuffing of ballot boxes with false papers, genuine voters being excluded; various forms of intimidation and violence, even murder; and false counting. It is clearly difficult to substantiate many of these charges; and they may well not apply everywhere. One has also to bear in mind that parties of the left with some claim to an ideology and a concern for the underprivileged may have to explain away their lack of success at the polls in many areas. But it is clear that in some areas at any rate violence and sudden death have increased and are increasing at election time; that, in a society with massive unemployment and underemployment, there are all too many men eager to be hired as members of a mob or of gangs of intimidators; and that the late Sanjay Gandhi and his Youth Congress were by no means innocent in this respect (perhaps through lack of confidence in populist appeals, and through the weakening or destruction, in factional struggles, of Congress' formerly efficient links downward to State and locality; it is also said that Mrs Gandhi unwittingly cut herself off from linkages by surrounding herself with sycophants who prevented unwelcome information from reaching her, and only substituted dubious and risky direct links with local bosses, bypassing State-level leaders). It may further be maintained that, as in other polities past and present, powerful people are all for elections because they know how to manipulate them to their advantage.

Now there have been those who have seen the Indian political system, particularly as it developed under dominant Congress rule, in terms of bargaining between factions whose power and patronage flowed down through the linkages with lower levels (whence pressures and information flowed upward), as a means by which the country, with all its diversity, its cellular structure, its tendency to separatism, its local and regional 'loyalties' was held together as a functioning political system. Blair has referred to this as 'the pluralist paradigm', and has cited Hardgrave, Kothari, Morris-Jones and others as political scientists who in their several ways subscribed to it.[31] In Kothari's hands, indeed, the paradigm became almost teleological: here was an instrument, wielded by Congress, *designed* to keep India together in a way that eluded less fortunate lands; and yet not by autocracy but by democracy, ever flowing down through 'political development' to remote places and lowly strata of society. Some of the pluralists failed to appreciate that vote-banks and electoral malpractice are hardly politically developmental (though one must repeat the caution that we need to know much more, in all parts of the vastness of India, about elections as they really are). Some of the pluralists changed their tune, or were horrified, by The Emergency and Mrs Gandhi's centralization of power. And meanwhile, as Blair shows, the Marxists and others were submitting India to class analysis and concluding that the whole political system was a means by which the national bourgeoisie and their allies in the dominant rural classes held urban workers and the rural poor alike in subjection. In favour of the pluralist view, it is indeed remarkable that India up to the 1970s had contained separatist pressures so successfully, most if not all of the potential separatists showing willingness to play the game according to the all-India rules, constitutional, neo-Congressional, or whatever; while last year's separatist reappears this year as a loyal ally of the central government, bargaining, patronage and claims of legitimacy having done their work. But whether the poor and the landless, the urban Muslims and the tribals would be better or worse off if India had not hung together is another matter. The Marxian paradigm gains some support from what is known of the effective electoral disenfranchisement of the poor; and much more from what is surmised by journalists who never leave the city. And some support, too, from the never-dismantled machinery for repression erected (or perhaps in part inherited) by the Raj and strengthened in The Emergency.

The fact that India has so far contained separatism does not of course mean that it will always do so. (Some see the 1980s as witnessing both increased separatist strains and a diminishing ability on the part of Mrs Gandhi to contain them, partly because of the weakness of linkages.) Nor does the fact (surprising to many who ask why the poor do not revolt against their so-evident disabilities) that India so far has not undergone a revolution, agrarian, or urban, or both, mean that it will never revolt. But (as has indeed been the case in the past) caste and its acceptance, cellular structure, and patterns of dominance may well see to it far into the future that revolts are local and extinguishable and not widespread and all-consuming.

Equally (or almost equally) the fact that India (like Sri Lanka but unlike Pakistan and Bangladesh) has so far not come under a military autocracy does not mean that it will never do so. But a number of factors work against a military coup: the vast size of the country the fact that officers in a number of different command areas would have to concur if military rule was to be more than local (and local rule would carry the risk of armed forces elsewhere moving in to suppress it); the relatively small size of the forces compared with the population and the fact that in some sense the central government has a legitimacy, or has been able to claim a legitimacy, never so widely accorded to governments in Pakistan.

The political system of Sri Lanka

When the Crown Colony of Ceylon slipped so quietly into independence on 4 February 1948 its constitution echoed Westminster very closely: King George VI remained King of Ceylon; and there was a bicameral legislature, and a Cabinet under a Prime Minister, initially D. S. Senanayake.[32] The first major change came in 1972, when Ceylon became the Republic of Sri Lanka (the country's ancient Sinhala name), with a single chamber (the National State Assembly). A much more drastic change followed the general election of 1977. After relatively short deliberation, a constitution much more like that of France or the United States was inaugurated, the President having wide executive powers and the Prime Ministership diminishing in power and importance (on paper, at least). (Mrs Gandhi seems to hanker after such a presidential system.)

Up to 1977 Sri Lanka held general elections at the proper intervals. But in 1983 President Jayawardene, who had been re-elected for a second term, held a referendum as a result of which the life of Parliament and therefore of his government was prolonged for six years. This, with the proscription of certain political parties following the 1983 riots (see p. 100), dismayed liberal opinion, which fears autocracy and is proud of the fact that Sri Lanka has had universal suffrage since 1931.

The political party that carried Sri Lanka into independence was the United National Party (UNP) under D. S. Senanayake, originally in alliance with S. W. R. D. Bandaranaike and his Sinhala Maha Sabha. Both groups in the new parliament consisted almost entirely of the English-educated upper and middle classes, relatively more numerous in Sri Lanka than in India; and, though dominated by affluent Goyigama families, also contained relatively wealthy members of the three coastal castes whose rise to economic and political importance has been outlined in Chapter 2. The UNP also held representatives of the 'Ceylon Tamil' community. Commentators at the time of independence may be forgiven for thinking that this peaceful little country was fortunate in the possession of a single, non-communal cross-caste élite (however comprador-like some of them thought it to be). Its UNP government seemed conservative and stable, though not without plans for economic development; and to wish to continue ties (including a defence agreement) with the United Kingdom (a great comfort to ex-proconsuls).

From 1948 until 1956 the UNP remained in office. On the death of D. S. Senanayake his son Dudley became Prime Minister, to be succeeded by his nephew, Sir John Kotelawala. (Not for nothing were the initials 'UNP' held to stand for 'Uncle and Nephew Party'.)

But in 1956 there was a traumatic general election. The UNP was reduced to a rump in the new parliament. The swing in votes was however much less than the swing in seats, as is usual in 'first-past-the-post' systems. The incoming government was formed by an alliance known as the Mahajana Eksath Peramuna (MEP), People's United Front, the dominant party in which was Bandaranaike's Sri Lanka Freedom Party (SLFP). The other component was the Viplavakari Lanka Sama Samaja Party (VLSSP, Revolutionary Socialist Party, a Trotskyite group). Bandaranaike had also negotiated a no-contest pact with the LSSP, another Trotskyite group, and the Communist Party: these two parties, however, went into opposition.

Since that time one of the features of the politics of Sri Lanka has been a tendency for the UNP and SLFP, with or without allies, to alternate in office (clearly a difference from the Indian situation): so much so that some authors have thought in terms of the firm establishment of a two-party system.[33] Certainly these two parties have been the most important contestants for power in Sri Lanka but others have also been of significance.

The UNP has stood for a generally non-ideological, pragmatic attitude to economic affairs, while leaning towards middle-class interests in such matters as industrialization. The UNP government that took office in 1977 has, for example, permitted the freer import of consumer goods likely to appeal to urban customers and (as we shall see) encouraged foreign capital. In international relations the UNP's 'non-alignment' has looked to the west. SLFP-dominated governments, on the other hand, whether under Bandaranaike or his widow (who succeeded him), have generally been seen as well to the left of the centre; though, as is implicit in the paragraphs to follow, it is simplistic to think of the SLFP as an ideology-based left-wing party as understood in the West. However, the SLFP's posture in foreign affairs has led it to seek friendly relations with the USSR and other Communist countries. Ideology is not surprisingly more clearly defined in the case of the Communist Party (or Parties); and of the LSSP and its derivatives.[34] Three leftist parties were proscribed after the 1983 riots. Yet other parties, like the Tamil Congress and the Tamil United Liberation Front (TULF) have represented constituencies with Tamil majorities in the north and east; the latter party supported secession and was also proscribed in 1983.

Communalism, intertwining language and religion, has indeed played a very important part in Sri Lankan politics, inside and outside of parliament.[35] Thus Bandaranaike fought the 1956 election largely on the language issue, promising to make Sinhala the national language and to support Buddhism. He thus found sympathizers in Sinhala Buddhist rural areas among groups frustrated by what they saw as the advantages in employment held by the English-educated, especially those among the 'Ceylon Tamils'; and benefited too from a wave of Buddhist revivalism associated with 'Buddha Jayanti', the 2500th anniversary of the Buddha. There was an inevitable Tamil reaction. The ensuing period of tension culminated in the serious communal disturbances of 1958. Sinhala–Tamil tension in Sri Lanka is indeed never far below the surface, and sometimes above it (as in violent disturbances in 1977 and 1983). The 'Indian Tamils', descendants of people who came over to work on plantations, were disenfranchised by an enactment of 1948, apart from those few granted citizenship. Some have been repatriated, but others remain to raise periodic Sinhala fears that they will make common cause with the 'Ceylon Tamils' (see pp. 126–9), who form one-eighth of the population.

Caste, as might be expected, has a role in Sri Lankan politics, very much as in India; and some factions and floor-crossings are caste-based. A strand not, however, represented in India, at national level at any rate, is the rivalry between two important families, the Senanayakes and the Bandaranaikes, both Goyigama and affluent, which is seen by some observers as a basic component in UNP/SLFP differences.[36]

What of the linkages we have discussed, in history and in recent politics, in the Indian case? In Sri Lanka, of course, the scale is smaller and the number of levels less. But it is clear that national parties have their links with localities. Bandaranaike, in particular, skilfully wove networks leading to the Sinhala groups whose grievances and frustrations he canalized and, some would say, in the process exaggerated. But genuine, grass-roots politicization seems to have gone further than in most parts of India.

Finally, the point must be made that not all political action in Sri Lanka since independence has followed orderly constitutional channels. Sri Lanka has had its share of violence and of states of emergency. Quite apart from communal riots and the assassination of Bandaranaike (apparently for personal, not political reasons, however) there was an insurrection in April 1971, when groups, mainly of frustrated unemployed youth, associated with the JVP (Jatika Vimukthi Peramuna, People's Liberation Front) and professing an ideology to the left of the 'old' leftist parties, played havoc for some time.[37] More recently there has arisen a terrorist movement among even more frustrated Tamil youth in the north; its acts set off violent Sinhala reaction in 1983. Sri Lanka has not yet done with the problem of youth unemployment, with or without a communal dimension.

The political system of Pakistan

If India and Sri Lanka have so far since independence maintained parliamentary government, albeit seasoned with emergencies and violent events, it has been very different with Pakistan, in which periods of uneasy parliamentary government have alternated with long spells of military rule.[38] Pakistan started with many handicaps. India inherited far more of the administrative machine left by the British Raj; Pakistan had in many respects to start *de novo*. True, it possessed at the outset a remarkable and charismatic leader, Mohammed Ali Jinnah, who was not only the first Governor-General but President of the Constituent Assembly and of the principal political party, the Muslim League. But Jinnah died very soon after independence, in September 1948; and the assassination, three years later, of Liaquat Ali Khan, the first Prime Minister, was another severe blow. India adopted its constitution (which, with amendments, has survived ever since) in 1950. Pakistan did not adopt its 'Islamic' constitution until 1956, carrying on in the meantime essentially under pre-independence enactments. Then, in October 1958 came the first period of military rule under Ayub Khan, who assumed the office of President and Chief Martial Law Administrator (CMLA).

It was Ayub Khan who in 1959 promulgated the Basic Democracies Order, under which electorates of 400 or so voters formed a 'primary constituency'. Eight to ten of these elected a Union Council or Town Committee, termed a 'Basic Democracy'. Above this was a hierarchy of councils at *tahsil*, district, division and provincial levels, to each of which members were elected by the level next below. There was also at all levels provision for nominated members. The scheme in some respects and at the lower levels recalls Panchayati Raj in India. It has variously been seen as a commendable, coercion-proof and politician-proof effort at political mobilization; as a means of widening Ayub's power base, 'democracy' at the higher levels at any rate being illusory because of the weight of officialdom and of nominated members; and as a means of silencing opposition. The experiment did not outlive the Ayub regime.

Ayub was succeeded in March 1969 by Yahya Khan, who a year later set in motion the machinery under which a new constitution might be framed and elections held. It was these elections, in December 1970, which led, as we have already seen (p. 72), to the victory of Mujibur Rahman in East Pakistan and of Bhutto's Pakistan People's Party (PPP), in the West; and so to the train of events that culminated in the secession of Bangladesh. In December 1971 Yahya Khan handed over the Presidency of Pakistan to Bhutto, who also became CMLA. Four months later martial law ended and the National Assembly adopted an interim constitution, superseded in April 1973 by what was described as the Permanent Constitution of the Islamic Republic of Pakistan. Under it Bhutto became Prime Minister. In March 1977 there were elections, handsomely won by the PPP amid allegations of widespread rigging. Four months later a new martial law régime, under General Zia-ul-Haq, assumed power, which it still holds at the time of writing after several promises of elections and subsequent postponements. Bhutto was executed in March 1979 for alleged involvement in a political assassination.

So much for the bare bones of the narrative, with its tale of military rule (tempered for a while, perhaps, by 'Basic Democracy'), from October 1958 to April 1971 and again from July 1977 to date; close on half of Pakistan's independent existence. In order to throw some light on the reasons for this state of affairs and for the contrast with India and Sri Lanka reference must be made to politicians and parties; to questions surrounding the shadowy concept of an 'Islamic State', and to the position of the armed forces. The reader will also need to bear in mind the separatist forces described earlier in this chapter (pp. 74–6), both before and after the secession of Bangladesh; and the landlord-dominated social structure (see p. 13).

The Muslim League was, of course, the embodiment of the movement that, under the leadership of Jinnah, carried the Muslim majority provinces of British India into partition and independence. It invites comparison, then, with the Indian National Congress. But such a comparison would be very superficial, for all the respectably long history of the League (it dates from 1906). Congress had roots in and links with all of the regions of what was to become the Republic of India; and a particular claim to legitimacy. The League had its strongest roots in UP, and either left them there to wither after partition, or (in the case of some of them, represented by migrants like Liaquat Ali Khan) tore them up and transplanted them to the arid lands of West Pakistan. It was the Unionist Party, not the League, that had been strong in Punjab until not very long before partition; while, as we have seen, the 'Frontier Gandhi' favoured Congress. The loss of Jinnah and Liaquat Ali Khan in quick succession bore hard on the League as well as to the new, struggling country. And Congress in India has not had to contend with the same array of rival parties with strong local bases and landlord-delivered vote banks that faced the Muslim League. From 1954 or so onwards, in fact, the Muslim League in Pakistan went into rapid decline; and has never since been the force that Congress, or rather its dominant faction, has remained in India; though factions of the League have fought subsequent elections.

Not much need be said of most other parties in Pakistan during the period when political activity was countenanced. After the death of Liaquat Ali Khan, and until the coup of 1958, even authors friendly to Pakistan see party politics as a matter of shifting alliances and of leaders of relatively small stature, a 'sorry tale' as one of them calls it, with civil servants twice intervening in advance of the first military coup in order, as they saw it, to bring some order out of chaos.[39] The reader must be reminded, however, of the Awami League, and of its roots in East Pakistan and role, under Mujib, in the secession of Bangladesh. And something must be said about the PPP and its leader, Zulfikar Ali Bhutto.

Bhutto first sprang to prominence in 1958, when he took charge of commerce in Ayub Khan's Cabinet as 'a young man new to politics'.[40] He subsequently held a number of other Cabinet offices, including that of Foreign Minister; but resigned at the time of the Tashkent agreement with India (see p. 112) and was for a time imprisoned by Ayub. Having rejected the possibility of establishing a 'forward bloc' within the Muslim League, and urged on, it is said, by leftist friends, he founded a new party, the PPP, in 1967. In the 1970 elections for the National Assembly the PPP won 60 per cent of all seats in West Pakistan; but, it should be noted, all but two of these represented either Punjab or Bhutto's native Sind (where his family were wealthy landowners). In NWFP four other parties divided the seats between them in not very unequal proportions. Then, as we have seen, Bhutto became successively President and Chief Martial Law Administrator; Prime Minister under the 1973 constitution; victor in the widely challenged 1977 elections; and a fallen leader, later to be imprisoned and executed, after the coup of July 1977. But the memory of Bhutto lives on, and is kept green by his widow and daughter and by many loyal supporters.

What manner of man, then, was this Bhutto? And what was, and is the appeal of the party so closely associated with him? Bhutto himself may fairly be described as charismatic, and his appeal as populist, overworked if not ambiguous though both words may be. His motives may be suspect in the eyes of those who emphasize his rise to power, not under democracy, but under an authoritarian régime; and who note his exploitation of hostility to India at the time of his resignation from the Ayub government, his attempt to eliminate all opposition, within and without the PPP, and his ban on the National Awami Party (NAP) in the last few years before his downfall. He certainly proclaimed himself a servant of the people; and the PPP's policy statements 'represent a blend of Islamic, socialistic, and liberal democratic values and vocabulary' which, like some of Mrs Gandhi's pronouncements, strove to appeal to 'the people', or some of them, over the heads of other leaders.[40] To some extent, by nailing so many planks to his election platform, he succeeded, especially among some groups in Punjab and Sind in 1970; and reminds one inevitably of similar tactics pursued by Bandaranaike in Sri Lanka — though Bandaranaike's patiently-forged links with the countryside may well have been stronger than Bhutto's. When in power, moreover, Bhutto and the PPP did initiate programmes of land reform and economic development (to be reviewed in Chapter 6) which suggest that, however pragmatic his approach, some sort of socialism, Islamic or otherwise, formed part of his ideological position. There are those, too, who see Bhutto and the PPP as mobilizers of the people, as purveyors of political modernization.

Why, then, the very mixed record in office that led to the debacle of July 1977? Anwar H. Syed suggests that one important factor was factionalism, not very different from that so familiar in the Indian scene, and related to personal ambitions, opportunism and nest-feathering on the part of some PPP leaders.[41] Syed suggests, too, that the PPP was a movement that failed to convert itself into a party; and that it suffered from 'organizational debility', an inability to manage the political process and, in particular, the 'participatory urges that mobilization had generated'.

Be that as it may, and in spite of the repressions of the tail-end of the Bhutto era, the PPP might well sweep the polls, at least in Punjab and Sind, if free elections were held. For other parties in these heavily-peopled provinces are apparently weaker (we have seen the factional disarray and decay of the Muslim League); though the Pakistan National Alliance (which helped to topple Bhutto in 1977, and temporarily co-operated with the military rulers in forming a civilian Cabinet) and various Islamic parties might provide some competition there amid a scene of shifting alliances recalling those of India. Baluchistan and NWFP would probably provide their own local parties with greater or lesser separatist flavour.

We now turn briefly to the Islamic dimension in the politics of Pakistan. Chapter 3 has shown that it was specifically *Muslim* separatism that led to the birth of Pakistan as an independent country, partitioned from India; and also outlined the nature of the controversy about the nature of an Islamic polity. In all the troubled post-inde-pendence history of Pakistan, before and after the loss of Bangladesh, rulers and politicians have proclaimed that Pakistan is an 'Islamic State' or 'Islamic Republic'. And in all that history there has been acute controversy and endless compromise because of the difficulty of reconciling 'modern' notions like democracy or socialism, to say nothing of the needs of a twentieth-century economy, with Islamic concepts of the state and of divine law in all their rich and confusing variety (variety, that is, given the many schools of thought within Islam, both modernist and traditionalist). Almost all politicians, not least Bhutto, equally with military rulers have with greater or lesser sincerity vied with each other in proclaiming their devotion to Islam and in well-publicized public gestures. The devout Zia-ul-Haq has gone further than most leaders in deference to Islam and in proposing or enacting legislation in tune with conservative Islamic thought. Yet Islamic parties have never made a very strong showing in elections, partly no doubt because of their disunity but also because of the success of Bhutto, initially at any rate, in appealing to populist sentiments.

As Peter Hardy has pointed out, there is a tendency to read into Pakistan's situation the Islamic fundamentalist revivalism that played such a spectacular part in the Iranian Revolution, and is clearly active elsewhere in the Muslim world.[42] But in Pakistan Islamic forces have on the whole supported governments, not swept them away; and fundamentalist Islamic fervour has succeeded, not preceded political change. Some would say that Pakistan is still looking for an Islamic ideology to justify its existence.

It must also be remembered that Islam in Pakistan is not monolithic. The majority of Pakistanis are Sunnis, but a substantial minority (20 per cent) are Shi'ah, some of whom were responsible for serious riots when Zia tried to impose *zakat* (the only tax countenanced by the Koran, and one which Shi'ites do not recognize). Another minority, the Ahmadiya community, are not even recognized as Muslims by orthodox Sunni.

Finally, the puzzle of Pakistan cannot be understood without reference to the special position of the military in the country. The British Raj included many groups in what is now Pakistan under the head of 'martial races'. There is still a strong pride in military service in many parts of Pakistan, and many ex-servicemen in such areas as the Punjab Canal Colonies. The Pakistan army has always represented a higher proportion of the population and taken a larger slice of the budget than has India's. Moreover, the establishment of military rule in Pakistan does not face such formidable difficulties in terms of the size of the country and the diversity of commands as does India (cf. p. 97); and is aided by the landlord-dominated social structure with its authoritarian ethos. (I remember a civil servant in Pakistan in 1956 bellowing at cowed villagers in a way which would have provoked at least sullen resentment, possibly a riot, in India.)

Pakistan, then, is not just Muslim India. Its politics and government reflect not only Islam, but a top-down society, and a regionalism much stronger than that in India. But, as in India, the higher judiciary has often shown a quite surprising independence and resilience.

Politics and government in Bangladesh

Bangladesh, as we have seen, started its independent existence in 1971 under the leadership of Sheikh Mujibur Rahman, whose Awami League had swept the polls in the 1970 elections in East Pakistan. Mujib took over a chaotic country devastated by war and full of armed bands apt to take the law into their own hands. But he also started with an enormous fund of goodwill within the country and internationally (with exceptions to be entered in the next chapter). But within a relatively short space of time much of this goodwill had been dissipated, within Bangladesh at any rate. For although Mujib came home as a hero and although he had qualities of crowd control that some would call charisma, others demagogy, he was no administrator. And although he himself may have been relatively uncorrupt, it became clear that his immediate entourage, including his family, were engaged in nest-feathering on a large scale. Moreover, there was widespread disillusionment and loss of morale among public servants and others: there was no incentive for honest men to toil for development. There had been a number of ill-judged and ineffective measures of nationalization. And anti-Indian feeling had surfaced (and, remember, Mujib could be represented as an Indian puppet).

In 1975, a period of great instability and uncertainty began. First, in August, came a military coup in which Mujib and most of his family were killed. Soon after, there was a pro-Indian counter-coup, hard on the heels of which came another military coup whose impetus was captured by General Ziaur Rahman and his supporters. In June 1978 he was endorsed as President in a nationwide plebiscite: executive President, that is, under a French-style constitution which provided for a single-chamber national assembly. In the elections to that assembly in February 1979 Zia's Bangladesh Nationalist Party

(NAP), of which he was president, won a massive victory, securing 250 seats out of a total of 330. The once-mighty Awami League (or, rather, a rump-like faction of it) was the second-largest party with only 39 seats, the Muslim League third with 12.

But in May 1981, Zia was assassinated by a rival general. Abdus Sattar, a judge, was constitutionally elected President; but was overthrown by yet another military coup in March 1982, as a result of which General Hossain Mohammed Ershad became chief martial law administrator, and suspended the constitution (he later declared himself Prime Minister).

Bangladesh, unfortunate country that it is, may well see yet more coups and counter-coups engineered by rival factions within the military, punctuated from time to time by periods of constitutional government during which corruption provides opportunity, or excuse, for yet another military takeover.

Politics and government in Nepal and Bhutan

Nepal was a monarchy throughout the British period, and remains a monarchy today. But the power exercised by the monarch, and his relationship to other political forces, has varied over the years, especially since 1950.[43] In that year the Rana family, who had over a century earlier come to hold a monopoly of power from their original base as hereditary 'prime ministers', were toppled by a palace revolt (a revolt by, not in, the palace) in which the king was aided and abetted by India. A constitutional monarchy was proclaimed and, in 1959, a constitution adopted. But successive kings have had an uneasy relationship with politicians, notably with B. P. Koirala and his Nepali Congress, which clearly has owed much to the Indian model (it also has had its factions) and, indeed, to Indian encouragement; and there has been much unrest. True, a general election was held in 1957, in which the Nepali Congress emerged as the dominant party; but three years later there was a coup engineered by the king, with army support, and Koirala and many other politicians (whom the king had come to distrust) were jailed. The king then tried to establish a party-less, five-tier *panchayati* democracy reminiscent of Ayub's efforts in Pakistan, and confirmed by a referendum in 1980. But the situation remains uneasy; the king is likely to be forced to manoeuvre constantly to retain power, confronted as he is by politicians, student and other rioters, and an army that may not always remain loyal to him; and enthroned as he is in a kingdom whose politics are of great concern both to India and China.

Bhutan also remains a monarchy that has toyed with popular government; and a member of the United Nations whose foreign relations are subject to the advice of India.[44]

Clearly, then, the affairs of Nepal and Bhutan cannot be divorced from those of India; while India itself, together with the other countries of South Asia, has crucially important international relationships within and without the subcontinent. These will be the subject of the next chapter.

References

1 Spear, P. (1972) *India: a Modern History*, rev. edn, Ann Arbor, 424–7; Schwartzberg, J. E. (ed.) (1978) *A Historical Atlas of South Asia*, Chicago, 75–7. See also Morris-Jones, W. H. (1982) 'The transfer of power, 1947', *Modern Asian Studies*, 16, 1–32.

2 Rushbrook Williams, L. F. (1966) *The State of Pakistan*, 2nd edn, London, 99–111; Michel, A. A. (1967) *The Indus Rivers: a Study of the Effects of Partition*, New Haven, 195–340.

3 Farmer, B. H. (1974) *Agricultural Colonization in India since Independence*, London, 36–42.

4 Ibid., pp. 280–9.

5 Stephens, I. (1968) *The Pakistanis*, London, 1.

6 Rushbrook Williams, L. F. (1975) *Pakistan under Challenge*, London, 14–16.

7 Stephens, I. (1968) op. cit., p. 95.

8 Hafeez Malik (1977) 'Nationalism and the quest for ideology in Pakistan', in Ziring, L. *et al.* (eds), *Pakistan: the Long View*, Durham, NC, 271–300, especially 286–7.

9 Ibid., pp. 286–8.

10 Ziring, L. (1977) Introduction to Ziring, L. *et al.* (eds), op. cit., p. 4.

11 Rushbrook Williams, L. F. (1975) op. cit., pp. 92–3. See also Ziring, L. (1981) *Pakistan: The Enigma of Political Development*, Folkestone, Chapter 6.

12 Chaube, S. (1973) *Hill Politics in Northeast India*, Bombay; Venkata Rao, V. (1976) *A Century of Tribal Politics in North-East India*, New Delhi. See also Taylor, D. and Yapp, M. (eds) (1979) *Political Identity in South Asia*, London; and Rustomji, N. (1983) *The Imperilled Frontiers*, Delhi.

13 Farmer, B. H. (1974) op. cit., pp. 13–15, 56–9.

14 Weiner, M. (1962) *The Politics of Scarcity: Public Pressure and Political Response in India*, Chicago, 41–3.

15 Farmer, B. H. (1974) op. cit., pp. 272–4.
16 Rao, G. R. S. (1975) *Regionalism in India: the Case of Telengana*, New Delhi; Ram Reddy, G. and Sharma, B. A. V. (1979) *Regionalism in India: a Study of Telengana*, Delhi; and Gray, H. (1971) 'The demand for a separate Telengana State in India', *Asian Survey*, 11, 463–74 and (1974) 'The failure of the demand for a separate Andhra State', ibid., 14, 338–49.
17 Parthasarathy, G., Ramana, K. V. and Dasaradha Rama Rao, G. (1973) 'Separatist movement in Andhra Pradesh', *Econ. & Polit. Weekly*, 8, 560–3.
18 Kothari, R. (1970) *Politics in India*, Boston, Mass., 7.
19 Some of the principal books on politics in India are: Carter, A. (1974) *Elite Politics in Rural India: Political Stratification and Alliances in Western Maharashtra*, Cambridge; Dasgupta, B. and Morris-Jones, W. H. (1975) *Patterns and Trends in Indian Politics*, New Delhi; Hardgrave, R. L. (1975) *India: Government and Politics in a Developing Nation*, New York; Hanson, A. H. and Douglas, J. (1972) *India's Democracy*, London; Hiro, D. (1978) *Inside India Today*, London; Kothari, R. (1970) op. cit.; Kothari, R. (ed.) (1971) *Caste in Indian Politics*, New Delhi; Mayer, A. C. (1967) 'Caste and local politics in India', in Mason, P. (ed.), *India and Ceylon: Unity and Diversity*, London; Mellor, J. W. (ed.) (1979) *India: A Rising Middle Power*, Boulder, Co.; Morris-Jones, W. H. (1971) *The Government and Politics of India*, London; Taylor, D. and Yapp, M. (ed.) (1979) *Political Identity in South Asia*, London. See also Brass, P. R. (forthcoming) 'National power and local politics in India: a 20-year perspective', *Modern Asian Studies*.
20 Morris-Jones, W. H. (1971) op. cit.
21 Low, D. A. (1980) *Emergencies and Elections in India*, Kingsley Martin Memorial Lecture, Centre of South Asian Studies, University of Cambridge (typescript held in the Centre).
22 Morris-Jones, W. H. (1971) op. cit., pp. 182–93.
23 Ibid., p. 120.
24 Hardgrave, R. L. (1975) op. cit., p. 156. See also Hart, H. C., (ed.) (1976) *Indira Gandhi's India: A Political System Reappraised*, Boulder, Co.
25 Mendelsohn, O. (1978) 'The collapse of the Indian National Congress', *Pacific Affairs*, 51, 41–66, especially 47–8.
26 Blair, H. W. (1980) 'Mrs Gandhi's Emergency, the Indian elections of 1977, pluralism and Marxism', *Modern Asian Studies*, 14, 237–71.
27 Farmer, B. H. (1974) *Agricultural Colonization in India since Independence*, London, 255–6.
28 For example, Brass, P. R. (1965) *Factional Politics in an Indian State*, Berkeley.
29 For example, Arora, S. K. (1969) 'Exploring political predisposition:

efficacy and cynicism in rural Andhra Pradesh', *Behavioural Sciences and Community Development*, 3, 126–38; Ram Reddy, G. and Seshadri, K. (1972) *The Voter and Panchayati Raj*, Hyderabad; and Seshadri, K. and Jain, S. P. (1972) *Panchayati Raj and Political Perceptions of the Electorate*, Hyderabad.

30 Maneshwari, A. C. (1980) 'Uttar Pradesh: rigging in practice', *Econ. & Pol. Weekly*, 15, 99–100; and Nalini Singh (1980) 'Elections as they really are', ibid., 909–15.

31 Blair, H. W. (1980) op. cit. referring to Morris-Jones W. H. (1971) op. cit.; Hardgrave, R. L. (1975) op. cit.; and Kothari, R. (1970) op. cit.

32 Some of the more important general works on the politics of Sri Lanka are: Wriggins, W. H. (1960) *Ceylon: the Dilemmas of a New Nation*, Princeton, NJ; Kearney, R. N. (1973) *The Politics of Ceylon (Sri Lanka)*, Ithaca, NY; Wilson, A. J. (1974) *Politics in Sri Lanka, 1947–1973*, London; and De Silva, K. M. (ed.) (1977) *Sri Lanka: a Survey*, London, especially Chapters 12–15.

33 For example, Woodward, C. A. (1969) *The Growth of a Party System in Ceylon*, Providence, RI and (1974–5) 'Sri Lanka's electoral experience: from personal to party politics', *Pacific Affairs*, 47, 455–71.

34 Lerski, G. J. (1968) *Origins of Trotskyism in Ceylon: a Documentary History of the LSSP, 1935–42*, Stanford, and (1970) 'The twilight of Ceylonese Trotskyism', *Pacific Affairs*, 43, 384–93. See also Blackton, C. S. (1974) 'The Marxists and the ultra-Marxists of Sri Lanka since independence', *Ceylon J. Hist. Soc. Studies*, New Series, 4, 126–33.

35 Farmer, B. H. (1963) *Ceylon: a Divided Nation*, London, and (1965) 'The social basis of nationalism in Ceylon', *J. Asian Studies*, 24, 431–9; Kearney, R. N. (1967) *Communalism and Language in the Politics of Ceylon*, Durham, NC; and Roberts, M., (1978) 'Ethnic conflict in Sri Lanka and Sinhalese perspectives: barriers to accommodation', *Modern Asian Studies*, 12, 353–76.

36 Jiggins, J. (1979) *Caste and Family in the Politics of the Sinhalese, 1947–76*, Cambridge.

37 Obeyesekere, G. (1974) 'Some comments on the social background of the April 1971 insurgency in Sri Lanka (Ceylon)', *J. Asian Studies*, 33, 367–84.

38 For politics in Pakistan see especially Rushbrook Williams, L. F. (1966) *The State of Pakistan*, 2nd edn, London; and (1975) *Pakistan under Challenge*, London; Stephens, I. (1963) *Pakistan*, London, especially Chapters 18,19; Korson, J. H. (ed.) (1974) *Contemporary Problems of Pakistan*, Leiden; Ziring, L. *et al.* (eds) (1977) *Pakistan: the Long View*, Durham, NC; and Manzooruddin, A. (ed.) (1980) *Contemporary Pakistan: Politics, Economy and Society*, Durham, NC.

39 Stephens, I. (1963) op. cit., p. 243.

40 Rushbrook Williams, L. F. (1966) op. cit., p. 196. For Bhutto and the

PPP, see Anwar H. Syed, 'The Pakistan People's Party', in Ziring, L. *et al.* (eds), (1977) op. cit., Chapter 4.

41 Ibid., p. 77.

42 Hardy, P. in a lecture at the Centre of South Asian Studies, University of Cambridge, 3 March 1980.

43 Rose, L. E. and Fisher, M. W. (1970) *The Politics of Nepal: Persistence and Change in an Asian Monarchy*, Ithaca; Baral, L. S. (1980) *Political Development in Nepal*, London.

44 Rose, L. E. (1977) *The Politics of Bhutan*, Ithaca.

SOUTH ASIA:
INTERNATIONAL RELATIONS

This chapter will be concerned, first, with bilateral relations between the several states of South Asia; and then with their relations with the wider world outside the subcontinent. In the pages that follow, 'India' will, except when the context requires otherwise, mean the Government of India at the time in question; and similarly with other countries. This usage must not be taken to imply unanimity of opinion within a country (see, in this context, pp. 117–18).

International relations within South Asia: India and Pakistan

The unhappy, indeed tragic, animosity between India and Pakistan has overshadowed international relations within South Asia for most of the time since independence; and has powerfully affected and in turn been affected by the relations of both with countries outside South Asia, notably China, the United States and the Soviet Union. Chapter 4 has shown that a series of crises and disputes has bedevilled Indo–Pakistan relations: Indian action in Hyderabad and Junagadh; the Kashmir accession crisis and subsequent imbroglio; the prolonged Indus waters dispute; contested boundaries in that worthless wilderness, the Rann of Cutch; and the secession of Bangladesh and attendant complications. Chapter 4 has also shown that on no less than four occasions the neighbours have taken up arms against each other. True, there have been rapprochements (though never closer than arm's length) on a number of occasions, as at Tashkent in 1966, through Russian mediation, and at Simla in June–July 1972, when Mrs Gandhi and Bhutto conferred and even agreed on a line of control in Kashmir (while reserving their respective irreconcilable positions on that territory). There have been other notable and welcome agreements, as eventually in the case of the Indus waters; and as an extension of the Simla agreement, in August 1973. But after every hesitant rapprochement, after every agreement, ill-will has broken out again, as have poisoned suspicion and loud recrimination, often after some incident that, to the outside world, seems trivial. True, we shall see that the atmosphere in the early 1980s has seemed a good deal better; it is not pessimistic, but realistic to view this development against a background of the mutual suspicion and ill-will of earlier years.

Why, then, this mutual suspicion and ill-will, obsessive and ineradicable as they have often seemed to be, when to many uncommitted observers and, indeed, to many intelligent citizens of the two countries there is every advantage in friendship and co-operation, not least in the interests of economic development and the attainment of national security? Why, when both countries are so desperately poor, have such enormous resources been spent on armaments for use by the one against the other, with resultant loss of life and of material assets? (Indian defence expenditure, according to figures in the UN *Statistical Yearbooks*, grew from Rs 1916 million in 1956 to Rs 11,047 million in 1970; the latter figure represents about 5 per cent of the national income. Pakistan's defence expenditure grew over the same period from Rs 821 million to Rs 2761 million, about 4 per cent of the national income. None of these figures includes the value of arms and other military assistance received from other countries.) The answers on the questions posed before the parenthesis differ with the nationality and vi̶ ̶ ̶ ̶ ̶ ̶ ̶ ̶ ̶ ̶ ̶nt;[1] and it is worth spending a little time l̶ ̶ ̶ ̶ ̶ ̶ ̶ ̶ ̶ ̶ ̶ ̶rces in Indo-Pakistan relations.

The first point to be made is the obvious one that Pakistan is very much smaller than India, both in area and population. This was true before it lost Bangladesh and is even more true now. Howard Wriggins, in contrast to most authors (who stress the uniqueness of Pakistan's position vis-à-vis India), has developed a general model seeking to explain Pakistan's foreign policy in terms of the anxiety to be expected when a smaller, weaker state borders a larger, stronger one.[2] 'Typically', he says, 'smaller states next to larger ones are rendered anxious by that larger neighbour'. He goes on to quote Thucydides' tenet that fear is a central driving force behind statesmen; to emphasize the special vulnerability of a small Pakistan consisting of two even smaller wings separated by Indian territory; and to claim that India's army was never less than twice the size of Pakistan's. The last point needs some qualification. Onkar Marwah has stated that after arms began to flow from the US to Pakistan in 1954 its army grew almost to the size of India's, and gained a superiority in armoured divisions that caused anxiety among Indian military planners faced with 'the spectre (historic) of an invasion from the northwest with Pakistan Patton tanks clanking down the Grand Trunk road to Delhi'.[3] Anxiety, then, was not altogether on one side. And a certain ambivalence was abroad in Pakistan because of the traditional contempt of Muslim for Hindu soldiers: a certain braggadocio, too (I remember schoolchildren in Pakistani Punjab in 1956 being taught a song about marching on Delhi). Moreover, in various ways Pakistan early on set itself ambitious goals and struck hostile postures before it had the strength to match words with deeds. Nevertheless, Wriggins has a point, and develops it convincingly in terms of 'the balancing process' practised by small states throughout the ages who are led to seek alliances with powerful outsiders for fear of a bigger neighbour (Pakistan's efforts in this direction will be explored in the second half of this chapter). Ziring, indeed, goes further and, writing after the loss of Bangladesh, sees Bhutto's foreign policy as 'predicated on maximizing fear of India in order to keep his detractors from further fractioning the state' by exploiting separatist tendencies.[4] However, Wriggins has to admit that the applicability of his general model to Indo–Pakistani relations is limited; and in concluding draws attention to a number of particularities in these relations. To such particularities we now turn; and begin by asking the question 'How far has special hostility sprung from unhappy relations between Hindus and Muslims before, during and after partition'?

Doubts may have been sown in the mind of the reader by the discussion in Chapter 3 of the extent to which Indian Muslims under the British Raj formed 'a community' with uniform ideology and attitudes to their Hindu fellow-countrymen and to the two-nation theory; and there were undoubtedly many instances of peaceful coexistence of Hindus and Muslims in a number of parts of the subcontinent, especially but not exclusively in the south. But for all that it is certainly possible to speak, albeit with reservations, of the 'traditional hostility' between Hindus and Muslims if one bears in mind the refusal of Islam to go the way of other religions and cults and to be absorbed into the ever-open-door of Hinduism, and the related contempt of its adherents for infidels, especially those who were notorious idolators; and remembers, too, the all-too-frequent outbursts of communal rioting and of carnage. Such outbursts occurred, of course, under the Raj. The fact that they were particularly violent just before partition and even more so as the millions of refugees crossed from Pakistan, East and West to India and vice versa did nothing to improve relations between Muslim-majority Pakistan and Hindu-majority India; and, indeed, saw to it that, quite apart from other considerations, those relations got off to a lamentably bad start. This was particularly the case because refugees rose to prominence in politics, especially in Pakistan. The situation was of course greatly exacerbated by the Kashmir crisis and the inclusion in India, on the Maharaja's accession, of a Muslim majority area.

But the Muslims of Kashmir were not the only Muslims who found themselves in the new India. Pakistan soon set itself up as the guardian, perforce absentee, of *all* Indian Muslims from the large communities of UP to the smaller, but still important ones of Hyderabad, Kerala and the south generally. Intercommunal incidents and examples of discrimination against Muslims were duly reported, and often exaggerated, in the Pakistan press, and the notion of independent India as a Hindu Raj faithfully maintained; while Indian Muslim groups anxious to show that they were good citizens of the Republic were ignored. India, for its part, sided with Hindus left behind in Pakistan: these were mostly in the East. India's concern for Hindu refugees from East Pakistan, while laudable on humanitarian grounds, was not unmixed with political calculation; while, on the other side of the coin, reaction in Assam to Bengali Muslim immigrants has ranged from smouldering jealousy at their real or alleged economic prosperity to severe disorder (as in 1980–1 and 1983) (see pp. 78–9).

Pakistan as it was left after the secession of Bangladesh has clearly less claim to be the guardian of all Muslims in the subcontinent than it had from 1947 to 1971; but, as we shall see, there have been attempts, not altogether unsuccessful, for Pakistan and Bangladesh to reach out to each other over the top of, or behind the back of India and present something of a common Muslim front. It was in Bangladesh in 1976 that I heard the subcontinent referred to as 'the Bangla-Pak subcontinent'.

It was, however, not only intercommunal troubles around the time of partition in 1947 that got relations between India and Pakistan off to a bad start. There was persistent squabbling over such matters as the distribution of assets, including sterling balances held in London; the transfer of official files and records to Karachi, the provisional capital of Pakistan; and the division of the armed forces, made all the more difficult for Pakistan because since the Rebellion of 1857 the British had been careful to ensure that there were no all-Muslim units in the Indian Army. It is indeed very remarkable, and a tribute to the tenacity of such founding fathers as Jinnah and Liaquat Ali Khan, that Pakistan was able to set up a civil administration and an army of its own as quickly and efficiently as it did. The handicaps were crippling: for example, the Pakistan Foreign Office had for some time only one typewriter — or so it is said.

The fact that India could be blamed for many of these initial handicaps did nothing to foster friendly relations. But behind it all lay the suspicion, burgeoning into certainty in some Pakistani minds, that the new rulers of India were not in the smallest degree reconciled to partition. It is of course true that it was with the greatest reluctance that Nehru and his colleagues, including Mahatma Gandhi, accepted partition as a solution to the problem of moving swiftly to independence; and true, too, that some Indian political parties and bodies of opinion have never accepted it. This is especially the case with parties of the right with strong roots in Hindu chauvinism, for example the Jan Sangh: such elements profess that their hearts bleed at the dissection of Mother India. And militant Sikhs do not forget that some of their holiest places lie west of the new frontier in Pakistani Punjab, whence nearly all of their coreligionists fled in 1947. The events of 1971, particularly the part that India played in the secession of Bangladesh, strengthened in many Pakistani minds the conviction that India was bent on the destruction of their country and its reabsorption into an enlarged India. India did, as we have seen, withdraw and leave an independent Muslim-majority Bangladesh. Perhaps one motive in this (which in its wry way ought to reassure Pakistanis) is encapsulated in William J. Barnds' assertion that most Indians 'want no more Muslims or Bengalis'.[5] Moreover, in the war of 1971 India did not press its advantage on the western front; and, after the cease-fire, withdrew to its former frontiers. Earlier, in 1958, India had made no move against Pakistan when its internal state was one of chaos. But Pakistan has not been reassured by such Indian actions, any more than it was earlier or later reassured by statements by Indian leaders to the effect that they have no territorial designs on Pakistan (for example, that by Nehru, who in refuting the allegation that a main aim of Indian foreign policy is to weaken and isolate Pakistan and eventually to undo partition said 'Anything more unrealistic and devoid of fact I cannot imagine.').[6]

If such an atmosphere of suspicion has lingered long in the smaller country, India for her part has had some grounds, based on statements by Pakistani leaders and the slant given to press reports, for believing that Pakistan has rejoiced in every report of disunity, separatism and potential secession in the enormous and highly variegated Indian body politic; thus echoing the view held by a number of Britons in the days of the Raj that India was too divided by community, caste and language (and 'race', they would say) for it ever to function as a single independent state. Pakistan, of course, has suspected that India does all it can to foment such divisive activities as those of the Pakhtunistan movement discussed in the previous chapter (see pp. 74–5).

It is, I hope, implicit in some of the points that have just been made, and indeed in one or two cases explicit, that it is wrong to talk of India and Pakistan in all the tragic history of their mutual suspicion, misunderstanding, hostility and conflict as though each was a person with a consistent, single view of the other. There have been many people in India who, I am confident, have harboured no strong ill-will to all the people of Pakistan (though few if any of them have departed from their government's line on Kashmir). And equally, though the evidence here is harder to come by, there have been Pakistanis who have felt no constant and generalized hostility towards all Indians and all things Indian. For example, and indeed as evidence, I can testify to the fact that throughout all the troubles, even in the depths of the 1971 war, Indians, Pakistanis (and Bangladeshis when their state emerged) have talked to each other without hostility and, indeed, with friendliness in such academic institutions as the School of Oriental and African Studies in the University of London and the Centre of South Asian Studies in the University of Cambridge. It is however clear that there have been groups in both countries, whether communally-minded politicians or religious leaders or interest groups, who did nothing to reduce hostility and in some cases actively fomented it. Howard Wriggins has written:[7]

> Most states are not monoliths in fact, but a congeries of competing and collaborating interests. What were the bureaucratic, professional or economic interest groups within Pakistan that have been most important in shaping the concept of "national interest" and the making of foreign policy in Pakistan? Did domestic political support at any one time depend as heavily upon a high degree of hostility towards India as many Indians argue?

These questions are almost impossible to answer from the information that has come out of Pakistan or from the secondary literature, largely because of the prevalence of authoritarian regimes (which do not take kindly to enquiry into their decision-making processes) and of a controlled press. Pakistani scholars have told us little, largely because they may not, about domestic influences on foreign policy. Questions like Wriggins' ought also, of course, to be asked about India. There some answers emerge: for example, about the role of Hindu communalist groups and certain political parties. But others must remain at present unanswered. All, in fact, that can be done here is to utter a caution about accepting sweeping statements that 'Pakistanis have this attitude to India' and 'Indians have that attitude to Pakistan'; and that both sets of attitudes are unshakeable whatever the changes in circumstance, whatever the shifts in the internal power and influence structure in the two states, and notwithstanding the passage of time.

Now, it is unfortunately the fact that both governments have wrapped themselves in cloaks (rather different cloaks) of moral self-righteousness. But, equally, it is vital that the outside observer does not himself become self-righteously critical: if tempted to do so, he should remember the wise words of William J. Barnds:[8]

> ... it would have required the foresight of genius and the selflessness of sainthood for the leaders of either country to have acted differently ... in the midst of one of the major upheavals of the twentieth century.

However, as I have said, the atmosphere between India and Pakistan showed improvement in the early 1980s, in a wider international context discussed below (see pp. 144–5). There was a series of meetings at high level (including one between Mrs Gandhi and Zia in November 1982); consideration of a treaty of peace, friendship and co-operation; and proposals for a joint commission to resolve outstanding issues between the two countries. It will not surprise the reader that it was a matter concerning Kashmir that caused the suspension of talks for some months, and it remains to be seen whether Kashmir will, as some have supposed, eventually fade into the background;[9] while it is of interest that ideas about joint bodies were mooted, but not implemented way back in the months before partition.

India and Pakistan have recently met also at periodical conferences of the Foreign Secretaries of South Asian countries, which began in 1981 and which have set up working groups on a number of possible areas of collaboration, while in 1983 they agreed to set up a joint commission which, it was hoped, would lead to 'multi-faceted cooperation'. But this leads us on to bilateral relations in South Asia other than those between India and Pakistan.

International relations within South Asia: India and Pakistan and their relations with Bangladesh

Chapter 4 has explained how East Pakistan seceded in 1971 to become the independent country of Bangladesh, and explored the not uncontroversial role of India in the process. It is the purpose of the present section to discuss the relationships between India and Pakistan on the one hand, and Bangladesh on the other, since December 1971. It will be shown that these have in general served to complicate and further to embitter Indo–Pakistani relations.

True, one of the rare and all too brief rapprochements between India and Pakistan was, as already mentioned, that which grew from the meetings between Mrs Gandhi and Bhutto at Simla in 1972, when affairs in Bangladesh, especially those arising from the then-recent war, were high on the agenda (though they did not dominate it to the exclusion of all else: an amendment of the ceasefire line in Kashmir and the restoration of pre-war boundaries elsewhere also issued, actually with quite astonishing rapidity, from the discussions). But at Simla itself there was a great deal of bickering and haggling about Bangladesh, then, of course, in great distress and disarray in the aftermath of the struggle against Pakistan and the ensuing war. There was the problem of the 93,000 prisoners taken in what became Bangladesh (some 15,000 of these were civilians).[10] India was slow to resolve the issue of their release because it did not wish to impair its relations with Sheikh Mujib and with a Bangladesh then dominated by a pro-Indian mood. Mujib's stance was that prisoners could not be released till Pakistan recognized his country; and he also wished to try the 1500 or so prisoners said to have been involved in war crimes. Bhutto would neither accept the need for trials (hinting that if they took place he could not be responsible for the safety of Bengalis held in Pakistan, estimated at no less than 400,000); stalled on the issue of recognition; and expressed unwillingness to receive the Biharis (see p. 73), then for the most part in a distressed condition in Dhaka and elsewhere in Bangladesh. Further, Pakistan with Chinese support succeeded for some time in keeping Bangladesh out of the United Nations. However, after further haggling and renewed negotiations an agreement was signed by India and Pakistan, with Bangladesh's concurrence, in August 1973. All Pakistani prisoners save a mere 195 still charged with war crimes were to be repatriated, as were all Bengalis in Pakistan. An unspecified number of Biharis who wished to settle in Pakistan were to be allowed to go there. Eventually, after a flurry of diplomatic activity, Pakistan recognized Bangladesh in 1974; and at a meeting of the foreign ministers of India, Pakistan and Bangladesh a little later the idea of war crimes trials was dropped altogether and the migration of rather more Biharis to Pakistan was approved. Bangladesh finally became a member of the United Nations in September, 1974; and joined the Security Council in 1978.

Up to a point, then, a satisfactory conclusion was reached on issues arising out of the events of 1971 in Bangladesh. But since 1974 the triangular relationship between India, Pakistan and Bangladesh has been far from a smooth one, for reasons arising basically from disputes between India and Bangladesh, some of which go back in time before the independence of the latter; from changing stances of successive regimes in Bangladesh towards the other two states; and from what India has seen, rightly or wrongly, as attempts by Pakistan to reach across to Bangladesh in order to embarrass India.

One of the principal disputes between India and Bangladesh, with highly important economic implications for both countries, has been that over the Farakka Barrage.[11] This, as Burke says, 'first appeared as a small cloud on the horizon in 1951, and progressively assumed major proportions in the nineteen-sixties'. It thus became one of the many bones of contention between India and Pakistan. The dispute rumbled on into the period of Bangladeshi independence. The physiographic basis of the problem lies in the contrast between the old and new deltas in Bengal, to which allusion was made in Chapter 2: the new delta in the east, and covering much of Bangladesh, still subject to active flooding rivers, to the accretion of silt, and to seaward growth; the former, lying mainly in West Bengal and so in India, moribund and not under active construction by its rivers which tend to clog with silt. One such river is the Bhagirathi, which becomes the Hugli (Hooghly) and passes through Calcutta. As long ago as the 1850s British engineers recommended a barrage at Farakka, upstream of the take-off of the Bhagirathi from the Ganga (Ganges), and a canal to the Bhagirathi to increase the flow through it and the Hugli and so to wash out silt from the port of Calcutta. The proposal was revived from time to time but plans were only finalized in the 1950s, by which time it was conceived that the increased flow in the Hugli would not only help to solve the problem of siltation and navigation at Calcutta but also improve drainage, sanitation and water supply to domestic and industrial consumers. Construction began in 1962 and was completed in 1971. Water began to be withdrawn from the Ganga and diverted to the Bhagirathi in 1975.

'Why', it may be asked, 'did Pakistan object to the Farakka scheme during the planning and construction stages, and Bangladesh after completion of the barrage, given that East Bengal's problem is an active delta subject to massive floods that a barrage upstream, albeit only some eleven miles from the Indo–Bangladesh frontier, might help to moderate?' The answer lies partly in the general tetchiness of relations between India on the one hand and Pakistan (and at times Bangladesh) on the other. It also lies partly in a dispute over international law, Pakistan (and later Bangladesh) contending that the Ganga is an international river, so that the lower riparian state has a legitimate interest in its waters, India contending that the Ganga is not an international river, but overwhelmingly an Indian river, given the high proportion of its course in Indian territory. But parts of the grounds of the dispute lie in practicalities. Flooded most of East Bengal may be in the south-west monsoon, but the waters of the Ganga are of great importance to agriculture and to irrigation, actual and prospective, in the dry season. It was maintained successively by Pakistan and Bangladesh that the volume India proposed to abstract at Farakka would be ruinous to cultivation and fisheries; and would lead to siltation and so increased flooding in the monsoon; and would make land at the seaward margin of the delta uncultivable through the upstream penetration of saltwater. It may be that consequences of this kind were painted in too black a colour.

Be that as it may, negotiations dragged on while Bangladesh was still East Pakistan, edging towards some measures of agreement, and narrowing the disputed issues down to the maximum volume India could abstract during the dry season, particularly in its most critical months. Argument broke out *de novo* following Bangladeshi independence, in spite of India's initial patronage of the new state. In November 1975 an agreement was signed on the sharing of the waters for a five year period and on a joint study on ways to increase the flow of the Ganga. Disputes have, however, continued, Bangladesh favouring storage reservoirs upstream of Farakka (which would, it seems, drown large areas of fertile Indian agricultural land) and India favouring a grandiose scheme to take Brahmaputra water across country into the Ganga above Farakka (shades here of the Triple Canals Project and the new construction in Pakistan following the Indus Waters Agreement: see p. 70). However, a new interim agreement was reached in 1982.

We must note briefly two other sources of disagreement between India and Bangladesh, both already in evidence before 1971. The first concerns minor boundary disputes, often due to changing river courses and the appearance of new areas of fluvial deposition known as *chars*. In 1974 a border agreement was reached, India giving up some small areas which it was more convenient for Bangladesh to administer and vice versa. But this did not prevent a dispute in 1979 over a *char* of only 40 acres in the Mujari river, bordering on Tripura; and in 1981 over a small piece of mud in the Sundarbans known as New Moore Island ('Talpati' to Bangladesh): here it was reported that oil as well as mud was at stake.

Secondly, and more serious, are cross-border incursions and movements: for example, of dissident Nagas and Mizos harboured in Bangladesh (as they were in East Pakistan before it) and re-entering hill areas of north-east India where, as we have seen, tribal separatist tendencies are prominent; or a two-way movement between Mizoram and the Chittagong Hill Tracts of Bangladesh; or the passage of Bengali Muslims into Assam, contributing to the tense situation in that state or the cross-border activity of the Amra Bangali movement noted earlier (pp. 73–4); or raids from India on Bangladeshi paddy-fields, reported frequently as incursions of 'armed miscreants' when I was in Dhaka in 1976. On the one hand, it may be argued that such movements of people are inseparable from such a long, artificial boundary. On the other hand, the seriousness with which these movements are taken clearly depends on their connexion, if any, with internal dissidence or separatism, and on the state of relations between the two countries (thus in August 1981, the Home Minister of Bangladesh voiced fears that those familiar figures, 'armed miscreants' from India, might be seeking to sabotage, subvert, and create disorder). To the general state of Indo–Bangladesh relations we now turn, subsuming in the discussion relations between Pakistan and Bangladesh (which clearly cannot have the immediacy of the disputes with India about water, land, and movements of mud and men).

Official relations between India and Bangladesh immediately after the war and 'liberation' of 1971 were friendly, and those between Pakistan and Bangladesh, so far as they existed at all, distant and hostile. In March 1973, India and Bangladesh in fact signed a 25-year Treaty of Friendship, Co-operation and Peace, which included a defence pact; and India was one of the countries supplying aid to restore the war-shattered Bangladeshi economy. Not surprisingly Pakistan was execrated in many quarters in Bangladesh, memories of atrocities during the period of repression in 1971 still being all too fresh and vivid. Few people whom I met in Dhaka in August 1973 admitted to a knowledge of Urdu, because of its Pakistani connotations, in spite of its having previously been the mother tongue of the old city élite and a *lingua franca* for others. Bhutto in Pakistan, for his part, spoke slightingly of 'Muslim Bengal' and, as we have seen, dragged his feet, nimble though they were in diplomatic matters, over the question of recognition. But signs were not lacking that anti-Indian sentiments were still present: slogans like 'quit, Indians' appeared on walls; and some Bangladeshis hankered after better relations with their fellow Muslims in Pakistan, and expressed anti-Hindu feelings. And even Mujib, the proclaimer of a secular state, attended an Islamic Summit.

Relations with Pakistan improved with recognition in 1974. Bhutto visited Dhaka and received what was described as 'an impressive welcome'. Ambassadors were exchanged at the end of 1975. By this time Sheikh Mujibur Rahman and the coup which displaced him from power had, as we have seen, been followed by a counter-coup, said to have been engineered by pro-Indian elements, only to be followed by yet another coup, the so-called 'Sepoy's revolt', which brought Ziaur Rahman to power. Pakistan clearly did not regret either the passing of the man they saw as the begetter of secession or the failure of the second coup; and welcomed the possibility of an 'Islamic State', seeking ties in the Middle East, with the arrival of the Zia regime. India, by the same token, viewed these developments with unease. Tension with India was increased dramatically when there was an attempt on the life of the Indian High Commissioner in November 1975. However, a high-powered Indian delegation renewed offers of friendship, and (as we have seen) the short-term Farakka agreement was soon signed. Relations deteriorated again in 1976 with renewed haggling over Farakka and raids on northern Bangladesh by allegedly 'pro-Mujib' forces which, Zia claimed, had received Indian assistance.

During the remaining years of the Zia regime in Bangladesh it remained broadly true that friendly relations with Pakistan were maintained, there being no outstanding issues between the countries. (Significantly, many more people admitted to a spoken knowledge of Urdu when I was in Dhaka in 1976.) By the same token, relations with India have been less happy; and mistrust has been fuelled by the issues mentioned earlier. Given the poisoned relations between India and Pakistan, it follows that any rapprochement between Dhaka and Islamabad has been viewed with suspicion in New Delhi, and (though less often) vice versa.

International relations within South Asia: Sri Lanka's relations with other South Asian countries

This section will be mainly concerned with Sri Lanka's relations with India, its giant neighbour, at the nearest point only twenty-odd miles away and with over forty times its population.[12] Chapter 2 has shown that Sri Lanka has seen an alternation of governments dominated on the one hand by the United National Party (UNP) and on the other by the Sri Lanka Freedom Party (SLFP). Its policy towards India has tended to alternate in sympathy, SLFP governments under Bandaranaike and his widow tending to show more friendliness towards India, and in certain important respects to follow the Indian line in international affairs more closely, than UNP governments under D.S. Senanayake and his successors. Some observers see something of a recent convergence towards a national consensus in foreign policy in general and in attitudes towards India; but we shall have reason to question this view. Indian attitudes towards Sri Lanka have, it should be said, been generally more consistent than Sri Lanka attitudes towards India.

In the early years of independence, from 1948 to 1956, D.S. Senanayake and his advisers were in process of formulating a policy towards foreign affairs and defence: no such policy had, of course, been necessary while their country was still a British Crown Colony, albeit one that enjoyed internal self-government and one whose citizens and politicians played a notable part in the Second World War. One strong motive in this process of formulation was undoubtedly a fear of India, for various reasons. One reason was, of course, the sheer size of the giant neighbour: if, on the Wriggins model (see pp. 113–14) small Pakistan feared huge India, so *a fortiori* should even smaller Sri Lanka. Moreover, Sri Lankans, and particularly intellectuals and members of the politicized élite, were able to quote influential Indian authors who drew attention to the importance of the Indian Ocean, and of Sri Lanka as a strategically placed island with a superb natural harbour at Trincomalee, to an India no longer able to rely on British sea-power to deter a possible maritime aggressor. There was, for example, the view of K. M. Panikkar that the Indian Ocean must '... remain truly Indian'; and his dictum 'It is the oceanic space that dominates the strategy of India's defence'.[13]. It is not surprising that the intelligentsia of an island that possessed a magnificent natural harbour and that had played a great part in the late war should be highly conscious of the sea and of seapower (and, for that matter, of airpower too). Some of them were aware, too, of remarks like that made by Nehru who, writing in 1945, drew attention to the cultural unity of India and Ceylon (as it then was) and forecast that Ceylon would be drawn into closer political union with India 'presumably as an autonomous unit of the Indian Federation'.[14] And there were Indian visitors, as I have personally witnessed, who made no secret of their sense of superiority over the Sinhalese. Nehru later repudiated the remark just quoted; and in any case soon had his hands full with the consequences of partition, with conflict with Pakistan, and with the Chinese on and over his border: though these problems did not prevent India from remembering that there was an oceanic dimension to its defence, or from building up a navy; or, one may presume, from drawing up contingency plans in case of the occupation of Sri Lanka by a power hostile to India.

However innocent Nehru and his successors were of designs on Sri Lanka (which could, however, draw attention to Indian action in Hyderabad and, later Goa), it does seem to have been largely anxiety about India that led Senanayake at the time of independence into a defence agreement with Britain (later terminated by Bandaranaike), under which *inter alia* a British base remained in Trincomalee. A related fact of his foreign policy was its decidedly pro-western and anti-Communist stance. This did not prevent, however, either protestations of anticolonialism or the refusal of transit facilities to the Dutch when they were clashing with Indonesian nationalists. Nor did it prevent the forging of bonds of unity with Asian and later African countries, as at the Bandung Conference in 1955. All this might have made India less irritated by its small and, some said, neocolonialist neighbour. But it was at Bandung that Sir John Kotelawala, by then

Prime Minister, and a more forthright and less tactful man than D. S. Senanayake, came out with some extremely strong anti-Communist statements (on the occasion of one of them Chou-En-lai left the conference hall) and exacerbated friction with Nehru, the arch-prophet of non-alignment and neutralism.

But there was a further cause of acerbity in Indo–Sri Lankan relations: one of long standing that is, in some ways, still with us. This was the problem of persons who had come from India, or were the descendants of those who had so come, to work on the coffee, tea and rubber plantations established in British days, or to work in Colombo port or elsewhere in connexion with the colonial export economy (see p. 44). Even before independence the Government of India had been concerned over these people, most of whom were classed as 'Indian Tamils' and whose presence had aroused hostility among some of the Sinhalese, especially the Kandyans. This ethnic reason for friction with India was, in fact, not distinct from the first, the generalized fear of a giant neighbour. For although they form a majority in the island, the Sinhalese (or some of them) were and are conscious that they are a minority in relation to the tens of millions of Tamils in South India who, they fear, might make common cause with their own Ceylon Tamil and/or Indian Tamil populations. They are, then, a majority with a minority complex.[15]

Now one of the first deeds of the parliament of Sri Lanka after independence was to pass the Ceylon Citizenship Act of 1948, which was soon followed by the Indian and Pakistani Residents (Citizenship) Act of 1949. The results of these enactments was effectively to deny citizenship to the vast majority of Indian Tamils except where they were able to become 'citizens by registration' under conditions that few of them could satisfy, and subject to cumbersome bureaucratic procedures. Moreover, non-citizens were disenfranchised, and subject to various disabilities: for example, they could not obtain grants of land in government land settlement schemes.

Indian reaction, both official and unofficial, was not surprisingly to denounce the acts, not least because they were not the fruit of any sort of prior agreement between the two countries. The Government of India, in fact, found the citizenship laws completely unacceptable; while *The Hindu*, the prominent Madras newspaper, called the bill that issued in the second act 'The Indian Ejectment Bill'. The Government of India did persuade the Government of Sri Lanka to amend the 1949 Act; but continued to be dissatisfied with the legislation as a whole and with the very slow progress of applications for citizenship by registration. Behind all the controversy and a whole series of meetings lay a fundamental conflict of principle. As Kodikara puts it:[16]

> The Government of India and Indian opinion generally have contended that the majority of the Indian population in Ceylon are permanently settled in the island. The Government of Ceylon, on the other hand, has regarded most Indians as 'birds of passage' without a permanent interest in Ceylon, whose sojourn on the island generally coincides with the duration of their employment.

The Government of India's policy was, in fact, to discourage overseas Indians from applying for Indian citizenship, to which they were not in fact entitled as of right. The Government of Sri Lanka's attitude was clearly not favourable to the registration as citizens of more than a small proportion of persons of Indian descent resident in the island. The spectre of statelessness thus hung over a large part of the Indian Tamil community. There were, however, a number of occasions when Nehru and successive Prime Ministers of Sri Lanka met in order to try to solve the problem; but, although various agreements and compromises were reached, the problem remained; and was complicated by continuing illicit immigration from India.

A change in Sri Lankan Government attitudes to India came, as already stated, when Bandaranaike led his SLFP to power in 1956. Fear of India, on at least the generalized ground, seemed to recede into the background. Instead came admiration for Nehru's policies of non-alignment and neutralism, and hostility for any policy of relying on one power bloc or the other for defence. The British defence agreement, with its provision for British use of bases, was terminated (amicably); and even-handedness was demonstrated by the establishment of diplomatic relations with Communist countries. Bandaranaike argued that Sri Lanka should follow the Swiss example of neutrality and the Indian example of non-alignment; and argued too that friendship with India and close relations with other countries in the region were a better insurance against involvement in war than membership of an alliance. The policies did much to promote good relations with India. After Bandaranaike's assassination similar policies were pursued by his widow in her dealings with Shastri and Mrs Gandhi.

Some progress was made too, on paper at any rate, in dealing with the problem of the Indian Tamils. Here the new atmosphere of friendliness was of some help. In October 1964 an agreement was reached in New Delhi between Mrs Sirimavo Bandaranaike and Lal Bahadur Shastri: this became known as the Sirima–Shastri Pact. The agreement provided *inter alia* that, of the estimated 975,000 non-citizen persons of Indian origin in Sri Lanka, 525,000 would be granted Indian citizenship and repatriated over a 15-year period; 300,000 would become Sri Lankan citizens; and the remaining 150,000 were to be the subject of a separate and future agreement. Fifteen years were allowed for the implementation of the agreement (i.e. to 1979).

The Sirima–Shastri Pact did not produce a wholly favourable reaction in India, notably among members of opposition parties and particularly in the the DMK of Tamil Nadu (see pp. 80–1); while *The Hindu* thought that concessions had mainly been on the Indian side, and viewed with apprehension the number to be repatriated and the absence of clarity as to whether repatriation was to be voluntary or whether there would be an element of compulsion.

The UNP government that came into power in 1965 announced that it would honour the Pact. In 1967 the Indo–Ceylon Agreement Act was passed, on the basis of a ratio of four persons of Indian descent to receive Sri Lankan citizenship to four to be repatriated and given Indian citizenship. But implementation soon ran into trouble over various matters, particularly the question of compulsory *versus* voluntary repatriation. It proved impossible to please both governments and all parties in both countries, and friction and recrimination continued. However, the doctrine of the convergence of the UNP and the SLFP in their relations with India is borne out to some extent by the fact that governments of both complexions have continued to honour both the broad outline of the Sirima–Shastri Pact and the act of 1967; though this has not prevented each party when in opposition from criticizing relevant actions of the other in power. And the issue remains a live one in domestic politics because of its communal overtones (in August 1981 a State of Emergency was proclaimed because of intercommunal violence largely directed against Indian Tamils). It was long not such a live issue in the domestic politics of India, except in Tamil Nadu. The 1983 riots in Sri Lanka, grievously affecting Ceylon Tamils and their property, brought a very strong reaction in India, especially in Tamil Nadu and its regionalist government. Mrs Gandhi assured a delegation from Tamil Nadu that her government saw the issue as a national one. This complex situation, compounded of the communal troubles of Sri Lanka and of the troubled relationship between Centre and States in India, may give a new twist to relations between the two countries. Meanwhile the Indian Tamils remaining in Sri Lanka constitute one of the most disadvantaged groups in the country, a pawn in politics and a target for abuse and worse.

Sri Lanka being an island, boundary disputes between it and India obviously cannot arise as they have arisen on India's land frontiers. There has, however, been a minor dispute over the ownership of a small island in the chain, known as 'Adam's Bridge', linking the two countries. This was settled in 1968, with an associated adjustment of fishing limits.

To return finally to the question of a consensus between the two main political parties in their attitude to India, we have seen that both have accepted the broad terms of the Sirima–Shastri Pact, though there have been differences of emphasis and interpretation as each government adjusted itself to the forces of internal politics. UNP governments, moreover, have not attempted to re-introduce British or other western bases. Up to a point, non-alignment has survived changes of government; and this, *a priori*, should make for good relations with India. But UNP governments have tended to favour links with the west, SLFP governments to cultivate good relations with China: neither posture is altogether pleasing to India. Moreover, perhaps rather incompletely formulated concepts saw Pakistan and China before 1971 as a counterpoise to India, or at any rate to the surviving fear, for all the generally friendly relations, of absorption by India.[17] But the events of 1971 clearly altered the balance of power in South Asia; and Sri Lanka noted that China did not leap to Pakistan's defence. Perhaps it is in this context, and also given the admiration shown by the UNP government formed in 1977 for all things Singaporean (see p. 226), that one should take suggestions that Sri Lanka might seek to join ASEAN, the Association of South East Asian Nations.

What of Sri Lankan relations with Pakistan, before and after the independence of Bangladesh; and with Bangladesh? Apart from the somewhat vague view of Pakistan as a counterpoise that has just been mentioned, and that never issued in any sort of pact or agreement, there is not much to be said. So far as Pakistan is concerned, relations are perhaps best described as correct and friendly, if for obvious geographical reasons less immediate than those with India. Pakistan did, however, at certain periods pay attention to Sri Lanka, as it did to other Asian states, as a counterpoise to India. Boundary disputes there could be none; fear of a giant neighbour was absent, and even though the act of 1949 referred to Pakistani as well as Indian residents in Sri Lanka, its enactment and subsequently chequered implementation raised hardly a ripple on the surface of Pakistani–Sri Lankan relations — for there were but few people involved, and they mainly members of various merchant groups who knew how to look after themselves and to make themselves useful to the politicians. Sri Lanka did, however, grant overflying rights to Pakistan's civil and military aircraft in mid-1971, when they could not cross over Indian territory in flying from one wing of their country to the other. Indian suspicions were, of course, thereby aroused.

One facet of Bandaranaike's 'Switzerland of the East' concept is worth a mention here. He, and his widow after him, saw their neutrality as a good basis on which they could offer to mediate. One of the conflicts in which Mrs Bandaranaike offered to mediate, having declared her strict neutrality, was that between India and Pakistan over Bangladesh in 1971.

As for Sri Lanka's relations with Bangladesh since its independence, nothing need be added here except to say that Ziaur Rahman paid an official visit in 1979; and that Sri Lanka and Bangladesh, like Sri Lanka and India, share a Commonwealth link, whereas Pakistan left the Commonwealth in 1971.

An official visit by King Birendra of Nepal in 1980 may be seen as an attempt to strengthen ties with a South Asian country other than India — one, moreover, with a substantial Buddhist population.

International relations within South Asia: relations of Nepal with other South Asian countries

We have seen in Chapter 3 (see p. 49) that under the Raj the independent but fossilized kingdom of Nepal was seen by the British as a buffer-state; and in Chapter 4 (see pp. 107–8) that the internal politics of Nepal are of great concern to both India and China. It is the function of the present section to pick up these threads and to discuss Nepali relations with other South Asian countries, particularly (indeed overwhelmingly) with India. Not much need be said about the other Himalayan territories: Bhutan's foreign relations are subject to the advice of India, while Sikkim, formerly possessing a special protected status vis-à-vis India, became a State of the Indian Union in 1975 (see p. 67).[18]

In the early years of India's independence its relations with Nepal were close. Nehru made it clear that, while recognizing the independence of Nepal, India would not brook foreign interference in that country, well aware as he was that it stretched for 500 miles along India's northern frontier. He showed blindness, however, to the geography and history of a mountain state that, for all the dominance of Hinduism in the culture of many of its peoples, had had longstanding relations with Tibet and so with China: for he said 'One cannot go to Nepal without passing through India.'[19] Perhaps he was here, as in a wider context, lulled into a sense of false security by the weakness and passivity of Tibet (and for that matter of China) during the British period, and by illusions of lasting Chinese friendship. To say this is, however, to anticipate.

India's relations with Nepal were the dominant element in the Himalayan kingdom's foreign contacts during the period up to 1955 or so. Nepal, indeed, relied on Indian help in a number of internal crises: notably, India allowed King Tribhuvan asylum in New Delhi when he fled his country during his conflict with the Ranas (see p. 107), and aided his successful return. The two countries signed a mutual assistance pact: and India sent troops to Nepal to assist in suppressing an uprising. India continued to recruit Gurkhas from Nepal as the Raj had done (and as Britain continued, and continues to do); an Indian military mission reorganized the Nepali army. Indian aid steadily increased in amount and scope. Indian dominance in this period was not without its critics in Nepal and outside. It could be argued, and was, that India's treatment of Nepal was inconsistent with recognition of its independence and with protestations of anticolonialism. And the relationship between the two countries was constantly punctuated by crises and uneasiness: when Nehru visited Kathmandu in 1951 he was greeted by a hostile demonstration.

In 1950 Communist China established its control over Tibet, on which its immediate predecessors had had so loose a grip. Ironically, in view of subsequent events, it was India that encouraged Nepal both to 'regularize' relations with Tibet (implicitly recognizing at last that Nepal could be approached otherwise than through India); and Nehru declared publicly that it was for Nepal to establish diplomatic relations with China if it so desired. In 1955, Nepal did in fact establish such relations, the two governments declaring that their basis was Panch Shila, or the five principles governing peaceful dealings between nations of which Nehru was the archprophet (see p. 135).

In retrospect this new relationship between Peking and Kathmandu marks a turning point in Indo–Nepali relations and, indeed, in Nepali foreign policy. This was by 1957 directly in the hands of King Mahendra, a more formidable figure than his father and predecessor, though a monarch who could not but be aware of the shakiness of his position inside his little state and of his weakness in dealing with larger powers, whether those on his borders or those farther afield. There is something of a parallel with Pakistan's efforts to balance one power against another, and therefore some justification for seeing here the working of Wriggins' model (see p. 113). But there was much less consistency in Mahendra's quest for a counterbalance to India; for, whatever the strength of anti-Indian feeling among some of his subjects, he and most of his élite lacked the special reasons for fear and hatred of India that so unfortunately operated in Pakistan.

True, the establishment of diplomatic relations with Peking were followed by offers of aid to Nepal from China which occasioned a sonorous ringing of alarm bells in New Delhi (Russia, incidentally, also offered aid at about the same time). But B. P. Koirala, a professedly pro-Indian and anti-Chinese Prime Minister, was appointed in Nepal in 1957 (see p. 107) and, not for the last time, Nepalese policy veered back towards India. Meanwhile, India's honeymoon period with China was at an end and Panch Shila had gone sour, with Indian realization that China had established itself in territory that India claimed as its own. The Himalayan frontier, dormant in British days, came alive and grew intensely dangerous. Not surprisingly India looked once again at its relations with Nepal (and with Bhutan and Sikkim); and in 1959 Nehru affirmed that any attack on Nepal would be construed as an attack on India. Indian troops were, in fact, sent at the request of the Nepal government to man a number of posts on their northern frontier. Indian economic aid increased. But anti-Indian feeling surfaced once again, in spite of joint declarations on the preservation of Nepal's independence and integrity.

Nepali policy was, in fact, by 1960, shifting towards neutrality in the Indo–Chinese dispute, and deliberate efforts were made to establish closer relations with both China and Pakistan, both of them eager to embarrass India. Nepal and China came to a frontier agreement (though there were some border clashes too); and China also agreed to build a road north from Kathmandu through the Kuti Pass in the Himalaya to Koderi (much to India's chagrin, though it continued its aid, which also include roadbuilding). So it was that, in the Chinese incursion into India in 1962, Nepal went unscathed but, equally, did not come to India's assistance. One Indian author sees the period 1960–3 as one of a 'widening gulf' in Indo–Nepali relations.[20]

The same author sees 1963–72 as a period of improving relations between the two, and credits India with a more realistic, mellow and sympathetic policy towards its tiny neighbour. It is, however, probably sounder to see this period as one in which Nepal continued to veer now towards India, now away from it, constantly seeking to maintain some sort of balance amid the shifting sands of its international relations; taking aid from an astonishingly wide range of donors, from India (usually the largest single source) to China, from America to the Soviet Union, from Britain to Switzerland. And disputes with India were not absent in the period.

Since 1972, a new factor in Nepal's calculation is the strengthening of India's dominance within the subcontinent following the Bangladesh war and the dismemberment of Pakistan. No longer is there much to be gained by playing off Pakistan against India. It is arguably more important for this land-locked state to seek good relations with Bangladesh, whose northernmost point is only some 20 miles from Nepali territory and whose port of Chittagong presents Nepal with a potential alternative to Calcutta (though still not accessible by land except by crossing Indian soil).

Since 1973 the swings to and from India have continued. Thus in 1973 a peace and friendship treaty with India was revived and seemed to take on the guise of a defence pact. But in the following years relations were described as 'estranged' because of Nepali hostility to what was seen as the Indian 'annexation' of Sikkim; while efforts were made to please China by taking a firm line on refugees from Tibet. In 1978 the Nepali Prime Minister went, evenhandedly, both to New Delhi and Peking. In 1979 it was Pakistan's turn to excite a demonstration in Kathmandu, because of the execution of Bhutto; and King Birendra went both to India and China.

Nepal, then, offers an interesting variant on methods on survival adopted by small South Asian states, seeking friendship now more with India than China, now more with China than India; and in the past with Pakistan too. In its willingness to receive aid from both sides of the iron curtain it invites comparison with Afghanistan before Russian influence came to dominate there, though Nepal has of course spread its net even wider, particularly in the direction of India and China. The King of Nepal has called for withdrawal of all foreign troops from Afghanistan, perhaps acutely aware that his own kingdom could easily go the way of that one-time buffer-state, or of Sikkim. In its political and strategic balancing act there is a parallel with Pakistan. But its most consistent posture has been non-alignment, particularly between India (itself ironically the arch-exponent of non-alignment) and China. Events in 1980 suggest that Birendra sees this still as the path ahead. Indeed, he called for non-alignment for the whole of South Asia; and, just as Sri Lanka has proposed a Peace Zone in the Indian Ocean, so he proposed a Zone of Peace for his own unhappily-sandwiched little state (and in 1982 was reported to be annoyed that India, unlike Pakistan, Bangladesh, Sri Lanka, and a number of non-South Asian countries, was reluctant to accept the proposal).

South Asia's relations with external countries: China, Afghanistan and Burma

We now turn to an examination of the relations between South Asian countries and states external to the subcontinent as it is defined for the purposes of this book. We begin with relations with the three countries bordering the subcontinent: namely, China, Afghanistan and Burma, in that order (Iran also has a border with Pakistan: see p. 75). It has, of course, been impossible to omit reference to states external to South Asia in the earlier sections of this chapter, since relations between the countries of South Asia are not conducted in subcontinental isolation; and Chapter 4 has demonstrated that there is an external dimension to politics *within* some if not all of the countries of South Asia. To some extent, then, the sections that follow involve an exercise in the pulling out and tying together of threads. They should also help to answer questions, factual and otherwise, that may well have occurred to the reader of preceding sections.

China is an obvious candidate for treatment here in some detail. Even if it did not border on our subcontinent, its enormous area and huge population, the largest of any country in the world and even larger than India's, would qualify it for inclusion. It has indeed come to play a major role in the international politics of South Asia, as we have already seen in discussing the foreign relations of Pakistan and Nepal.

While the Indian Empire and the Crown Colony of Ceylon were moving towards independence after the Second World War, the Chinese Communists were successfully establishing themselves in their own country (they were firmly in control in Peking by October, 1949); and were winning the sympathy of Nehru and other South Asian leaders, who saw in the Chinese Revolution something of a parallel with their own struggle against imperialism. True, 'China proper' never had its whole territory occupied by European colonizing powers. But it did suffer the indignity of the Treaty Port system[21]; and much of its territory had been occupied by the Japanese in the years before and during the war. The Chinese Communists invaded Tibet in October 1950 and quickly occupied the whole of that remote area, putting an end to its near-independence and to that of its theocratic ruler, the Dalai Lama (who submitted to Chinese sovereignty in return for provisions purporting 'to guarantee Tibetan autonomy and religious freedom' in an agreement signed in Peking in May 1951).[22]

The Chinese action in Tibet did arouse some anxiety in India. But this was the era of 'Hindi–Chini bhai-bhai', the proclaimed brotherhood of Indians and Chinese in their common struggle against imperialism and underdevelopment. So it was that in 1952 India implicitly recognized Chinese sovereignty in Tibet and was allowed to open a Consulate-General in Lhasa (China opened a similar office in Bombay). In 1954 a more comprehensive agreement was signed. India had already announced its intention to give up the extra-territorial rights in Tibet it had inherited from the Raj; and the treaty was largely concerned with facilities for merchants and pilgrims in both countries. In the preamble the Panch Shila, or five principles of peaceful co-existence were declared to be the basis of Sino–Indian relations. These were: mutual respect for each other's territorial integrity and sovereignty; mutual non-aggression; mutual non-interference in each other's internal affairs; equality and mutual benefit; and peaceful co-existence. The treaty was greeted in India and more widely as a great achievement and a victory for Nehru and his policy of non-alignment.

But hopes of eternal friendship with China and, for that matter, of a non-colonial, regionally-autonomous status for the Tibetans, were soon dashed. Alarming reports began to reach Nehru (though not the educated Indian public, or that articulate and irrepressible body might have reacted sooner) of intense Chinese military activity and road-building which left no doubt that Tibet was under heavy military occupance; and in 1959 the Dalai Lama fled to India. The People's Republic, Marxist though it might be, was losing no time in reoccupying in strength the marchlands of the Chinese imperial order. And it was not long before India was locked in a border dispute with China whose roots go back to British days and indeed earlier (it is not proposed to disinter those roots here).[23] Even before the flight of the Dalai Lama Indian patrols discovered Chinese incursions into territory that was believed in New Delhi to be Indian. In 1958 the Chinese were found to have built a road linking Tibet with Sinkiang (in Central Asia) across an area known as Aksai Chin which India claimed.

By that time the Sino–Indian border dispute was in full swing, and relations between the two protagonists had rapidly worsened, to the great perturbation of the Communist Party of India, which had begun from the position that China, as a Marxist state, could do no wrong.[24] It would be wearisome, and it is unnecessary, to recall the protracted arguments and futile negotiations that constituted the dispute. Suffice it to say here that it centred not only on Aksai Chin and other areas on the border of Kashmir, but also on small areas bordering Uttar Pradesh and, of great importance, on the then North-East Frontier Agency, now Arunachal Pradesh. In the last-named area India claimed a boundary along the McMahon Line, following broadly the Himalayan crest-cum-watershed, which had been agreed to by Tibet in 1914, but never ratified by China; whereas the Chinese claimed a line on the edge of the plains of Assam. India increased its military forces in the border areas, establishing a number of forward posts; and allowed the treaty of 1954 to lapse without asking for renewal, thus greatly offending China.

In 1962, the Chinese swept in force across the McMahon Line (which, as India correctly pointed out, was the *de facto* boundary) and, after a temporary respite, were poised to threaten the plains of Assam. Indian defence turned into a notorious debacle (contrasting strongly with the brilliant campaigns against Pakistan nine years later). Then, when India and the world were wondering what was to happen next, the Chinese announced a unilateral ceasefire. But India did not capitulate to China's demands as to where the ceasefire line was to be; and the border dispute remained unsettled. An attempt at mediation by six countries meeting in Colombo in December 1962, on Sri Lankan initiative, ran into the sand: Nehru was apparently willing to 'forgive and forget', though not at the expense of what he conceived as India's territorial integrity; but China's attitude was equivocal.

Two questions emerge from this bald narrative of events up to 1962. First, why did Nehru rely for some years on friendship with China, only to find himself and his country engaged in acrimonious dispute and eventually open warfare with the Chinese? Partly, no doubt for reasons already mentioned: his conception of revolutionary China as engaged in a common struggle against imperialism — whereas Chou En-lai and other Chinese leaders saw him as a bourgeois nationalist, if not a lackey of the imperialists, who had kept his country in the Commonwealth. Moreover, Nehru for all his political sagacity was an idealist who, as Dorothy Woodman put it, 'romanticised policy towards China'.[25] The actions of the Chinese in Tibet and in the border dispute, and finally the war of 1962, disillusioned him and perhaps hastened his end (he died in 1964). By then many sections of public opinion in India saw in Communist China no more than the old Chinese Empire wrapped in a red flag and determined to occupy all that it saw as the protective marchlands of the Middle Kingdom; some went further and thought China had, in Nehru's bitter words, 'profoundly inimical intentions toward our independence and institutions'.

The second question asks 'Why, then, did the Chinese invade in 1962 and so quickly declare a unilateral ceasefire?' One motive for the attack was perhaps to show up India's military feet of clay and so deal a severe blow to a bourgeois government and to a Prime Minister who aspired to leadership of the non-aligned and anti-colonial world. But a more specific motive was probably to bring limited pressure on India in order to achieve a compromise on the border issue that would concede Aksai Chin to China (which had good reason, given the mounting hostility of the Soviet Union, to hold its strategic road) in return for the acceptance of the McMahon Line in the north-east. But even though, or so it is said, Nehru began to think of a compromise along these lines, no such solution emerged.

Between 1962 and 1968 relations between India and China remained bad. Neither country suspended diplomatic representation in the other, but it remained at chargé d'affaires level. There was a long series of border incidents, frontier violations and protest notes; and claims that China was helping, and indeed training Naga and

Mizo dissidents. In 1968 China exploded an atomic device, to India's great alarm: this may have had much to do with India's own preoccupation with nuclear devices and its own explosion in the Rajasthan Desert, declared to be for peaceful purposes, in 1974. In the years 1969–72, India made cautious hints to China on a possible rapprochement, fortified at the end of that period by its success in the 1971 war and by confidence (or illusion) that north-east India was now secure so far as Bangladesh was concerned. In 1976, however, relations were 'normalized' after 14 years and ambassadors were exchanged. From 1977 onwards the Janata government gradually improved relations with Peking; and in 1979 its Minister of External Affairs was in China discussing a wide range of issues, not excluding the border dispute, when the news came of the Chinese invasion of Vietnam, by then in the Soviet orbit. The Minister immediately returned to New Delhi; and his government heavily criticized Peking. However, in August 1981, with Mrs Gandhi back in power, talks on the border dispute and other issues were resumed. It remains to be seen whether the two giants of Asia will settle their differences or whether détente will be prevented by their own intransigence or by the complications introduced by the relations of each of them with other powers.

One of the greatest complications in this context has been the rift between the Soviet Union and China, already wide by 1960. It is well beyond the scope of this book to unravel the reasons for the rift, beyond saying that they appear to be a combination of ideology and power politics, or perhaps the second masquerading as the first. Be that as it may, Khruschev was already denouncing China in 1960 for its attitude to India; though (with the Cuban missiles crisis hanging over it) the Soviet Union appeared to lean towards China when the latter made its ceasefire proposals after the 1962 incursion. But thereafter Russia and China drifted ever further apart and India and Russia nearer. It thus became possible for Pakistan to look to China as part of its balancing act (see p. 114) and, amongst other things, to build jointly with China the strategic road over the Karakoram, completed in 1978, linking Islamabad with the Chinese Tibet–Sinkiang communications system.[26] And China settled its boundary with Pakistan in 1963, to India's annoyance, for the area concerned lay in Azad Kashmir, claimed by India. But, it should be noted, China did not come to Pakistan's assistance in the Bangladesh war of 1972, perhaps deterred by Russia's treaty relationship with India, though it did twice veto the admission of Bangladesh to the United Nations.

Similarly, though with less impact, Sri Lanka has sought closer relations with China, at least when the SLFP was in power, as we have seen; and it was China that donated and constructed a large international conference centre in Colombo. We have just seen how Nepal has used China as a counterpoise to India and to some extent to Russia. China also settled its boundary with Nepal without much difficulty, though there was a temporary setback when China claimed the whole of Mount Everest (the international boundary, it was later agreed, runs through the highest point in the world).

Relations between Afghanistan and the South Asian countries need not detain us long, though it must be strongly emphasized that they are of great significance. The reasons for brevity at this point are, first, that troubled relations with Pakistan, because of the Pakhtunistan and Baluchistan agitation, have already been discussed in Chapter 4 (pp. 74–5), where the suspicion of some authors that India had not been slow to fish in these troubled waters has also been voiced; and secondly that more recent relations with Afghanistan are best dealt with when, very shortly, we are discussing superpower relations with South Asia, since it is Soviet military intervention there in 1979 that has greatly complicated the issues involved. It is perhaps worth mentioning, however, that in 1972 Afghanistan, then still a kingdom, was proclaiming its belief in a policy of 'active neutralism', accepting aid both from Moscow and Peking, and receiving visits both from Bhutto and from the President of India; and that in 1976 a trade agreement was concluded with Bangladesh.

Relations with Burma need detain us even less, even though it has land frontiers with both India and Bangladesh. On the whole, relations with India have been correct and reasonably friendly. In 1967 an agreement was reached for the delimitation and demarcation of their common boundary. Earlier, in 1964, some strain was occasioned by an exodus of Indians from Burma, following the nationalization of various enterprises: India had to resettle them on arrival. Burma, it should be noted, professes independent neutralism and has a Treaty of Friendship and Non-aggression with China which may, like Chinese relations with Pakistan, Nepal and Sri Lanka, be seen as part of the People's Republic's effort to oppose India.

And little need be said of relations between Burma and, first, East Pakistan and then Bangladesh. Potential irredentism may, however, have to be reckoned with in the future; and an incursion of Muslim refugees from Burma into Bangladesh caused some anxiety in 1978; but the problem was soon settled and the refugees returned.

South Asia's relations with external countries: the superpowers

If one of the tragedies of international relations in South Asia has been the animosity between India and Pakistan, another and not unrelated tragedy has been that a subcontinent, one of whose greatest leaders was the leading prophet of non-alignment, should have become so heavily involved in the friction and the conflict between the United States and the Soviet Union.[27] An observer at the time of independence, at least if he were an optimist of liberal disposition, might have thought the auguries good for the preservation of the subcontinent from Great Power conflicts, especially if he underestimated the poisonous evil that was to spread from the Indo–Pakistan estrangement. Certainly neither the United States nor the Soviet Union played more than a minor role in South Asia for the first few years after independence. True, just as there were those in the US who were sympathetic to what they saw as an anticolonial struggle in South Asia, so there were those after independence who saw India in particular as a poor country struggling to develop within a 'democratic' framework contrasting starkly with the authoritarian methods of Communist China. And the Russians, forsaking the role that they had played, or in which they had been cast as the great peril north of the mountains, confined their attention, before and immediately after independence, to relations (not very effective in early days at any rate) with the Communist Party of India (CPI).

The false calm of the 'Hindi-Chini bhai-bhai' period in Chinese relations with South Asia was in fact part of a wider calm in the relations of the outside world generally with the subcontinent. But soon the government of the US was shaken by the Korean War, which started in June 1950, and by other involvements with the Russian and Chinese, into the firm belief that the Communist powers were both bent on aggressive expansionism, and that the only way to protect the 'Free World' was to construct a network of strategic alliances backed by superior force. The 'Cold War' had arrived. Nehru, from his stance, was convinced that such a policy would, far from containing aggression, merely serve to provoke it. His sermons on this theme often annoyed the Americans. Pakistan, starting from a not dissimilar neutralist position, preached less, and differed less from the United

States over Korea and other issues, although it was and is very critical of the US and of the west generally over their support for Israel. Sri Lanka, under UNP rule and particularly under Kotelawala, took a staunch pro-western stance till Bandaranaike led his country into neutralism.

So one moves to the American notion that Pakistan might be a useful military ally, strategically placed in relation to the Soviet Union, a kind of enlarged North-west Frontier Province; to Pakistan's search for both arms and allies; to an arms and mutual security agreement between the US and Pakistan in 1954; and, eventually, to Pakistan's adhesion to two of the networks of alliances built up by the US as part of the policy of containing the Communist powers. These were the Central Treaty Organization (CENTO) linking the arc of countries from Turkey to Pakistan; and the South East Asia Treaty Organization (SEATO).

Meanwhile, Nehru (who had travelled in the Soviet Union as a young man and was most impressed by the Soviet model of industrialization; and who always wished for friendship with that country and, as we have seen, with China) had warned the US that if it armed Pakistan he would seek to improve India's relations with Russia. In fact he moved with some caution because of the part Russia had played in manipulating that thorn in the Congress flesh, the CPI. The Soviet Union, after an initial period of heavy-handed criticism of India's 'bourgeois nationalism', and after assessing the failure of the CPI's revolutionary activities (for example, in the Telangana revolt in Hyderabad), had in the post-Stalin era reappraised the South Asian scene and perceived, amongst other things, the benefit of cultivating and aiding India and so embarrassing and opposing Pakistan and thus also its western ally. Perhaps, also, Russia was already apprehensive about its relations with China and appreciated the geopolitical position of India in that context. India, reacting to Pakistan's arms deal with the Americans, not only reached with China the agreement on Tibet already discussed, but responded to Russia's apparently somewhat tentative overtures and offers of economic aid, very desirable given the ambitious content of the Indian Second Five Year Plan (1956–61) with its move towards heavy industrialization. To begin with, however, India stopped short of taking Russian arms. In 1955 Bulganin and Khruschev visited India and created a favourable impression. Before long, as we have seen, the Sino–Soviet rift appeared and widened. Pakistan was able to establish links with

China as a further step in its efforts to counterbalance India, while in the last decade or so, since President Nixon's visit to Peking, we have seen a notable rapprochement between the United States and China. So, it might be thought, all of the principal players had chosen their side.

But it would be simplistic to see the international relations of the major states of South Asia with the superpowers and with China, in the recent past as well as at present and in the foreseeable future, as characterized by complete polarization, with India and Russia on one side, and Pakistan, the United States and China on the other (but with Nepal swinging from side to side in its efforts at balance, and Sri Lanka changing sides as it changed governments).

To take India's relations with United States as a starting point for a venture into greater complexity, these relations have, it is true, frequently reached a point of shrill annoyance. If Nehru's sermonizing annoyed Americans, Indians (and their friends) have if anything been even more annoyed by American politicians and 'experts' who were tactless in their remarks and shamefully ignorant of India's justifiable pride in its history, civilizations and modern achievements. But the US had some notable friends of India among its ambassadors. And America did not crow over India's discovery of the hollowness of China's friendship or over the military defeat of 1962: in fact, this summoned forth rapid shipments of arms from America and Britain, but none, not even a condemnation of the Chinese attack, from Moscow. American economic aid continued to increase for many years, and was sometimes crucial in terms of food supplies. Again President Kennedy set out to achieve more friendly relations with India; and his assassination caused deep shock in New Delhi. But his success was limited, partly because of his continued support for Pakistan, to which India reacted by considering the purchase of fighter planes from Russia. And by 1965 (when Russia mediated between India and Pakistan at Tashkent) the US was more doubtful about the possibility and the utility of cultivating good relations with India, which persisted in criticism of the American role in Vietnam. This role and the preoccupation that went with it, on top of the doubts, led to diminishing American interest in South Asia in general, and in India in particular. Nixon continued this trend, though he tried to create an impression of even-handedness as between India and Pakistan.

In August 1971 India and the Soviet Union signed a twenty-year treaty of friendship and co-operation. Indo–American relations became more distant; strained when in 1971 Nixon's 'even-handedness' was extended to Pakistan even when it was suppressing the Bangladeshi revolt; and reached a low during the last stages of the Bangladesh war, when the US sent a naval taskforce into the Indian Ocean. I well remember the spluttering indignation of an hotel receptionist in Jaipur as he heard news of this over the radio. The US and USSR did, however, both join other countries in helping Bangladesh in the daunting task of postwar reconstruction.

With India's military success and rise to dominance in the subcontinent in 1971, America and India once again reappraised each other. Indeed, Nixon before his fall spoke of India as a major country with 'new stature and responsibilities'. But some observers see a contradiction between this degree of recognition and what they regard as America's self-characterization as regional security manager entitled to make an alliance with Pakistan and to think of the Indian Ocean as a legitimate area for the development of its naval power, using the base at Diego Garcia. Baldev Raj Nayar in fact sees *containment* of India as a US objective.[28] This may well be an exaggeration; but certainly suspicion of American motives is of long standing in India. However, in 1977, following the arrival of President Carter in the US and of the Janata government in India, cordiality once again entered into Indo–American relations, and some degree of coolness into Indo–Soviet relations. But at Christmas 1979 the Russians invaded Afghanistan; and India fell short of the immediate, outright condemnation that was forthcoming not only from the West but also from many non-aligned states — though it was certainly dismayed at the invasion, and did not endorse the Russian action, in spite of pressure brought to bear.

As is only to be expected, whenever the United States appeared to look with some favour on India, suspicion or worse was aroused in Pakistan. Thus arms aid to India in 1962 caused a reappraisal of foreign policy and an anti-western swing in Pakistan. A little later came American reappraisal of the value of the alliance with Pakistan, given the evolving situation in the subcontinent, the strengthening bond between Pakistan and China, and some of the pronouncements of Bhutto. And whatever Nixon's view of events in Bangladesh in 1971, a strong section of American public opinion was hostile to what it saw as Pakistani oppression. But since then there have been dramatic changes in the scene that have profoundly affected the environment in which America and Pakistan relate to each other. The rapproachement between America and China reduced the former's fears of the consequences of Pakistan's ties with the latter. The containing belt of alliances collapsed, first with the fading away of CENTO in the late 1970s and the demise of SEATO in 1975, then with the Iranian revolution (nothing if not anti-American) in 1979, which placed a higher value for the US both on the Indian Ocean and on Pakistan as at least a potential ally. Now in the 1970s there was some hostility to the US in Pakistan for reasons that included the failure of America more effectively to support Pakistan in the Bangladesh war; Carter's coolness to Zia's military takeover; and the strengthening of links between Pakistan and the Islamic world, which carried with it hostility to the US as a friend of Israel. In 1979, in fact, a mob burnt down the American Embassy in Islamabad. But later the same year the Russian invasion of Afghanistan brought great difficulties for Pakistan. Not only had it to face an influx of millions of refugees but, willy nilly given the nature of the frontier, it became the base from which guerilla activity might be launched into Afghanistan. Inevitably the Afghan crisis brought offers of American arms and economic aid to Pakistan, eventually accepted after a period of bargaining. But Pakistan has also not neglected to listen to the Russians on the Afghan situation; and remains a member of the non-aligned group. Inevitably, American arms for Pakistan once again brought hostile reaction and a Moscow-ward lurch in India.

Clearly, then the relations between India and Pakistan on the one hand and America and Russia on the other are not constant, but ebb and flow with a variety of factors: domestic politics, links with other countries and preoccupations of the superpowers elsewhere, oceanic *versus* continental strategy, and so on. All that one can safely predict for the future is that India and Pakistan, and for that matter the other countries of South Asia, are unlikely to be free from the everchanging calculations and interventions of the superpowers, even though the subcontinent is in most imaginable circumstances of less vital importance than, say, Western Europe to the US or Poland to the USSR; nor will the countries of South Asia cease to include the superpowers in their assessments of the means by which they may order their own, intra-South Asian relations.

In the early 1980s it is possible to discern a certain convergence in the foreign policies of India and of Pakistan in the direction of a reassertion of neutralism or, at any rate, depolarization. Mrs Gandhi visited Washington as well as Moscow (and, for that matter, London and Paris) in an ostensible (or even ostentatious) display of even-handedness and, as regards the western capitals, in a desire somewhat to distance India from Moscow. And, as we have seen, India's talks with China continued. Zia visited Peking, but also asserted a desire for neighbourly ties with the USSR; and, of course, continued to receive aid from the USA.

It is in this convergence on depolarization, in common realization of the dangers to both from the situation in Afghanistan, and even more from the return of the 'Cold War' (to say nothing of the effect on that war of a possible détente between Russia and China) that I believe one must view the concurrent rapprochement between India and Pakistan, already noted; although of course many things could halt that rapprochement or lead to a new polarization.

South Asia's relations with external countries: Britain and the Commonwealth

Since conceding independence to its former imperial territories in South Asia, on whose economy, society and institutions it had had such a great impact, Britain has not surprisingly played a far smaller part in the external relations of the successor states than have China, Russia and the United States. Indeed, its role has tended to decline in importance over the years. But this is not to say that it has been, or is negligible. For instance, Britain, as a permanent member of the Security Council of the United Nations, has been far from inactive in utilizing its experience both of diplomacy and of South Asia in advising on and influencing discussion of issues affecting the subcontinent; not least Indo-Pakistan disputes. And as an ally of the United States it also been able to exert some influence on that power.

A not insignificant link between Britain and the successor states of South Asia has been that through the Commonwealth of Nations. Before independence it had been generally supposed that India at any rate would reject Commonwealth membership when independence dawned, particularly because it was then on offer in the form of Dominion Status, unacceptable to many ardent Indian nationalists. After independence, with Britain's continued alliance with the United States and membership of the North Atlantic Treaty Organization (NATO) it seemed to some that Commonwealth membership would imply taking sides in the Cold War. But it became clear to Nehru and his colleagues that there was no necessary implication of this sort, and that there were many advantages in continuing links, given *inter alia* the ties of so many kinds with Britain and the information and consultative service that the Commonwealth provided. And when it was agreed that India could remain a member though a republic, Commonwealth membership was assured, and has been maintained.

This is not to say that relations with Britain have not from time to time been somewhat strained: as, for example, at the time of the Suez crisis; and when it became clear that the British South Atlantic island of Diego Garcia was to be made available as an American base. But on the whole Indian relations with Britain have been a good deal more harmonious than those with the United States. And India has played a notable and constructive part in Commonwealth matters. Indeed, its membership has made it much easier for other colonial territories to remain in the Commonwealth as they gained independence.

It will not surprise the reader that, although many of the arguments for continued Commonwealth membership applied with equal force to Pakistan at independence, the fact that India was to be a member caused heart-searching in Pakistan. In the event, however, Pakistan became a member, and retained its membership until it resigned following British recognition of Bangladesh. It may yet wish to rejoin. Bangladesh, of course, became a member of the Commonwealth.

Sri Lanka joined the Commonwealth at independence, as a kingdom: the Queen was Queen of Ceylon until a republican constitution was instituted in 1972. Sri Lanka, following the Indian precedent, retained its membership on becoming a republic.

It is a general opinion that the Commonwealth is less of a force in international affairs today than it was thirty years ago. Certainly it plays a declining part in the calculations of South Asian countries, for whom the alliances, balancing acts and neutralism discussed in this chapter are far more of the stuff of everyday diplomacy and of strategic planning. But relations with Britain, and with other Commonwealth countries, are still important in terms of economic aid and in terms of cultural links. Indian scholars and research students still in many cases wish to read British books and to come to British universities, where they are welcome (though one might not think so from recent policies of the British government). As an Englishman I have never met anything but friendliness in all parts of the subcontinent. And one of the remarkable features of India after so many years of close relations with Russia is, in Baldev Raj Nayar's words, 'the curious lack of impact in India domestically'.[29] This may in part be due to problems of language and culture, reinforced by the tendency of Russians like those in the MIG fighter factory at Koraput in Orissa to keep themselves to themselves (as many British people did in the heyday of the Raj), and perhaps because India really does not wish to be dependent on the Soviet Union. But the relationship between the South Asian countries and the United Kingdom, which many of us, South Asian and British, cherish, has been eroded, as Michael Lipton and J. Firn have emphasized; and conscious efforts will have to be made if they are not to decline further, to mutual disadvantage.[30]

South Asia's relations with external countries: the Middle East and other Third World countries

I was once asked by a Pakistani when the Centre of South Asian Studies in Cambridge would be transferring its books on his country to the Middle East Centre. Pakistan has, indeed, consistently hankered, not only after being an Islamic state, but also after being a country having more in common with the Islamic countries of the Middle East than with those of South Asia. It has consistently, too, striven to establish good relations with those countries and to proclaim its solidarity with them, and theirs with it. But, as Palmer has said, most of its efforts have 'proved to be abortive ... and produced disillusionment and frustration in Pakistan'.[31] The disunity of the Islamic world, and of the Arabs within it, is notorious — except in their hostility to Israel and its supporters, in which Pakistan has usually joined enthusiastically. Other states with predominantly Muslim populations did not share Pakistan's view, somewhat shadowy though it was, of the relationship between a nation and its interests on the one hand and religion on the other. None of them wanted, moreover, to become involved in the endless disputes between Pakistan and India: indeed, Nasser and his successors in Egypt seemed to be closer to India and to its policies of non-alignment than to Pakistan. More recently, however, there has been talk of Arab arms aid to Pakistan. One 'Islamic' country, Afghanistan, has, as we have seen, been a thorn in Pakistan's flesh, first because of its support for the Pakhtunistan agitation, and then because of the rise of Soviet influence in it, culminating in the occupation of 1979. On one level, however, relations with South-west Asia have been less frustrating and indeed positively beneficial: the oil-producing countries have provided large numbers of jobs for Pakistanis, contracts for contractors and remittances to benefit the home economy. In this benefit Bangladesh also has joined (but so have India and Sri Lanka).

As for the Third World more widely, India, of course, aspired to its leadership (especially so far as Asia and Africa were concerned) during the Panch Shila period. Indeed, the five principles were widely quoted in agreements and statements at the time. But they were much less frequently put into practice; and disillusionment soon set in, not least because of the events of 1962 in South Asia. Nehru was, indeed, upstaged by Chou En-lai earlier, at the Bandung conference in 1955. And one can hardly claim that India now has the moral authority of those early years.

Conclusion

What India does have, however, as this chapter has shown, is a position of dominance in the South Asian subcontinent broadly commensurate with its size, population and relative internal stability; and deriving from its victory over Pakistan and its role in the liberation of Bangladesh in 1971, which apart from everything else showed that the military debacle of 1962 had been redeemed and its lessons thoroughly learnt. But that position, too can be exaggerated, for example by those who saw India after 1971 as a 'rising middle power', with great potential even if its image of poverty and disunity still prevailed: potential that would make the superpowers, especially the United States, sit up and take notice.[32] However much India might continue to receive economic aid because of its manifest need, it would negotiate politically on a peer basis. But, dominant within the subcontinent though India is and will probably remain, events in recent years have shown how limited India is by external forces: China hovers over the high Himalaya, with border issues within them yet unresolved; the Afghanistan crisis has meant American arms for Pakistan and renewed American coolness towards India, not mitigated by the accession of the hard-line Reagan administration; the Indian Ocean is far from being either India's *mare nostrum* or a Zone of Peace; and continued weaknesses in the Indian economy provide an insecure home base. To that economy, and those of other countries of South Asia, we now turn.

Notes and references

1 See, for example, Nayar, K. (1972) *Distant Neighbours*, Delhi, and Gupta, S. (1966) *Kashmir: a Study in Indo-Pakistan Relations*, Bombay, for Indian points of view; Choudhury, G. W. (1968) *Pakistan's Relations with India*,

London, for the view of a Pakistani who was close to Ayub Khan; Burke, S. M. (1973) *Pakistan's Foreign Policy: an Historical Analysis*, London, for a more recent analysis, also by a Pakistani; and Barnds, W. J. (1972) *India, Pakistan and the Great Powers*, Durham, NC, for an American viewpoint, by no means uncritical (the book was written for the American Council on Foreign Relations). See also Ziring, L. *et al.* (eds) (1977) *Pakistan: the Long View*, Durham, NC.

2 Wriggins, W. H. (1977) 'The balancing process in Pakistan's foreign policy', in Ziring, L. *et al.* (1977), op. cit.

3 Onkar Marwah (1979) 'India's military intervention in East Pakistan', *Modern Asian Studies*, 13, 549–80, especially 552–3.

4 Ziring, L. (1974) 'Bhutto's foreign policy, 1972–3', in Korson, J. H. (ed.), *Contemporary Problems of Pakistan*, Leiden.

5 Barnds, W. J. (1977) 'Pakistan's foreign policy: shifting opportunities and constraints', in Ziring, L. (1977) *et al.*, op. cit.

6 Quoted by Choudhury, G. W. (1968) op. cit., p. 227.

7 Wriggins, W. H. (1977) op. cit., p. 576.

8 Barnds, W. J. (1977) in Ziring, L. (1977) *et al.*, op. cit., p. 373.

9 Onkar Marwah, (1979) op. cit., p. 576; Morris-Jones, W. H. (1982) 'The transfer of power, 1947', *Modern Asian Studies*, 16, 1–32, especially 25–31.

10 Barnds, W. J. (1977) op. cit. pp. 379–81.

11 Burke, S. M. (1973) op. cit., pp. 381–3. See also Sawvell, R. D. (1978) 'Crisis on the Ganges: the barrage at Farakka', *Geography*, 63, 49–52 (with map).

12 See Wriggins, W. H. (1960) *Ceylon: Dilemmas of a New Nation*, Princeton, NJ, especially Part 3; Kodikara, S. U. (1965) *Indo-Ceylon Relations since Independence*, Colombo; Wilson, A. J. (1974) *Politics in Sri Lanka 1947–1973*, London, especially Chapter 6; and Samaraweera, V. (1977) 'Foreign policy', in De Silva, K. M. (ed.), *Sri Lanka: A Survey*, London, Chapter 14.

13 Panikkar, K. M. (1945) *India and the Indian Ocean*, London, especially p. 84.

14 Quoted by Wriggins, W. H. (1960) op. cit., p. 399.

15 See Farmer, B. H. (1963) *Ceylon: A Divided Nation*, London.

16 Kodikara, S. U. (1965) op. cit., p. 11.

17 Wilson, A. J. (1974) op. cit., p. 277.

18 See Kavic, L. J. (1967) *India's Quest for Security*, Berkeley, *passim*; Mihaly, E. B. (1965) *Foreign Aid and Politics in Nepal*, London, and Rose, L. E. and Dial, R. (1969) 'Can a ministate find true happiness in a world dominated by protagonist powers? The Nepal case', *Annals of the American Academy of Political and Social Science*, 386, 89–101 for varied western viewpoints: Jha, B. K. (1973) *Indo-Nepalese Relations (1951–1972)*, Bombay; Jha, S. K. (1975) *Uneasy Partners: India and Nepal*

in the Post-Colonial Era, New Delhi; Ramakant (1976) *Nepal-China and India (Nepal–China Relations)*, New Delhi, for Indian views: and Shaha, R. (1978) *Nepal's Politics: Retrospect and Prospect*, Delhi, Chapters 3,4 for the views of an experienced Nepali politician.

19 Quoted by Mihaly, E. B. (1965) op. cit., p. 16.

20 See Jha, B. K. (1973) op. cit., Chapter 5.

21 See Murphey, R. (1977) *The Outsiders: The Western Experience in India and China*, Ann Arbor.

22 Fisher, M. W. *et al.* (1963) *Himalayan Battleground: Sino–Indian Rivalry in Ladakh*, London, 82.

23 For the border dispute and Chinese incursion of 1962 see, for example, Kirk, W. (1962) 'The inner Asian frontier of India', *Transactions of the Institute of British Geographers*, 31, 131–68; Fisher, M. W. *et al.* (1963) op. cit.; Lamb, A. (1964) *The China–India Border*, London; Maxwell, N. (1970) *India's China War*, London; Woodman, D. (1969) *Himalayan Frontiers: a Political Review of British, Chinese, Indian and Russian Rivalries*, London; and Barnds, W. J. (1977) op. cit., Chapters 7–9 and passim.

24 Varkey, O. (1974) *At the Crossroads: The Sino–Indian Border Dispute and the Communist Party of India*, Calcutta.

25 Woodman, D. (1969) op. cit., p. 303.

26 Miller, K. J. (1981) 'The International Karakoram Project, 1980', *Geographical Journal*, 147, 153–63, especially 156–8 (with map).

27 See Barnds, W. J. (1972) op. cit. and (1973) 'India and America at odds', *International Affairs*, 49, 371–84; Burke, S. M. (1973) op. cit.; Ziring, L. (1977) *et al.*, op. cit.; and Mellor, J. W. (ed.) (1979) *India: a Rising Middle Power*, Boulder, Col.

28 Baldev Raj Nayar, (1979) in Mellor, J. W. (ed.) op. cit., Chs 5,6.

29 Ibid., p. 154.

30 Lipton, M. and Firn, J. (1975) *The Erosion of a Relationship: India and Britain since 1960*, London.

31 Palmer, N. D. (1977) 'Pakistan: the long search for foreign policy', in Ziring, L. *et al.* (eds), op. cit., Chapter 14, especially p. 424.

32 See, for example, a number of the contributions in Mellor, J. W. (ed.) (1979) op. cit.

6 ECONOMIC DEVELOPMENTS IN SOUTH ASIA SINCE INDEPENDENCE

It is the purpose of this, the final chapter of this book apart from a brief envoi, to outline the changes that have taken place in the economies of the South Asian countries since independence. It will, however, begin with sketches of the state of those economies at the time of independence, and of the immediate consequences in India and Pakistan of the partition of the former Indian Empire. There will follow an indication of the context in which those active in economic affairs, whether as cultivators, or entrepreneurs, or politicians, or planners, found themselves operating at the dawn of independence. This will partly be a matter of reminding the reader of a number of points already made in the preceding chapters of this book; but it will also be appropriate to dwell at rather more length on a very important part of the context of economic change, that related to population, not only as it stood at independence, but as it has grown in the ensuing years.

There will then follow, and fill the bulk of the chapter, a country-by-country survey of policies, achievements and problems in economic matters.

Economies at independence: India and Pakistan

The economy that India and Pakistan inherited from the British Indian Empire at independence was, of course, predominantly, indeed overwhelmingly an agricultural one. Over 80 per cent of the Indian population lived in villages, nearer 90 per cent in Pakistan, and some 65 per cent of the population was engaged in agriculture. Most cultivators were engaged in growing food crops, for themselves and their families or for sale for consumption within the imperial economy. Rice was by far and away the dominant food crop, grown in *kharif* in the Indo-gangetic plains, and in other seasons as well, especially where there was irrigation, in the Bengal delta and in the plains and deltas of both coasts of the peninsula.[1]

Wheat was a crop of the *rabi* season of the northern parts of the plains; while the various hardy grains commonly lumped together as millets were the main food crop of the drier, unirrigated parts of the peninsula. In many areas pulses, and in some groundnuts, were subsidiary food crops. As we have seen, the British period saw the massive construction of new irrigation canals in the Punjab, in western UP, and to a lesser extent elsewhere; while village tanks had grown in numbers, especially in the South, and were beginning to put a strain on water resources; and wells had been sunk in many areas, above all in the plains, the water being extracted from them almost everywhere by devices operated by human or animal power. In contrast to the state of affairs in Ceylon (or, for that matter, in Malaya or parts of the then Netherlands East Indies) a comparatively small proportion of the total cultivated area of the Indian Empire was in what are usually, but misleadingly referred to as 'cash crops' (misleadingly because rice, wheat and other food crops had long, and increasingly been sold for cash). These included such non-food crops as jute, cotton, tea and sugar (though it may be thought that the last two are 'food crops'). Locally however these were important if not dominant: for example, tea in parts of Assam and what was soon to become the State of Kerala; jute in Bengal; sugar in parts of UP and of the hinterland of Bombay.

In many parts of the Indian Empire in 1947 growth of population, especially since 1921, had led, in the absence of either sufficient uncultivated land or of sufficient outlets in non-agricultural livelihoods, to severe pressure of people on land. This was especially the case in northern Punjab, outside the canal colonies; in eastern UP, Bihar and Bengal; and in the south. With this pressure had come subdivision of holdings till many of them were too small to support a family at subsistence level; and, increasingly, severe poverty, undernourishment, indebtedness, and landlessness, and, less certainly, declining soil fertility. It will be remembered, however, that landlessness was no new phenomenon in Indian caste-bound society (see p. 41); and recognized that the plight of the small cultivator and the even more pitiable plight of the landless labourer cannot be understood merely in terms of population pressure, but also demands consideration of other factors in the Indian social scene, especially land tenure.

We have seen in Chapter 3 (pp. 39–41) that Indian systems of land tenure were very complex before the impact of the west and that whatever else the British contributed it did not consist in simplification. It is no more proposed to enter that jungle which is Indian land tenure at this point than it was in Chapter 3. Suffice it to remind the reader that, at independence, landlordism of one sort or another, and often capping a pyramid of rights to land, was characteristic of many parts of the Indian Empire, whether under *zamindari* or *raiyatwari* tenure. With that state of affairs went gross inequalities in land holding, income and power. Particularly was this so where landlords held large amounts of land, as in parts of what was to become West Pakistan (compare figures for 1959 cited in chapter 2, p. 13). Not even there, however, were there absentee landlords holding vast amounts of land. Most landlords were village-based (indeed, certain legislation enacted in British days was designed to prevent land passing to 'non-agricultural classes'; and a 'big man' in such areas as Bengal or Madras Presidency was one who owned a score or so of acres (when the small farmer held a fraction of an acre).

In terms of their agriculture and agrarian structure, then, India and Pakistan inherited a state of affairs to which there are parallels in many other parts of what was soon to be known as the 'Third World': particularly in terms of a high degree of dependence on agriculture, of production mainly for internal consumption, of population pressure; and of inequalities of income, intense poverty afflicting a major part of the rural population, and an ever-growing landless class. But the Indian Empire on the eve of independence differed from many of its contemporaries among less-developed countries in a number of important respects. First, it possessed a respectable infrastructure in the shape not only of the irrigation works already mentioned but of railways, roads, commercial and other institutions; and an administrative and legal system almost without parallel in the colonial world, at least as far as British India and the more progressive princely states were concerned.[2] Secondly it was producing considerable quantities of minerals: notably coal which, at some 30 million tons per annum, placed India seventh in the world table of producers; and iron and manganese ore (though it produced but little oil). Thirdly, although part of the mineral production was exported, as in so many primary producers in the Third World, part (especially of the coal and the iron ore) was used at home, notably in the giant Tata steelworks at Jamshedpur in Bihar, claimed to be the largest in the Commonwealth at independence, when India was making about three-quarters of its requirement of steel.[3] Tata, it should be noted, was an entirely indigenous enterprise, though it used foreign expertise with great skill and discretion. Fourthly, and in addition to the surviving, and in some cases reviving handicraft industries whose fate in the British period we have discussed in Chapter 3, there were modern textile mills in Calcutta (notably for jute), Bombay, Nagpur and Ahmedabad (cotton), and also in Kanpur, Madras and Coimbatore (also cotton). At independence installed capacity in these mills was second only to that in the United States. Fifthly, there were also many sugar factories, a number of cement works, several railway works, and the beginning of the factory manufacture of consumer goods. So it was that at independence 50 per cent of exports by value were of manufactures.

But considerable and noteworthy though these industrial develop-ments were (and we have seen in Chapter 3 that there are those who consider that they would have been much greater but for imperialism) their impact on the Indian Empire must assuredly not be exaggerated. India was still heavily dependent on imported manufactures, especially of consumer goods, and on the metropolitan market in the United Kingdom. Factory industry only employed some 2 per cent of the labour force, and was highly localized geographically: virtually confined, in fact to Calcutta and Hooghlyside, with an outlier in Jamshedpur; to Bombay and axes running thence north to Ahmeda-bad and east to Nagpur; to Kanpur in UP; and to Madras and Coimbatore in the South. In such areas modern urbanization was most rapid. Over vast areas of the plains and of the Deccan, over most of what was to become Pakistan, little sign of modern industry or mining was to be seen: everywhere, there was nothing but the endless fields of innumerable villages, with the occasional ancient city or town (sometimes sheltering craft industries). The same was true of much of the Deccan. In tribal areas like the north-east Deccan fields gave way to jungle. Clearly, then, the new states were to face highly uneven regional development, not surprising given the vast size and varied geography of the subcontinent. But that is not to say that such spatial inequalities were more important than interclass and intercaste inequalities.

Bhagwati and Desai draw attention to two other attributes of manufacturing industry at independence: the tendency for industrial enterprises to congeal into large groups or 'empires', which they relate to the origins of the entrepreneurs in tightly-knit merchant caste and kin networks, reinforced by the vertical integration facilitated by the managing agency system and the lack of attention to research and development, which they also relate to the merchant origins of the entrepreneurs.[4]

The overall poverty of the Indian Empire and the limited impact of the modern industrial sector is further demonstrated if one looks at some of the principal indices of development quoted in such works as Norton Ginsburg's *Atlas of Economic Development* which, though published in 1961, is based on data relevant to the early 1950s and thus to the years before post-independence changes had made much impact.[5] (A warning must be issued on the reliability of certain of the data for India and Pakistan, as for most developing countries.) These show a Gross National Product per capita of $84 for India and of $56 for Pakistan, placing them respectively 84th and 91st (equal) of the 96 countries ranked by Ginsburg. The calories per capita per day are cited as 2125 for Pakistan and 2000 for India, respectively 66th and 78th out of 93 countries. To take one more index, gross energy consumption is given as 2.7 megawatt-hours per capita for India and 2.4 for Pakistan, respectively 86th and 87th (equal) in a list of 124 cases. And these aggregated national indices tell us nothing, of course, about interregional disparities, or about income and consumption inequality in this region of fabulously rich Maharajas and unbelievably poor rural Harijans and city slum-dwellers. And the claim that manufactures composed 40 per cent of the Indian Empire's exports at independence is placed in perspective if one notes that Ginsburg cites India's trade per capita as $0.7 and Pakistan's $0.9, both very near the bottom of the list (though it must be remembered that other things being equal a large country may be expected to register a much lower index than a small because of the possibilities of internal trade).

The immediate consequences of partition on the economies of India and Pakistan[6]

Chapter 3 has shown how the boundary between India and Pakistan was drawn to effect the partition of 1947. Pakistan secured almost all of the land irrigated by the Punjab canals, though, as the same chapter indicates, India retained the headworks of some of them, and the Indus waters dispute ensued; while the Pakistan Punjab, often a food surplus area, was cut off by the new frontier from its previous markets. The raw cotton of West Pakistan and the jute of East Pakistan were similarly, though more disastrously severed from the mills that had processed them; for there were very few cotton or jute factories in Pakistan at partition. West Pakistan retained its natural port in Karachi; but East Pakistan and its intricate and well-developed network of waterways were cut off from Calcutta. The same was true of Assam; as late as 1968 I saw many barges laid up, idle, at Gauhati in that State, which suffered considerably because its only link with India through Indian territory consisted of a narrow corridor round the north of East Pakistan. It will be appreciated, too, that the economy of Pakistan, divided as it was until the emergence of Bangladesh by a thousand miles of India, was fundamentally difficult to manage. The consequences of partition would, of course, have been less severe if the two successor states had not been, right from the outset, such bad friends, so that economically logical measures like a customs union or rights in each other's ports were out of the question.

Partition, with its dislocation and vast exchange of populations (see p. 62), also spelt short-term consequences in terms of the resettlement and rehabilitation of refugees (see pp. 168–9); not so short-term in the case of continued migration from East Pakistan to India.[7] Altogether, these consequences included a great taxing of resources, administrative and financial. But there were, of course, wide areas of both countries that were not affected directly by migration, devastation and resettlement.

The economy of Ceylon at independence

There are ways in which the economy of Ceylon at independence was similar to that of the Indian Empire across the water. Over 80 per cent of the population was rural and over 50 per cent of the workforce engaged in agriculture (though strict comparisons are impeded by differences of definition). The principal food crop was rice, as in south India. Pressure of population on cultivated land, with its concomitants, was evident in the Wet Zone in the south-west of the island and in the hills. And the economy was beyond dispute that of a less-developed country.

But that economy, unlike that of the mainland, was essentially an export economy; or, as exponents of dependency theory would hold, an economy dependent on that of the metropolitan imperialist power.[8] Trade per capita is cited by Ginsburg as $8.3, placing Ceylon about halfway up the rank order for this index. Ceylon in fact exported the products of its tea, rubber and coconut plantations and small-holdings, largely to Britain; and in return imported foodstuffs (especially rice) and manufactures. The sector of the economy producing and handling these export crops is often called 'the plantation sector', but this is to ignore the substantial contribution of small-holdings, especially of coconuts and rubber. The other sector, the 'traditional' sector, is seen as that producing rice and other foodstuffs, and long neglected (though the colonial government, hampered by malaria, had begun the restoration of ancient Dry Zone irrigation works).[9] Writers like D.R. Snodgrass see the two sectors as the separate parts of a dual economy, pursuing their own paths with very little contact. But many links between them had developed by the time of independence: for example, through the employment of local capital and labour, not only in commerce associated with the export crops, but also in plantation ownership; and through the ownership by 'peasants' of both paddyfields and holdings of rubber or coconut. But Ceylon at independence did have its problems of regional disparities, if only because of the generally sparse population of its malarial Dry Zone.

Also in contrast to the Indian Empire, Ceylon had few modern manufacturing industries (though some handicrafts survived): but there was a fair amount of repairing and indeed making of machinery for the plantations. And it had a higher proportion of its workers in transport and commerce — with a good road network in the West Zone and Up-country plantation areas. Its GNP per capita as cited by Ginsburg was $122, almost twice that of India and more than twice that of Pakistan round about the time of independence. Ceylon's higher figure was mainly due to the productive export sector. But, as in the case of India and Pakistan, an aggregate national figure conceals gross disparities between groups of people, notably in Ceylon those between affluent Colombo citizens, grown fat on the export economy, and the poor Tamil labour on the plantations, or the poor Sinhalese peasant.

The economy of Nepal in 1947

Nepal was, of course, never formally part of the British Raj; but we have seen that the small Himalayan state was protected and fossilized by the British, whose *pax* created conditions in which population grew and pressed heavily on land resources. But when the Raj passed into history in 1947 Nepal was still an almost entirely agricultural and pastoral country, approximating closely to the stereotype of a peasant 'subsistence economy'. There was very little industry, just a few miles of railway running into the country from India, and hardly any metalled roads. Quantitative data for the period are either lacking or of even more doubtful authenticity than some we have already quoted. Ginsburg, however, puts it at the bottom of his table of GNP per capita, at $40; and also quotes a very low adult literacy figure (1–5 per cent).

The context of economic activity

The context in which economic activity began to take place in South Asia at the coming of independence consisted not only of the state of the several economies at independence, and of the demographic situation to be discussed in the next section, but also of a number of phenomena that have been touched on in earlier chapters. It may be useful at this point to remind the reader of some of them.

The earlier part of Chapter 2 dealt with the resources and limitations of the natural and man-modified environment, especially its soils and climates in their enormous variety (a variety not always sufficiently recognized by economists and other social scientists). The second part of the same chapter approached the South Asian social environment through the caste system. Here one would highlight what may be seen, in spite of caste mobility in Hindu society and the brotherhood of Islam, as the built-in inequality of South Asian society: indeed, the present chapter has already drawn attention to gross inequalities of land holdings and incomes. Chapter 2 has also shown that 'tribals' as well as Harijans tend to be among the notoriously disadvantaged; that certain castes tend to be dominant in land-holding, wealth and power in many villages; that 'village republics' are of doubtful authenticity and utility as a basis for rural development; that the urban élites are detached from their rural roots, which they despise; and — very important — that the force of linguistic regionalism is such, in India at any rate, that States formed under its impact are the only effective units at the immediately subnational level, whether in politics or in planning (if indeed, the two are not the same thing).

From Chapter 3 I propose only to draw one or two threads here. First, the existence of change in these supposedly changeless oriental societies, even though it was not at the pace predicted by nineteenth-century observers, makes it unrealistic if not downright foolish to see South Asian economies and societies in 1947–8 as a static tableau, awaiting the magic touch of independence before it could spring into life. Secondly, the relatively high levels of education and of literacy in the Indian Empire and Ceylon (though not, as we have seen, in Nepal) provided the successor states with a very different base from that of many less-developed countries.

The latter part of Chapter 4 outlined the evolution of politics in South Asia. From the discussion there it will be evident that government intervention in economic affairs in India has to operate in a federal system in which both the Centre and the States are constitutionally concerned with economic planning (not without friction), the central Planning Commission being extraconstitutional. The chapter also showed that the Congress party, so long dominant, covered with its umbrella a diversity of ideologies and interest groups. So, in a different way, did the Janata coalition briefly in power from 1977 to 1980. Other political parties, notably those of the left, have had a clearer ideology in relation to economic policy, which they have from time to time been able to deploy in state governments. Behind all this has lain the factional fighting, the uncertain linkages from Centre to State and, eventually, to the organs of Panchayati Raj and power groups or individuals at village level: all not without influence on the actuality of economic change (or lack of it), sometimes even making an impact on policy by linkages back up the hierarchy. And, at the bottom of the pile, there ever struggling for survival the poor and landless, deprived for the most part of political influence.

In Sri Lanka the alternation of parties in power, to which Chapter 4 drew attention, has meant certain oscillations in economic policy; though at times, particularly those of communal conflict, thinking on economic policy has taken a back place. Meanwhile, as we shall see, the economy as a whole has been in decline; and the disenfranchized Indian Tamils, and the ever-growing army of unemployed, have been the worst sufferers.

Pakistan, Chapter 4 reminds us, has seen long periods of military rule interspersed with bouts of uneasy politics: and has developed various concepts of an 'Islamic State'. It is in this context that Pakistan has taken an economic course generally very different from that of India, though with some superficial convergence of declared policies (some would say rhetoric) in the Bhutto era.

Bangladesh, since its secession from Pakistan in 1971, has, we have seen, suffered long spells of instability and military government which, following Mujib's introduction of a somewhat unrealistic 'socialism', have provided the political context for the country's struggle to survive. Finally, Nepal has precariously remained a monarchy with much unrest amongst some of its interest groups.

So much then for a reminder of some of the strands in what many would call the 'political economy' of South Asia.[10] Finally, the international relations of the several South Asian countries have affected economic change, not least through foreign aid policies and programmes. But there remains a part of the context of economic change, population, which deserves a separate section that will deal, not only with the situation at independence, but with change since that time. And, since population, particularly in its interaction with society and the economy is a not uncontroversial subject, something will have to be said on differing viewpoints and conclusions.

Population in modern South Asia

Before discussing population growth in South Asia since independence, something must be said about the reliability of data. The countries of the subcontinent, with the exception of Nepal, have a sophisticated census organization:[11] it has, indeed, increased in sophistication, and one may assume in general accuracy, since independence. More reliance may therefore be placed on census data, especially in terms of total population and its distribution, than in most Third World countries. But censuses have sometimes taken place under disturbed conditions that must have affected their accuracy: for example, in West Bengal in 1971 and Assam in 1981. In any case, the census is conducted by a vast army of enumerators (1½ million in India in 1971) of varying skill and conscientiousness who are supposed to visit every house and fill in their forms by questioning the occupants. But houses may be missed (as my host's was in Colombo in March 1981) and questions misunderstood, especially by the illiterate. In these and other ways, then, errors may occur. In fact, when a post-enumeration check was conducted, on a sample basis, in Bangladesh in 1981, 3.3 per cent underenumeration was revealed: an appropriate correction has been applied in Table 6.1. The fact that some tabulations take account of underenumeration, while others do not, is one of the reasons for differences between figures cited in

Table 6.1   Population of South Asian countries, 1941–81 (in millions)

	1941	1951	1961	1971	1981
Bangladesh	42.0	41.9	50.8	71.5[a]	89.9[b]
India	318.7	361.1	439.2	547.8	683.8[b]
Nepal	6.3[c]	8.7[d]	9.8	11.5	14.2
Pakistan	28.3	33.8	46.1	65.3[e]	83.8[b]
Sri Lanka	6.7[f]	8.1[g]	10.6[h]	12.7	14.6[b]

Notes:

[a] 1974
[b] Provisional figures
[c] Estimate
[d] 1954
[e] End of 1972
[f] 1946
[g] 1953
[h] 1963

Sources: Reports on national censuses and:

Bangladesh — Entirely based on *Preliminary Report on Population Census, 1981* (Dacca, 1981), Appx A;

India — Cassen, R.H. (1978) *India: Population, Economy, Society*, London, and Unwin, P.T.H. (1981), 'The census of India 1981', *Geography*, 66, 221–2;

Nepal — Karan, P.P. (1960) *Nepal*, Lexington, Kentucky; Macfarlane, A. (1976) *Resources and Population: A Study of the Gurungs of Nepal*, Cambridge, especially p.204;

Pakistan — Johnson, B.L.C. (1979) *Pakistan*, London, 14;

Sri Lanka: Balakrishnan, N. and Gunasekara, H.M. (1977) 'A review of demographic trends', in De Silva, K.M. (ed.), *Sri Lanka: A Survey*, London, 109–27.

different sources. Not all sources, for example, agree that the population in Bangladesh declined slightly from 1941–1951 (by 65,000 according to official sources): it must be remembered that 3 million are estimated to have died in the Bengal famine of 1943.

For such reasons as these, data on populations for Bangladesh, India, Pakistan and Sri Lanka must be treated with some reserve (data for Nepal are much more suspect). To quote populations other than in millions and tenths (as in Table 6.1) or growth rates other than to the nearest 0.1 per cent may give a spurious appearance of accuracy, at least for the more populous countries (strictly, of course, one should quote all populations to a constant number of significant figures).

Censuses are usually taken at ten-year intervals in the second year of a decade; hence the headings in Table 6.1. But the notes to that table indicate that there were a number of variations from this pattern,

Table 6.2   South Asia: average annual compound rate of
population increase

Bangladesh	%	Nepal	%
1941–51	0.0	1941–54	2.5
1951–61	2.0	1954–61	1.7
1961–74	2.7	1961–71	1.6
1974–81	3.3	1971–81	1.4
India	%	Pakistan	%
1941–51	1.3	1941–51	1.7
1951–61	2.0	1951–61	3.1
1961–71	2.2	1961–72	3.0
1971–81	2.2	1972–81	2.9
Sri Lanka	%		
1946–53	2.8		
1953–63	2.7		
1963–71	2.3		
1971–81	1.4		

Source: Derived by the author from data in Table 6.1

notable in Sri Lanka, but also in Pakistan and Bangladesh after the
disturbances and war of 1971. Since, however, Table 6.2 has been
calculated in terms of average *annual* compound growth rates, sound
comparisons may be made (subject always, of course, to accuracy of
underlying data).

Demographers rely for analysis and for projections on data
additional to population totals: in particular, on the age and sex
composition of the population. These are even less reliable than
population totals, for a number of reasons. Thus people rarely know
their age in a society in which birthdays are not commemorated; while
details about females may well be less accurate than those about males
in a male-dominated society. Again, in countries like those of South
Asia in which registration of births and deaths is incomplete,
published birth and death rates tend to be inaccurate; so that
estimates of population in intercensal years may go wildly astray.
Hence planners have from time to time found with dismay that the
census reveals a considerably higher population than had been
projected. Thus in India in 1961 the census registered a population 8
million higher than had been projected only two years earlier.[12]

In 1971, on the other hand, the expectation was some 12 million more than were in fact recorded.

Tables 6.1 and 6.2 taken together give a fair picture of what can be said about absolute populations in South Asia and about rates of growth, provided that due caution is exercised. Thus in South Asia as a whole in 1981 there were 886 million people. Of these some 77 per cent were in India. It will be clear, too, that the populations of Bangladesh and Pakistan have doubled since independence, while those of India and Sri Lanka have not fallen very far short of doubling. This at once gives some measure of the burden that population growth has placed on the several national economies.

Table 6.2 shows that from 1951 to 1961, and excluding Nepal with its doubtful data, each country experienced an average annual compound population growth rate equal to or greater than 2 per cent. Bangladesh, it would appear, has seen its growth rate rise since 1961 to reach, for the period 1974–81, a frightening annual rate of 3.3 per cent; and this in a country with one of the highest densities of rural population in the world which has been seen as an actual or potential Malthusia.[13] India, with a rate for 1971–81 approximately the same as that for 1961–71, gives some indication to the optimist at any rate that a plateau has been reached in terms of growth rates, and the hope that 1981–91 will see a significant decline. But it cannot be too strongly emphasized that there is still a steep upward slope, not a plateau, in terms of total population. An annual growth rate of 2.2 per cent means that India enters the decade 1981–91 with an annual increase of population of over 15 million; and that this annual increment will itself increase at compound rates unless the growth rate falls sufficiently. Pakistan demonstrates the steadiest compound growth rate at around 3.0 per cent. The Sri Lanka case is, however, different. Here one can with reasonable safety discern a descent from a plateau at 2.7–2.8 per cent in the periods 1946–53 and 1953–63 to 2.3 per cent in 1963–71 and 1.4 per cent in 1971–81. As for Nepal, it is clearly hard to draw any firm conclusions about trends, uncertain data being piled on unknown migration.

Average annual compound growth rates vary considerably from area to area within countries. In some regions, as in the Dry Zone of Sri Lanka, rates above the national average are mainly to be accounted for by internal migration. Elsewhere, other factors are clearly at work. Thus in India from 1971 to 1981 rates for the States of Haryana, Karnataka, Kerala and Tamil Nadu were respectively 2.6, 2.3, 1.7 and 1.6 per cent.

Overall, one is justified in asserting that population growth and its consequences have overshadowed all of the countries of South Asia and most of the states of India in the years since independence; and that none of them, with the possible exception of Sri Lanka, Kerala and Tamil Nadu, can look forward for the immediate future to a certain and significant decline in their rates of population growth, still less to a stabilization of their absolute population levels.

Population increase in a country is, of course, due to an excess of births over deaths, plus net international immigration. Such immigration has not been of great importance in South Asia since independence once the immediate consequences of partition were over and done with, except from Nepal (though there was an intermittent stream of refugees from East Pakistan, as it then was, accelerating in 1971; and in recent years Sri Lanka has seen a small net out-migration of persons of Indian origin). As in many other parts of the Third World, the countries of South Asia have seen a declining death rate, mainly as a result of the reduced impact of famine, disease and infant mortality. Crude death rates per 1000 persons fell in India from 27.4 in 1941–51 to 14.8 in 1971–81.[14] There were comparable falls in Pakistan (from 23 in 1960 to 14 in 1979) and in Bangladesh (from 23 to 16 between the same two years). In Sri Lanka there was a more spectacular fall to a level as low as that of some 'advanced' countries: from 13 at independence to 7 in 1979. In Nepal the crude death rate is quoted as having fallen from 29 in 1960 to 20 in 1979 (clearly still much higher than in other countries of South Asia). All this is not to say that malnutrition and disease do not still stalk the countries of South Asia, nor that death rates and infantile and maternal mortality are not still unacceptably high among poorer people and in poorer regions: the data cited are national averages.

While death rates were falling in these ways, crude birth rates have continued to run at a much higher level, hence the high rates of natural increase. But crude birth rates do appear now to be falling, though differentially, and still at a level far above crude death rates. At independence crude birth rates in India were running at around 45 per thousand: between 1971 and 1981 they were of the order of 37. In Pakistan and Bangladesh the birth rates have fallen from 48–9 in 1960 to 44 in 1979; in Nepal, for what the figures are worth, from 46 to 42 over the same period. In Sri Lanka, again the odd man out, crude birth rates fell from 39 at independence to 28 in 1979. The decline in recent years has been attributed mainly to an increase in the age of marriage.[15]

One important consequence of the 'population explosion' or 'demographic revolution' occasioned by the huge surplus of births over deaths has been, for all of the South Asian countries, a very high proportion of children and young people in their populations. In India in 1971 some 135 million, or nearly a quarter of the total population, were under twenty years of age. Over 20 per cent of Sri Lanka's population in 1971 were under the age of 24. Many results flow from the age composition of South Asian populations: for instance, the enormous resources that have to be, or ought to be, devoted to education; the vast numbers clamouring for land and employment, and the increasing size of the reproductive age groups as today's juveniles become tomorrow's mothers and fathers (so that even if the birth-rate stays constant, or falls, but inadequately, the annual number of births will increase).

Future increases of population obviously depend on the balance between births and deaths; so there are a great many imponderables in the assumptions that must be made as a prelude to population projections.[16] It seems very likely that death rates will continue to decline, barring a Malthusian disaster of the sort that might overwhelm Bangladesh or those parts of India that have very dense rural populations pressing hard on available land; but at what rate, and when, they will flatten out and at what level, must remain uncertain. Birth rates seem set to decline slowly. Many authors envisage that the decline will be, or would be helped by increasing urbanization; by economic development and raised income levels; and by improvements in female literacy and the social and economic position of women in society. And there is some evidence that a declining birth rate is indeed correlated with these economic and social phenomena, and that they may lead the countries of South Asia slowly towards 'the widespread voluntary adoption of the small family norm'. But these forces are slow-acting at best; and are likely to act differentially on different parts of South Asia's segmented society. For instance, Muslim women are likely to benefit less compared with their Hindu and Buddhist sisters; and the poor less and last (if ever). For what they are worth, amongst the plethora of projections, recent projections at the national level by the World Bank may be of interest.[17] These show the year of attaining a stationary population as 2105 for Bangladesh, 2115 for India, 2130 for Nepal, 2100 for

Pakistan and 2065 for Sri Lanka. The 'hypothetical size of stationary population' in millions is cited as 338 for Bangladesh, 1621 for India, 44 for Nepal, 340 for Pakistan, and 31 for Sri Lanka, a total of 2374 million. These are indeed frightening figures; and will, to many minds, conjure up the Malthusian nightmare.

Not surprisingly, then, South Asian governments have pursued conscious population policies with more or less vigour and success, and in the face of formidable difficulties.[18] Thus the Indian Third Plan of 1961 set the stabilization of population within a reasonable period as a firm objective; and in the early 1960s an organization was designed to spread methods of family planning. The difficulties, it should be emphasized, were not so much that there were religious or ideological objections as administrative and technical problems; and also, Cassen believes, that 'the socio-economic conditions for widespread voluntary acceptance of birth control did not exist'. But, writing in 1978, he concluded 'it is difficult not to believe that family planning has not prevented something like an average of one million births annually'. But the excesses of The Emergency, which included compulsory sterilization, did nothing to improve the image of the programme. The impact has probably been less in Bangladesh and Pakistan (though in the former at any rate there is a vigorous organization) and much less in Nepal. Sri Lanka long lacked a clear population policy, though voluntary agencies were at work and received a government grant. In the 1970s, in spite of fears that its differential impact would alter ethnic balances, a clearer policy emerged; but family planning has probably had less effect on diminishing the birth rate than delayed marriage. Hence the birth rate could rise again if employment prospects improve.

So far, the discussion and the views of the authors cited have been generally consistent with a neo-Malthusian position: with, that is, a fear of population growing faster than the means of providing for it; though we have cited a number of socio-economic conditions as tending to influence birth rates. Marxist and Marxian analysis takes this last point further. In some hands at any rate it plays down 'the so-called population explosion' as a cause of such ills as unemployment, whose origins it sees as structural.[19] In others, one argument for population limitation, that fewer children will mean less poverty for the family, is stood on its head; and it is argued that poorer rural people firmly believe that a *large* family is an economic advantage, primarily because sons at any rate can earn from a quite tender age.[20]

One does not need to be a Marxist to see, if one knows the Indian village, that there is something in this point. But, in a wider context, a Marxist would probably not see population, still less overpopulation, as overshadowing South Asian development since independence, viewing overpopulation as 'an imperialist myth'[21] and the more significant overshadowings as those of colonial and neocolonial dependency externally and class structure internally.

Be that as it may, it is time to turn to the broad strategies adopted by South Asian countries since independence, to what has been achieved by way of economic development, and to what problems have emerged. The reader will find that there is a great deal of interest in the contrast between the policies and strategies of the several countries of South Asia; indeed, the interest is such that an enormous literature has been built up.

India: strategies and policies since independence

Of none of the countries of South Asia is this more true than of India, for a number of reasons specific to India.[22] One reason, is of course, the vast size of the country, with a population second only to that of China. Moreover, India, unlike China, has generally speaking been directly accessible to foreign, and especially western research workers; while it has produced a number of economists and others of world stature and great prolificity. Again, the data on which scholars, whether Indian or foreign, are able to work are voluminous, and in English. A final and very important reason for interest is that Nehru and his sympathizers in India and abroad saw as a unique contrast, both to the capitalism of the west and to the communism of China, his vision of a democratic socialist India which should have a mixed economy, with central planning and public sectors co-existing with private enterprise, and which should improve the condition of the poor without revolutionary upheaval.

Now in 1938, and in anticipation of independence, Congress had created a National Planning Committee, which in turn set up a number of sub-committees. Given what has been said about the all-encompassing nature of the Congress in Chapter 4, it will be no surprise that the Planning Committee included persons of widely diverging interests and ideologies: Gandhians, western-style social- ists, communists, industrialists and others, all under Nehru's consensus-seeking chairmanship;[23] and that there were contradictions between the recommendations of different subcommittees, and even within a single report of the same committee. Thus the Subcommittee on Land Policy, Agricultural Labour and Insurance took up a socialistic Congress resolution of 1936 in favour of co-operative farming and recommended that land should be compulsorily distributed for cultivation among collective or co-operative organizations. But later, in a somewhat confused passage, the report envisaged co-operative cultivation 'without sacrificing the element of individual property', cultivators sharing produce according to the labour *and* capital provided by each.

In many of the reports one can discern the influence of Nehru and his fellow western-style socialists, impressed by the Soviet model and whole-heartedly in favour of central planning of the economy, as opposed to the Gandhians who, looking back to their idealized Indian co-operative village, were not against communal land tenures, but *were* hostile to central planning and the establishment of heavy industries.

Bhagwati and Desai[24] put it:

This basic opposition of rival ideologies and political forces was to continue into the post-independence period. While sentiments continued to be expressed in favour of radical reconstruction of the social and economic order, the actual programmes to be recommended, and even more the attempts at implementing them, were to represent compromises between different ideological positions on these questions.

Immediately after independence the attention of the Government of India was not surprisingly directed towards these areas and sectors of the economy most affected by partition and the associated movements of people (see p. 62). The greatest disruption was felt from Punjab eastward to Delhi and westernmost UP, and again in West Bengal and Calcutta. The south felt hardly any effects at all. Resettlement of refugees was, as we have seen, a major problem, and for many years large numbers languished in squalid camps in already grossly overcrowded Bengal. Many agriculturalists were however settled on land abandoned by Muslims in Punjab; and numbers were rehabilitated in colonization schemes, particularly in the UP Tarai and in the plateau area in the eastern Deccan known as Dandakaranya.[25] Delhi and Calcutta bore the brunt of the influx of urban refugees, but other towns and cities also grew rapidly because of their arrival.

But meanwhile the government under Nehru's leadership, was preparing a number of strategic measures designed to bring about a 'socialist pattern of society', albeit with a mixed economy. The Planning Commission in New Delhi has been of prime importance in the government's efforts to give central direction to the economy. It was established in March, 1950 under Nehru's chairmanship; and has always been an extraconstitutional (and in theory purely advisory) body. It has been responsible for the formulation of successive Five Year Plans, the first in respect of the years 1950–5 and the sixth, only finalized in February 1981, in respect of the years 1980–5. The Planning Commission, especially in its early days, was able to call on the advice of a number of distinguished Indian and foreign economists. More important, almost certainly, was its association with the National Development Council (NDC), set up in 1952 and also initially under Nehru's chairmanship. The Council consisted of the Prime Minister, the Chief Ministers of States, and the members of the Planning Commission. The NDC had a number of formal initial purposes, but in practice became a sounding-board which could be used to try out on the Chief Ministers (and therefore on State governments and politicians) the political feasibility of various proposals and alternative lines of economic policy. It has played a crucial part in Centre–State linkages in the planning field, all the more important as the States came to develop their own, at first rudimentary planning machinery and to formulate their own Five Year Plans; and also to chafe at the power of the Centre (see pp. 30–1 and 96).

The Planning Commission has always had two basic tasks: first, to decide on the amount of plan investment in the economy; and, secondly, to allocate that investment between alternative sectors and uses. The amount to be invested in the public sector derived by 'state accumulation' from taxation, government revenues, and foreign aid, and in the private sector from non-government sources; and was not all plan investment handled by that Planning Commission: in the allocation of foreign aid, for example, the Ministry of Finance has always played a key part, and grew in power after Nehru's death. Increasingly, too, debates on economic policy came to involve current expenditure (e.g. on agricultural extension) as well as capital investment.

In the development strategy formulated by Nehru, his government and the Planning Commission, industrialization took a central place: especially was this true of the establishment of heavy industries. There were a number of reasons for this emphasis on industry in the thinking of Nehru and of his associates, who in this context notably included P.C. Mahalanobis, a statistician with socialist leanings. Modern medium- and large-scale factory industry was seen as progressive, as essential to the construction of a viable state able by its own efforts to escape from the shackles of colonialism. Here, the reader will remember what has been said earlier (pp. 42–3) about the 'nationalist' view that the colonial impact had nipped an incipient and endogenous industrial revolution in the bud. Moreover, the vision was of an independent India, not only self-reliant but able to defend itself and to play a leading role in the affairs of the subcontinent and of the wider world: and this meant that India must be a modern industrial state. Again, rising living standards for the masses would depend, once needs for food were satisfied, on consumer goods from textiles to electric torches that were seen as inevitably the products of modern industry.

Important sectors of manufacturing industry were to be reserved for the public sector. Thus an Industrial Policy Resolution of 1948 reserved new iron and steel plants and new production of ships, mineral oil, coal, aircraft and telecommunications equipment for public enterprises. The resolution rejected the nationalization of existing private businesses for a ten-year period. Here one can readily discern the influence of the industrialists' lobby within Congress. A second Industrial Policy Resolution of 1956 essentially repeated the list of reservations for the public sector, adding heavy electrical goods and heavy castings and forgings; envisaged a progressive interest by the public sector in further industries; and generally conformed to the adoption by the Lok Sabha in 1954 of the goal of a 'socialist pattern of society'. But there are those who see movement towards this goal in subsequent years, especially since 1965, as slow and erratic, not least in the industrial field (this in spite of the continuing importance of the public sector in industrial development); and who look back to the Nehru–Mahalanobis era as to a golden age.

The emphasis on heavy industry within the public sector was particularly evident in the Second Five Year Plan (1955–60) and Third Five Year Plan (1960–5), when the influence of Nehru and Mahalanobis was at its height. The reasons for this were a conflation of ideology, prestige and pragmatism. Both Nehru and Mahalanobis were impressed by the Soviet achievement, which they saw as development into a socialist society, through the choice of heavy industry as a leading sector, of a country that had been backward and ravaged by war and revolution. Further, heavy industry, and not just manufacturing, seemed necessary to the vision of a modern, progressive, self-reliant and influential India, as it had been to its imperial master. And, if the prime assumptions of the need for industrialization were accepted, then it was difficult to see how sufficient of the capital and intermediate goods necessary to the production of the requisite consumer goods could be imported, since a large enough expansion of traditional exports like cotton textiles and tea was out of the question: capital and intermediate goods had to a large extent, then, to be made in India; and this necessarily entailed heavy industries. Prudence, as well as the attainment of a socialist pattern of society, demanded that these be in the public sector; and so they have remained to this day.

But the private sector, with its powerful interests springing from what we have seen as the considerable industrialization of India at independence (see p. 43), had also to play its part in the development of modern industry, outside the sectors reserved for the public sector under the Industrial Policy Resolutions. But it was to be subject to strict government control, notably under a system of industrial licensing which sprang from the Industrial Policy Resolution of 1948 and from the Industries Act of 1951; and which was designed to ensure that industrial investments were consistent with plan priorities and targets; that 'small' industries were protected and encouraged; that concentration of ownership was prevented; and that 'balanced regional development' of the various regions of India was secured. No new industrial undertaking, and no substantial extension of an existing undertaking, could be made without a licence.[26] Indian industrialists have never ceased to complain that the system lacked rational economic criteria, and introduced delays and inefficiency. Observers from outside India have variously seen the system, with attendant import licensing and other official measures, as a constraint on free capitalist enterprise, a means of distorting the Indian economy, and an exemplification of the impossibility of turning a public service, excellent though it may be as a 'steel frame' for the administration of an enormous country, into a dynamic agent of development.

What, amid all this planned development of modern industry, heavy and light, public sector and private sector, of Gandhian notions of decentralized cottage industries? It is clear that, generally speaking, these notions as a broad strategy fell by the wayside as the juggernaut of the industrialization policy, and especially its heavy-industry manifestation, ground on. True, the early Five Year Plans dutifully contain a section on village and small industries. And a plethora of bodies such as the Village and Small Scale Industries Committee, the All India Khadi and Village Industries Board, and the All India Handloom Board, were established in the early years of planning; and, as we shall see, handlooms and small-factory cloth production has increased very substantially (p. 196). Some attention was also given to the establishment of industrial co-operatives, and of industrial estates to assist small-scale industries by such means as the provision of power and other infrastructure, and of technical assistance. But only 3.6 per cent of the planned public sector outlay in the second plan was allotted to village and small-scale industries, compared with 17.5 per cent to large-scale industrial and mineral development. Moreover (as is indeed implicit in what has just been said) not even this relative small amount of effort was in line with Gandhian ideals of village handicrafts; for industrial estates and other measures are intended for modern, machine industry, albeit on a relatively small scale, and in the private sector (to government *control* (and perhaps constraint) of that sector, just stressed, one must therefore add a modicum of government *assistance*). Very modest provision and encouragement for the small-scale industrial sector, incorporating both village-traditional and modern has continued through all the ensuing plans, up to and including the sixth (1980–5). Only during the time of the short-lived Janata Government of 1977–9 was there a policy declaration that all that could be made by village industry should be so made; that as much as possible of the remainder should be the preserve of the (modern) small-scale sector; and that only the residuum be allotted to large-scale industry. Here one can see the influence of old-style Gandhians like Morarji Desai. But the policy, if that is what it was, was soon overtaken by political events, and was never implemented.

Notwithstanding the occasional mention of 'balanced regional development' and the inclusion of a chapter under this title in the third plan,[27] Indian planning has from the outside been overwhelmingly sectoral in character and hinged to a great extent on sophisticated models of the economy as a whole. It is true that, as India settled down to a more stable internal pattern of political geography; as the States involved in this grew into more powerful means of mobilizing regional opinion; and as, particularly in the post-Nehru era, some States came to have non-Congress governments unwilling to accept all that New Delhi decreed and, in particular, resented the 'interference' of the extraconstitutional Planning Commission: it is true that as these and other developments took place the bargaining power of the states grew at the expense of the centre, and that in a very real sense each State became effectively a planning region in its own right. Uneasy Centre–State relations in the economic sphere had in fact a great deal to do with the so-called 'holiday from planning' from 1966 to 1969, as a result of which the fourth plan did not come into force until the latter year. But for a State to press for, let us say, a steel works to enhance its own prestige, and because of the opportunities for patronage that would arise from such a massive development within its borders, is a far cry from 'balanced regional development' aimed at the uplift of backward regions, which anyway rarely coincide with State boundaries. We shall see, however, that some attention has been given, in the plans at least, to 'multi-level planning' and to special schemes for 'target areas' and 'target groups' (see pp. 200–2). Formulae were also devised to weight central grants to the States under the provisions of the plans in favour of remote and relatively backward areas like Jammu and Kashmir and Assam. But the sixth Five Year Plan (1980–5), like all of its predecessors, remains overwhelmingly sectoral, and only to a minor degree spatial or regional, in general thrust.

Indian planning, especially during the heyday of the Nehru–Mahalanobis strategy, has often been criticized for its relative neglect of agriculture, and to a considerable extent the charge is justified. The second plan thus allotted considerably less to agriculture and community development than to (large-scale) industries and minerals. It is also true that, for all the resolutions before and after independence on co-operative and communal organization and for all the stated objective of a socialist pattern of society, government tended to regard agriculture as essentially in the private sector, the preserve of myriads of cultivators spread throughout the length and breadth of the land. Nevertheless, ever since independence government agencies have continued to build and to maintain major irrigation works and rural roads; to undertake agricultural research and to organize extension agencies; and in many other ways to foster agricultural production. We shall return to agricultural and agrarian matters at a later stage in this chapter (see pp. 176–95).

Finally, in this review of strategy and of the content of successive Five Year Plans, it must be emphasized that the government has also made itself responsible for very considerable infrastructural invest-ment, notably in roads and railways and in power; and also for expenditure on education, health services (including family plan-ning), and housing (rural and urban). In the sixth plan many of these sectors are seen as contributing to the Minimum Needs Programmes.

Now, it will be clear from the account just given that Indian planning has, during its operation over more than three decades since independence, demonstrated a number of apparent continuities: notably in its emphasis on central planning and on industrialization in the public sector. But it is important not to give the impression of an unchanging grand strategy, still in the 1980s running smoothly and reflecting that of Nehru and of Mahalanobis. A number of observers, some writing near the time, some more recently, date a certain faltering in the strategy to the mid-1960s; though it was to some extent presaged by difficulties during the period of the second plan (1956–61), particularly in terms of a shortfall in public sector investment and in food supply.[28] A number of reasons may be, and have been adduced for this faltering and for subsequent changes of strategic emphasis, though some of them are not uncontroversial and not all can be cited here. Nehru, it will be remembered, died in 1964 and his successor, Shastri, insisted that more resources be devoted to agriculture, following severe droughts and the need for food imports and food aid. Even more disastrous droughts struck in 1965–7 and, as we shall shortly see, contributed to a reappraisal of agricultural policy, especially given alarming population growth (which also gave new urgency to family planning). Heavy industry, as we shall see, ran into recession. As Chapter 4 has shown (see pp. 80–1) Centre-State relations became more strained with the election early in 1967 of a number of non-Congress governments, which resented the extra-constitutional power that had accreted to the Planning Commission, whose macro-economic models and data had, moreover, been heavily criticized by economists. Morale in the Commission fell; and it found its strategic influence reduced; Treasury orthodoxy tended to prevail. In terms of financial resources, too, troubles came thick and fast. The halcyon days of the first plan, when India still had sterling balances built up during World War Two, were over and gone. A yawning gap between planned outlay and available resources surfaced in the second plan period and became even more evident during the third plan period, compounded by inflation. Pressure has come from Chief Ministers to reduce the overall size of the plans while increasing State outlay at the expense of the Centre; from industrialists to limit taxation and provide incentives; from ever more powerful rural interests to diminish or to abolish land revenue and to resist proposed new taxes like agricultural income tax. The yawning gap, and associated foreign exchange shortages, have meant large-scale use of foreign aid, notwithstanding original and constantly proclaimed goals of self-reliance.[29] Now pipers call tunes: for example, in 1965 the United States changed its aid policy and began to require 'specific aid offers contingent upon the institution of particular adjustments in indigenous rural policy';[30] pressure from the World Bank and from the International Monetary Fund (IMF) had much to do with the Indian devaluation of 1966, which of course had repercussions for the economy and the planning process; while as I write (Spring 1982) controversy burns about the conditions attached to the latest IMF assistance. Again, American aid was suspended during the wars with Pakistan in 1965 and 1971. (Less can be said about pressures from the USSR in return for its aid, which is in any case much smaller in amount than that of the USA.)

One reaction to these and other difficulties has been, in the opinion of some observers, to make the central planning process increasingly unrealistic and increasingly distanced from implementation and from the pressing problems of real life as it is lived, especially in the countryside. Perhaps one can see here the equivalent in planning terms of the decaying political linkages with lower levels to which Chapter 4 has drawn attention (see pp. 87–8). Another reaction has been a failure sufficiently to redefine objectives (hence some at least of the apparent continuities in planning); though Streeten and Lipton see a shift in aims at the time of the gestation of the fourth plan and of the so-called 'holiday from planning' (1966–9) from self-sustaining growth to rapid growth, from railways and heavy industry to roads, light industry and improved seeds.[31]

Francine Frankel, among more recent authors, views the Indian scene rather differently, though not altogether inconsistently.[32] She highlights what she sees as 'the emerging contradiction' between Nehru's two main aims: 'accomodative politics', to include under the

Congress umbrella and within a parliamentary democracy all of the diverse interest groups of India; and the achievement of a social transformation which should gradually and peacefully uplift the masses economically, socially and politically. She regards post-independence history, especially since 1965, as a retreat from socialist objectives that has gathered momentum with the years, leaving only the rhetoric of *gharibi hatao* (see p. 87) and the protestations of successive plans about the war on unemployment and poverty.

But it will be fairer to try and reach a conclusion on these matters after we have reviewed what has been accomplished and not accomplished in India since independence. This will be done under the heads agriculture; agrarian structure; mining and manufacturing; regional and 'target group' planning; and foreign trade.

Indian agriculture since independence

In terms of aggregate agricultural production, India can record notable achievements since independence. Official statistics are neither completely reliable nor invariably consistent as between different sources; and cannot be taken to indicate more than rough orders of magnitude (all tons quoted are metric tons). They show that total food grain production increased from about 60 million tons in 1949–50, to nearly 90 million tons in 1964–5, before the great drought and also before the so-called 'green revolution'. It rose to about 118 million tons in 1960–71 and 127 million tons in 1977–8, and may be 134 million tons in 1981–2. Both before and after the great drought, however, there were bad years, some necessitating food imports and food aid, as we have seen; but buffer-stocks have been built up in good years. The general trend of aggregate food grain production has kept ahead, even if only just ahead of population. Up to about 1962, it would appear that about half of the increase in food grain production came from increased yield per hectare (and this, it should be noted, before the 'green revolution' of the late 1960s) and half from increased area. After about 1962, increases in yield became more important than increases in area.

Not all food grains have participated equally in this aggregate growth. Rice, the most important food grain, climbed from about 24 million tons in 1949–50 to a peak before the great drought at 39 million tons in 1964–5, with setbacks in poor years. Its production then plummetted to only just over 30 million tons in 1965–6 and

1966–7; regained its pre-drought levels in 1967–8; and since then has risen, with shortfalls in poor years, to something over 50 million tons per annum in the late 1970s and early 1980s: not a spectacular rise given the expectations of the 'green revolution', but of this more in a moment.

Wheat production climbed, with the expected oscillations, from some 6.6 million tons in 1949–50 to 12.3 million tons in 1964–5; and, after the lean years, rose spectacularly to 26.4 million tons in 1971–2 and then, after a relapse, to 35 million tons in 1978–9. The rapid rise in the last fifteen years or so is undoubtedly to be associated with the 'green revolution', subject to the reservations to be entered shortly.

No other food grains are as important to India as rice and wheat. But one must not neglect the so-called 'coarse grains', which comprise millets like *jowar* (sorghum), *bajra* (bulrush millet) and *ragi* (finger millet), very important in dry, unirrigated areas, especially to poor people; maize; and barley. Some of these crops are also used as fodder. On the whole, production of these 'coarse grains' registered a relatively slow rate of increase from the first plan period (when they averaged 15.9 million tons per annum) to the fourth; but climbed from 22 million tons in 1972–3 to over 30 million tons in 1978–9. As a whole they have been less affected by the 'green revolution' than rice or wheat. But average yields for *jowar* and maize have roughly doubled since independence.

Pulses are of nutritional importance as a source of protein, especially for vegetarians. But production has only increased by about 50 per cent since independence, to some 12 million tons in 1978–9. One reason for this is that in some regions the area under pulses has fallen as farmers have taken to high-yielding varieties of cereals. Much the same is true of oilseeds, which totalled 9 million tons in 1978–9. The sixth plan judges increased production of both pulses and oil-seeds as 'a most urgent requirement'. Sugar cane production has doubled since independence, to over 150 million tons (of cane).

Turning to non-food crops, cotton production has risen from 3 million bales in 1949–50 to nearly 8 million bales in 1978–9; and jute production from 3 million to over 6 million bales in the same period.

Since population increased by about 90 per cent between 1951 and 1981 (see Table 6.1), a doubling of production between independence or the first plan period and recent years means that, roughly speaking, average production per capita has stood still. Moreover, average figures conceal areas and groups that suffered a decline in per capita terms. And it must be remembered that *average* nutritional levels are still very low in India: calorie intake is only about two-thirds of that in the UK.

Government agencies, whether responsible to the central or to State governments, claim, and can take some of the credit for increases in aggregate production, just as they must accept blame for certain shortcomings. Now, official agricultural research in India did not begin with independence, but has been considerably strengthened since and has included some distinguished and highly important work. But it has nevertheless been somewhat uneven (thus rice-breeding has, until recently at any rate, and relative to the importance of the crop, tended to lag behind wheat-breeding); and feedback from the farmer's field to the research stations has been inadequate, while links between research and extension are sometimes tenuous and obstructed by bureaucracy (I remember one extension officer in Kerala who would not profit from the useful work of a research colleague literally over the fence, insisting that the fruits of research could only reach him *via* the Department of Agriculture in the State capital).

Again, agricultural extension and schemes for rural uplift are not new arrivals on the Indian scene. However, in 1952, inspired by the newly-created Planning Commission, and with American assistance, fifty-five 'community projects' were started to stimulate agricultural development in areas with good water supply: each had a staff of extension and other workers.[33] But Nehru objected to the concentration on already-favoured areas and to an exclusive emphasis on production; though he agreed with the partial reliance on self-help. So it was that, under the second plan, community development (CD) was born, with the purpose not only of agricultural improvement but also general rural uplift, especially of the poor. The whole of India was to be (and eventually was) divided into blocks of a number of villages, each under a block development officer (BDO), under whom were generalist village level workers (VLWs (= Gram Sevaks)); and specialists, notably agricultural extension workers.

Another, and very important parallel development was that of Panchayati Raj, essentially the re-creation of what were, or were thought to be ancient village councils, seen by Nehru and his like-minded colleagues as a means of shifting power in the village towards the poorer classes (see p. 96); and to be associated with village-level co-operatives and, originally, that elusive goal, co-operative or collective cultivation.[34] In 1958, the control of community development at block level was moved from appointed officials to elected block Panchayat Samitis (though technical personnel still came under bureaucratic control); while later a further body, the Zila Parishad, was established at district level. All were to be associated, in the minds of Nehru and his planners, with land reform (see pp. 134–91).

What can be said about the effects of these new or revived or modified institutions on agricultural production and on the distribution of income and power in the countryside? First, while one can appreciate the motives behind the rapid spread of community development to the whole country, its impact was thereby necessarily diluted; and it not surprisingly proved difficult to find enough able and dedicated officers to fill the ranks of BDOs, VLWs, and associated extension staff. I remember visiting a training institution in 1956 and finding that all those accepted for the course were automatically 'passed out' at its termination. Again, while one has appreciated the motivation and effectiveness of some CD officers, particularly those who work without exploiting or condescending to less privileged classes, one has frequently met BDOs who allowed themselves to be submerged in the mountain of paperwork that all too readily accretes in India (where all institutions, including universities, tend to become bureaucracies) and rarely visited their villages. And I have been to villages, as late as 1973–4, that have never received the ministrations of CD or NES officers. However, in our survey of North Arcot District of Tamil Nadu, John Harriss reported that 'the effectiveness of some extension activities in information dissemination appeared quite strong', a conclusion borne out by other surveys on which, however, as on the operation of the extension service, Robert Chambers and B.W.E. Wickremanayake have critical comments to make.[35] The fact is that the effectiveness of agricultural extension is very difficult to measure objectively and accurately; not least because information can reach farmers in so many ways: e.g., through the vernacular press, through the radio, and through conversations with other farmers.

What is quite clear, however, is that a tendency is at work in the Indian countryside that is even more universal than the tendency for every institution to become a bureaucracy. Given what has been said in earlier chapters it will be no surprise to the reader to learn that, whatever the wishes of Nehru and the planners in terms of the uplift of the poor and their growth in political power, there is a very strong tendency for institutions, whether panchayats or co-operative societies or other bodies, to be captured and turned to their own use by the dominant castes in the villages (who are, moreover, politically important to politicians at higher levels).

Now already in Nehru's day seeds had been sown that were to grow into a new agricultural strategy which had profound, if selective and controversial effects, on Indian agriculture.[36] In 1959 a Ford Foundation team advocated an approach to the problem of sufficiently increasing Indian food production that, *inter alia*, involved a reversion to concentration on areas with good water supply; and the intensive advocacy to farmers in them of a 'package of practices' to include fertilizers, improved methods of cultivation, and improved varieties. So was born the Intensive Agricultural District Programme (IADP), deployed in seven districts in 1960–1 and later extended, but still on a highly selective basis;[37] while the less intensive IAAP (Intensive Agricultural Area Programme) was applied to certain other areas. In the mid 1960s Shastri's concern for agriculture,[38] advice from the World Bank and USAID, and changing US aid policies (see p. 175) converged to associate IADP and IAAP with a 'new agricultural strategy' that also involved strengthened research and more reliance on incentives to farmers; though they were still to be assisted by improved credit facilities. Now, while IADP and IAAP recognize inter-regional differences (as economists, planners and even agronomists rarely do to a sufficient extent) they equally clearly tended to exaggerate spatial differences in average income levels, and to contrast with the (theoretically) uniform spread of CD. Indeed, there are those who see the new strategy as a triumph of the technocratic and production-orien-ted over the distributive and socialist policies of early independence.

But the new strategy, by the time that it had been more completely formulated in the mid-sixties, involved yet another programme, the High Yielding Varieties Programme (HYVP), which leads us on to the so-called 'green revolution'.[39] This is, of course, the popular (and misleading) title for the introduction and spread from the mid-1970s onward of high-yielding varieties (HYVs) of cereals in association with chemical fertilizers in specific doses at specific stages; with insecticides and pesticides; with controlled watersupply (usually envisaged in terms of irrigation); and with improved cultural methods. These together were usually seen, in IADP terms, as a 'package' to be adopted as a whole by the cultivator. The HYVP was originally planned to be applied to the IADP districts, in the expectation that it would spread outward from them.

To evaluate the effects of the 'green revolution' on aggregate production we must clearly look at the years after the great drought of 1965–7. We have already seen that wheat production leapt upward: in fact it nearly trebled between 1963–4, just before the great drought, and 1971–2; and, with oscillations, has climbed upward since to its present level of over 30 million tons per annum. Wheat has, indeed, been the crop that has benefited most from the new technology, which in terms of varieties has been based on dwarf wheats derived, many of them recently in India itself, from Mexican progenitors. At first, adoption of these HYVs was mainly a matter of Punjab, Haryana and western UP; but it later spread down the plains to eastern UP and Bihar and even to West Bengal. In these more eastern states (and indeed elsewhere) increase in area under wheat has been partly responsible for increased production: but this trend has been made possible by the HYVs. Over the whole plains region, increased production has been underpinned by a massive increase in the sinking of tubewells for irrigation. Many of these have been the result of private action on the part of farmers (in Bihar, where the watertable is near the surface, enterprising cultivators have developed a method of sinking bamboos in place of the usual, and much more expensive steel tubes). Another crucial factor has been the very extensive use of chemical fertilizers (consumption in Punjab increased from 25,000 tons in 1966 to 565,000 tons in 1970–1). But the HYVs and the associated technology have so far had much less impact south of the plains, in the drought-prone areas of the western Deccan, except locally where well irrigation is feasible.

Aggregate rice production has, as we have already seen, told a very different story: indeed, while wheat production was nearly trebling rice production rose only by some 16 per cent. True, there have been success areas — or, rather, success seasons in specific areas. Most of these have been those that bear out the old school geography-room dictum that rice flourishes when its feet are in the water (at controlled depth, one should add) and its head in the sun. Thus HYV adoption has reached high levels, and yields increased markedly, in such areas as Punjab in *kharif* (the south-west monsoon season of light rains and much sunshine under canal and tubewell irrigation); West Bengal in the *boro* or winter (north-east monsoon) season, given irrigation; and dry seasons, again given irrigation, in the south.

But HYV adoption has been much lower, and increases in yields much less marked, in two contrasting areas: those characterized by waterlogging or deep flooding; and those prone to drought unalleviated by irrigation. The first of these is quantitatively very important, constituting some 80 per cent of Indian rice-growing areas — where, moreover, no other foodcrop can be grown, but where a wide range of traditional varieties, each suited to a particular environment and length of growing season, have been selected by cultivators through the millenia. A number of factors contribute to this situation. The HYVs are dwarf, so easily submerged by relatively shallow flooding; they cannot survive such submergence; they are of short duration and non-photoperiod sensitive or 'date-fixed' (so that if sown early in the monsoon they come to maturity while the rains are still all too evident); they, or many of them (especially the 'miracle rice', IR.8, for which such foolishly large claims were made) are very susceptible to the pests and diseases that proliferate under hot, humid monsoon conditions; and some of them are vulnerable to the soil toxicity that may build up under anaerobic conditions when fields are flooded or waterlogged. Clearly, in terms of most of these considerations, the deeper the flooding, the greater the problem; and, while there are traditional deep-water or floating rices that will produce small though acceptable yields in depths of one to six metres, the problem of producing HYVs to boost yields under these conditions is an intractable one, though attempts are being made. Less intractable, though still difficult, are the problems of land subject to less deep flooding and to waterlogging. Here Indian research has of recent years made some progress by breeding a new range of medium-tall or semi-dwarf varieties, some with notably greater resistance to pests and diseases.

As for drought-prone without adequate irrigation, research is also in progress to produce water-sparing varieties of rice: this is a need emphasized in the sixth Five Year Plan. So is the enhancement of the irrigated area.

We have seen in Chapter 3 (see p. 38) that irrigation in India has a long history (indeed, it seems that the ancient Harappan civilization of about 2500 BC made inundation canals, through which water flowed when rivers ran high; while the massive Grand Anicut on the Kaveri dates from the eleventh century AD); and that the British added substantially to the irrigated area, especially by the construction of perennial canals. According to official statistics, independent India had in 1950–1 a net irrigated area of nearly 21 million hectares.[40] By 1975–6 this had increased to 34.5 million hectares, an increase of some 64 per cent. Over the same period the canal irrigated area grew from

8,295,000 hectares (40 per cent of the total) to 13,775,000 hectares (still 40 per cent of the total). The area irrigated from tanks (small reservoirs) grew from 3,613,000 hectares (17.3 per cent) to 3,986,000 hectares (only 11.6 per cent). Well irrigation was responsible for 5,978,000 hectares (28.7 per cent) in 1950–1, and for 14,348,000 hectares (47.6 per cent) in 1975–6. The well irrigated area thus grew by 140 per cent. Most of this astonishing growth was accounted for by tubewells, many of which are now pumped by electric motors or diesel engines. In fact, the sinking and mechanization of tubewells sometimes under government auspices, often as we have seen accomplished by the cultivators, has had a greater impact on Indian agriculture than many of the spectacular post-independence schemes like the Bhakra–Nangal project, the Rajasthan Canal and the Kosi project.[41]

Again according to official figures, 18 per cent of the net sown area was irrigated in 1950–1 and 24 per cent in 1975–6. (The net sown area is officially defined as 'the net area sown with crops and orchards, areas sown more than once being only counted once'.) But the irrigated proportion of the net sown area varied widely: to take only some of the larger States, from about 10 per cent in Kerala, Madhya Pradesh and Maharashtra and 13 per cent in Karnataka to 43 per cent in Tamil Nadu, 46 per cent in Uttar Pradesh, 48 per cent in Haryana, and no less than 75 per cent in Punjab. In some States, of course, a low figure results largely from lack of need — for instance, in well-watered Kerala and in the eastern parts of Madhya Pradesh. But it is clear that the need is great, but to a considerable extent unmet, in many of the dry Deccan districts of Karnataka, western Madhya Pradesh and Maharashtra. And there is, of course, a finite limit to the renewable water resources, whether surface or underground, of such drought-prone regions — and, for that matter, elsewhere. There are areas, like interior Tamil Nadu, where underground water is being pumped out faster than it is recharged by rivers and rainfall, so that the water-table is falling.[42] Grandiose schemes are from time to time mooted to take water to the Deccan from areas still in surplus, such as the lower Ganges; but the cost would be so high as to place many such schemes virtually in the realm of fantasy. For it cannot be too strongly emphasized that there are economic constraints, as well as hydrological limits, to the extension of irrigation in India. Estimates of a potentially irrigable area in excess of 100 million hectares must be treated with caution.[43] There are also political constraints in the shape on unresolved interstate disputes on the use of river water: for example, between Maharashtra and Andhra Pradesh over Godavari water, and between Gujarat and Madhya Pradesh over Narmada water.

Even those areas already irrigated have their problems. Irrigation, especially from unlined canals, can in the absence of adequate drainage works or sufficient pumping from tubewells lead to a rise in the water-table and eventually to waterlogging and, through capillary action from a near-surface water-table, to saline and alkaline deposits on field surfaces which may put land out of cultivation.[44]

In some major schemes, it has been found impossible to irrigate the original target area. Thus the original target of 1½ million acres (0.6 million hectares) for the Kosi canal system in Bihar has had to be reduced to just over 900,000 acres (some 360,000 hectares), for reasons that include here, as elsewhere, over-optimistic assumptions about the area irrigable by a unit volume of water; inadequate appreciation of topography and soils; and channel siltation.[45] In major schemes more generally, there has been official concern at the difference between area irrigable (in theory, at any rate) and area actually irrigated; hence the institution in the fifth plan period of Command Area Authorities charged with the integrated development of areas in major schemes through such measures as the construction of channels, the levelling of land, and the improvement of cropping patterns and input supply. This programme, extended under the sixth plan, may be seen, because of its concentration on areas already favoured with irrigation, as an extension of the IADP philosophy.

One of the depressing features of discussion of irrigation problems in official Indian literature is that the subject is seen dominantly in technocratic terms: the physical availability of water, dam and channel construction, and so on; and (though less often) in terms of economic costs and benefits. But the cultivators who use irrigation water, when they can get it, are not automatons, but people set in India's very unequal society and complex polity, on whom many socio-political constraints operate. This brings us to questions of equity in Indian agricultural development and, first, to land reform.

India: agrarian structure and related problems

Chapter 3 has shown that the distribution of land in pre-British India was already very unequal, and that the landless already existed; and that, however controversial the effects of British rule on agrarian structure, one consequence was certainly an increase in landlessness, while another was a strengthening of the power of *zamindars*, who became powerful landlords and revenue collectors for, and allies of the Raj. Not surprisingly, then, there was early agitation (in the 1890s) for the abolition of *zamindari*, which gathered strength with the nationalist movement. In the years leading up to independence there was a great deal of discussion inside and outside Congress which broadened from the *zamindari* issue into the reform, or even abolition of tenancy, the imposition of ceilings on holdings; and proposals for collective and co-operative cultivation (see p. 168). Some of this discussion was spurred on by a notable book, *Poverty and Social change: a Study in Economic Reorganisation of Indian Rural Society* published in 1945 by Tarlok Singh, a civil servant who was later Secretary of the Planning Commission.[46] After independence, in 1949, Congress appointed an Agrarian Reforms Committee which Frankel sees as 'a major product of socialist–Gandhian collaboration'.[47] Rejecting both a capitalist structure and wholesale collectivization the Committee, like Nehru in his grand strategy, chose a third and composite structure: the amalgamation of very small holdings for joint cultivation; the survival in individual tenure of holdings from one to three times the size of an 'economic holding'; and a ceiling pitched at three times an 'economic holding'. An 'economic holding' was defined as one which could afford a reasonable standard of living and provide full employment for a normal family and for at least a pair of bullocks. Not surprisingly, given the variegated nature of Congress, there was dissent from some members of the Committee, especially over compulsory co-operative farming. But opinion in favour of this was boosted by an Indian delegation who visited China and reported favourably, if naively, on agrarian co-operatives there; while in 1959 Congress passed its well-known Nagpur resolution in favour of co-operative joint farming, but such that property rights were maintained and a share of the net produce allotted to workers, whether they owned land or not.[48] (From dissent over this resolution sprang the Swatantra Party (see p. 90).)

What has actually been achieved by way of land reform in India since independence is but a pale shadow of these radical programmes. In the words of M.L. Dantwala, 'If you ask me what is the most important feature of land reforms I would say non-implementation'.[49]

True, *zamindari* abolition was accomplished fairly quickly by state legislation enacted between 1950 and 1954, in spite of a sturdy rearguard action by the *zamindars*. But it cannot be too strongly emphasized that this was primarily a change in the tax system. Tenants who formerly paid revenue and rent to *zamindars* now paid the same total amount direct to government. Though in some states the status of tenants was improved, the distribution of land was not affected. Indeed, *zamindars* retained land for 'personal cultivation' and received handsome compensation for the loss of their revenue-collecting status, with which many of them bought yet more land; while some former tenants of *zamindars* lost their rights and became labourers. Altogether, then, the much-trumpeted reform did not increase equity in land-holding, and indeed tended to decrease it.

What, then was the distribution of land as land reform moved into the next phase after the abolition of the intermediaries? Table 6.3 was derived by Doreen Warriner from the data of the National Sample Survey, 8th Round;[50] and has been slightly adapted for present purposes.

Table 6.3 needs interpreting with caution. First, the data are

Table 6.3 Distribution of estimated number of households and of total area owned/operated by size-level and household ownership (1954–5)

Size-group acres	Percentage of	
	Households	Area
0.00–0.005	22	—
0.005–1	25	1
1–2½	14	5
2½–5	14	10
5–10	13	19
10–15	5	13
15–20	3	10
20–25	1	7
25–50	2	19
over 50	1	16
	100	100

derived from a sample of 12,480 households throughout India, out of an estimated total of 66 million households; and information on holding size is notoriously inaccurate. Secondly, there is the ambiguity implicit in the words 'owned/operated'; for the area operated by a cultivator may differ greatly from the area he owns, even quite small owners tending both to lease in and to lease out. And the survey itself overtly classifies certain kinds of tenants as owners, though it is clear that the great mass of tenants-at-will and share-croppers are excluded. (It is, in fact, impossible to determine the number of such tenants in India or in most parts of it.) Thirdly, three acres of irrigated, double-cropped paddy land in the south is a prince's patrimony compared with 50 acres of land in Rajasthan yielding only when rare rains fall, soil fertility and climate both favouring the former.

However, it is clear that would-be reformers had to deal with a highly skewed distribution in the decade or so after independence. It will be noted that about a fifth of the households held no land at all, or less than 0.005 acres (i.e. less than 24 sq.yds). Another quarter held less than an acre. Here lies the bulk of the great mass of disastrously impoverished villagers who, unless they can find non-agricultural employment (and that is scarce in most parts of India) are dependent on tenancy, or agricultural labour, or (as is usual) some combination of the two. It will be noted, too, that no less than 75 per cent of the sampled households held less than five acres, covering 16 per cent of the land. Finally, India is clearly not a land of vast *latifundia*: a 'big man' in a South Indian village is a man with, say, 15 or 20 acres;[51] though there, and even more in the north, much depends on the nature and irrigability of the land. Clearly there cannot in logic be a uniform all-India ceiling.

In turning to the question of ceilings on land-holdings and the redistribution of surplus land in excess of ceilings (generally seen as the most obvious way of reducing if not removing skewness in the distribution of land ownership) it must at the outset be stressed that in India land reform is constitutionally a State subject. Whatever the recommendations of Congress committees or central government bodies like the Planning Commission, the enactment and implementation of relevant legislation is entirely a matter for State governments. In the vast majority of States, ceiling legislation was in fact enacted in the 1950s and 1960s; and in some of them subsequently amended with lower ceilings after prodding in 1969 from Mrs Gandhi, concerned at both agrarian unrest and her populist image. But generally speaking, and over and above foot-dragging in enactment, much legislation was so drafted as to ensure that, as Warriner puts it, 'a ceilings law was enacted in accordance with official (i.e. Central) policy, while its intentions were neatly by-passed' by other provisions in the Acts:'[52] for example, exemptions for particular categories of land such as orchards or tea plantations; a raising of ceilings for allegedly dependent relatives; the admissibility of transferring excess land to 'heirs' within a given period *after* enactment. Who has need of a lawyer to find loopholes when the legal draftsman has ingeniously built them into the Act? Not surprisingly, the areas of land declared surplus (i.e. in excess of the appropriate ceiling and available for distribution) were in most States only slowly assembled, and then totalled vastly less than had been anticipated by the would-be reformers (though data are hard to obtain). The sixth plan claims that up to 1980 some 1.6 million hectares (about 1 per cent of the total area of agricultural holdings) had been declared surplus but only 960,000 hectares had been resumed by the States and 680,000 hectares redistributed to 1,154,000 landless persons, of whom just over half were members of scheduled castes and scheduled tribes.[53] But redistribution appears to have been pursued with vigour only in a few States, particularly Jammu and Kashmir, Uttar Pradesh, Maharashtra and West Bengal (under left-dominated governments). But available data suggest that land reform has in most States not had more than a marginal impact, if that, on the skewness of the distribution of land possession. The number and proportion of landless and of very small landholders continues to grow as population moves inexorably upward and as for some at any rate the unequal effects of the 'green revolution' are felt (see pp. 191–2). The bold and radical programmes, the idea that distributive measures could and would be taken, and that they would not only promote equity and relieve poverty but also stimulate production (on the assumption that productivity per acre was higher on smaller holdings than on larger, the 'inverse relationship'): all of this has run into the sand, though local bosses may use ceiling legislation against political enemies.

Tenancy in India is of course extremely widespread, though variable in its incidence from area to area, and also extremely complex, given the prevalence of a 'pyramid of rights' (see pp. 40–1). The reform of tenancy, with the objects of achieving security of tenure for tenants, 'fair rents' and a right of purchase was a main plank in the platform of the would-be reformers at the time of independence. Tenancy legislation was, with the expected foot-dragging, passed in most states by the early 1960s; and there were many loopholes and evasions. Landlords were able to resume land for 'personal cultivation', ejecting tenants and reducing some of them to the status of labourers. Even where the law should have protected tenants, enforcement was absent or weak; and most tenants were either ignorant of their rights, or afraid to press them against powerful landlords who were also moneylenders to whom they were indebted. True, in West Bengal the government formed by the Communist Party of India (Marxist) has vigorously pursued 'Operation Barga' under which share-croppers (*bargadars*) are being registered (and ceilings firmly imposed), while observing some caution for fear of alienating 'middle peasants'. In some other areas tenants were able to improve their position, for example in parts of Uttar Pradesh, and in Maharashtra and Kerala; but in others their position worsened — notably in Thanjavur District of Tamil Nadu, known for its agrarian unrest. On the whole one can conclude that the equity goals of the would-be reformers have not been widely achieved, and that the position of some tenants has worsened; and that the production effects of tenancy legislation (on the assumption that insecurity is a constraint on the application of inputs) are hard to find.

On the land-reform programme as a whole, one must observe that if effective, it would weaken just those men on whom Mrs Gandhi's government has grown dependent (see above, p. 95).

What then of co-operative cultivation, so assiduously pressed in various forms by the would-be reformers, some of them with Gandhian notions of the re-creation of an idyllic village that never was? By 1968 there were apparently only 1347 co-operative farming societies in India, of which only 381 were collectives (in which land ownership subsists in the society), the rest being joint farming societies (in which ownership was merely pooled, and reflected in the 'dividend' of the cultivator).[54] Of these, some, perhaps many were bogus, like the one I visited in the Chambal Valley of Madhya Pradesh in 1963, where an extended family of Sikhs had formed a co-operative on paper and so secured land and government subsidies, but were in fact operating an estate growing long staple cotton, many of the 'members' being absentee and employed elsewhere. It is doubtful if there are now more co-operative farming societies than in 1968, probably fewer except in left-inclined West Bengal; and it is also unlikely that a higher proportion are genuine. The subject is in fact virtually dead, for all the zeal of the reformers and the controversy of former years, and the hopes (almost certainly ill-founded) that co-operative cultivation would increase production.

There are two further measures usually included in the Five Year Plans and other Indian official literature as government contributions to land reform. The first of these is land settlement, particularly of landless labourers on wasteland marginal to existing villages, or in entirely new villages (when it qualifies for the title 'agricultural colonization').[55] There are those who see such settlement as dodging the issue of radical land reform, since it does not affect the hold of dominant groups on land already in cultivation. But, in my experience, the process, especially when land is given to Harijans on the edge of villages, can provoke profound resentment among these groups, since it tends to remove the beneficiaries from a subservient role and to occupy land that they covet (and may, indeed, forcibly reoccupy). The process, however, goes on: the sixth plan claims that some 850,000 hectares of government waste were distributed to the landless during 1975–8. But probably far more waste was brought into cultivation, licitly or illicitly, by spontaneous action by cultivators who already held land. And, as I have shown elsewhere, agricultural colonization in India has not only benefited the landless, but also refugees, those who have lost land through the construction of irrigation works, and even ex-*jagirdars* (essentially *zamindars* with local administrative and judicial functions) in Rajasthan; and has had production as well as equity motives.

The other measure, land consolidation, is designed purely to increase production. Its aim is to rearrange each fragmented and scattered holding in a village into a compact block of equivalent area, due account being taken of land quality, under appropriate legislation (which may involve compulsory powers) and with central government subsidies. Considerable progress has been made in several States, including Punjab, Haryana and Uttar Pradesh (where consolidation is hailed as a factor in success with high yielding varieties) but the sixth plan reports that nothing at all has been done in the south and in Rajasthan. Care should, however, be taken in the blanket application of consolidation to paddy-growing areas, where the possession of land in a number of different categories (always irrigable, irrigable only if water is plentiful, liable to or free from flood, and so on) may be a positive advantage to the cultivator: though, I suspect, one that the holder of a small amount of land in few parcels (or only one) is unable to take advantage of.[56]

If we now turn to the equity effects of the 'green revolution', it is of course widely claimed that this is also something that rarely benefits the small cultivator because he cannot afford, or cannot manipulate the bureaucracy to procure, the necessary inputs and plant, especially fertilizers, tubewells, and electric pumpsets. There is a vast literature on these matters, some of it cited in note 39 to the discussion of production aspects of the 'green revolution' (see pp. 180–2). Certainly the early facile optimism that the new varieties and the associated technology would usher in an era of universal prosperity (which would, *inter alia*, keep 'red revolution' at bay) was soon falsified; and the shadows deepened when it was realized (by some, at least) that the spatial impact was so uneven, some of the poorest and most densely peopled rice-growing areas being (as we have seen) but little affected. Current orthodoxy, in fact, inclines to various shades of what may be called the 'red' view — that the effects of the 'green revolution' are so uneven, not only between areas, but between classes in the same area, that disparities of income and of wealth widen, the poor get poorer, and (in some views at any rate) agrarian unrest leading to revolution is or will be generated. On this view, it is the larger farmers who can take greater risks, who can procure the inputs and therefore the benefits, who can obtain credit, and who become (if they are not already) rural capitalists; small farmers and tenants lose out, not least because of the ineffectiveness of land reform, and in Marxist terms 'the peasantry is differentiated'; landless labourers are in even worse plight because, contrary to the claims made in the early, easy optimistic days, there is decreased employment for them (especially where there is mechaniza-tion or electrification); and their numbers are swollen by the impoverishment of the small farmers and tenants. So runs, in simple terms, the 'red' view.

I personally am sceptical of the all-India applicability of this scenario.[57] Careful field studies in some areas show that small farmers do adopt the HYVs and by hook or by crook, often by incurring increased indebtedness, acquire fertilizer, pumpsets and so on;[58] though they may well adopt later than big farmers, and to a smaller extent (though in certain circumstances they may adopt to a greater degree than 'middle' farmers). They may, then, benefit from the 'green revolution', though to a lesser extent than the big farmers; and may obtain lower yields per hectare than them, so that the inverse relationship between holding size and productivity is reversed (see p. 188). Labourers may find increased work (e.g. for women in the weeding needed by the HYVs) but lose employment because of whatever mechanization has been introduced: on balance, however, and generalizing rather wildly, they, as ever in India, gain less than any other class, and may well lose out in absolute terms. Their plight tends to be compounded by increases in food prices greater than increases in wage rates, where the old payments in kind have been replaced by payments in cash. But the poor, whether small landowners, tenants, or labourers, tend only to revolt sporadically (as, indeed, they appear to have done long before the 'green revolution'), sometimes where organized by parties of the left. I for my part do not think of rural India, for all its sufferings, as in, or entering a 'revolutionary situation', except perhaps in areas where the left is strong, as in West Bengal and Kerala. But this is not meant as a complacent conclusion. The plight of the rural poor, perhaps as many as 200 million of them, should indeed arouse compassion and prompt action: for it is very severe indeed.

Now it may be argued that, even if land reform has failed, other government programmes to assist the small farmer and the labourer have done something to ameliorate their condition and to make them more productive. Here one thinks in particular of credit provision on the one hand, and on the other special schemes like Small Farmer Development Agencies (SFDA) and projects for Marginal Farmers and Agricultural Labourers (MFAL).

Government intervention in the provision of credit has a long history in India, going well back into the days of the Raj; and it would be wearisome to recount its history in any detail.[59] Suffice it to say, first, that 'official' credit now (1982) depends on three main agencies: a country-wide network of co-operative societies; the nationalized commercial banks, which now have (with government encouragement) nearly 15,000 rural and special agricultural branches; and the newer regional rural banks. There are certainly areas in which these agencies, and especially the co-operatives, have played a large part in the provision of credit for agricultural purposes and in the 'green revolution': one thinks here particularly of co-operatives in the Punjab, and also in Maharashtra. But in other areas and states provision has consistently fallen short of targets; and recovery of loans has been lamentable: while the rate of growth in co-operative credit has slowed down. Secondly, many studies show that access to credit for the 'weaker sections' is far short of need: the 'big men' understand the system, tend to control the co-operatives, can manipulate the bureaucracy, and find the second and third agencies just mentioned far more closely attuned to their needs and knowledge than do the small men, who still tend to have to rely on traditional village sources — mainly the 'big men' themselves. Thus in our North Arcot study in 1973–4 only 10 per cent of the paddy cultivators with holdings between 0.4 and 1 hectare drew credit from co-operatives, compared with 62 per cent of those with more than three hectares.[60] Dependence on private sources of credit is of course, another name for indebtedness, and the chronic state of many small farmers in that regard is well known.[60] Altogether, it is clear that the improvement of the position of such farmers, whether absolutely or relative to their wealthier neighbours, is still a long way off.

SFDA were instituted, on a pilot basis, in the fourth plan in order specifically to assist with credit, services and supplies farmers whose economy was potentially viable, but specifically excluding even smaller farmers and agricultural labourers. For them MFAL schemes were set up under the same plan, and involved subsidies for improving agricultural practices and setting up auxiliary enterprises such as animal husbandry of various kinds. Dasgupta, reviewing a number of studies aiming to evaluate these programmes, concluded that both have had a limited impact, partly for administrative reasons; and that both have often helped, not those for whom it was intended, but larger farmers who have faked the land records or manipulated the bureaucracy.[61]

At this stage in the discussion, we strike off apparently at a tangent, and look briefly at the Indian cattle problem, confining our attention to bovines (including buffaloes) associated with agricultural villages. Now everyone knows, or thinks that he knows, that India has a 'cattle problem': that vast numbers of useless cows wander through town and village alike and pass into a decrepit old age because no Hindu will countenance their slaughter;[62] further, because of the acceptance of doctrines of non-violence and vegetarianism, there is no slaughter of beasts other than the cow. So runs the received wisdom. To it, some would add that there is no tradition of pasture management: that this contrasts with the care lavished on paddy and other terraces (though fodder crops are of course grown, perhaps over 4 million hectares of them, of which half are in Punjab and a quarter in Maharashtra — competing with food crops). However, the distinguished Indian economist, K.N. Raj, has concluded after an interesting piece of empirical work that, under population pressure (bovine and human), cows are underrepresented in the bovine population, most notably in UP and Bihar, strongholds of Hindu orthodoxy: so killing must be taking place, if only by infanticide and deliberate starvation. Are there, then, *no* cattle surplus to strict economic requirements? It would, I think, be unwise to give an unqualified negative answer: more data and analysis, by regions, are required. But at least the conventional wisdom stands challenged.

But what are the 'strict economic requirements'? Cattle play a very important part in the village economy, for some at least. Bullocks, and sometimes bulls, supply power for ploughing and other field operations, and for cart-pulling, as do buffaloes in wet rice areas. There are some splendid breeds for these purposes; for example the Kangayams of Tamil Nadu. Cows supply milk, though usually in pitiful quantities compared with western dairy cattle: only some 200 kg per cow per annum in rural areas, compared with some 3000 kg in the west. Yields are, however, higher in some areas like the Punjab and in some urban areas, where the animals are better fed altogether; and she-buffaloes also provide milk. Cattle in some areas (e.g. Gujarat) supply a useful income for poor people, even some of the landless, because they can scrounge some sort of living on roadsides and patches of waste. Some co-operative ventures help small producers to market their milk: those in Gujarat, which produce Amul cheese from buffaloes' milk, are famous. However, R. Crotty has demonstrated that 'operation flood', under which EEC dairy surpluses are transferred to the Third World, reduces the cost of milk for urban consumers while increasing the revenue of the Indian Dairy Corporation, who handle the operation in India.[63] This means that the Corporation can in turn pay a higher price for Indian milk and transport it to towns over longer distances, so that it becomes more difficult for the rural poor who have no female cattle (cows or buffaloes) to buy milk, their only source of animal protein. Moreover, there is at the same time an inducement to those who have such cattle to keep more, thus putting increased pressure on communal pastures and on fodder prices, so making it harder for the poor and landless to keep them. In short, a programme of food aid has perverse effects which bear hardest, like so many other things, on the rural poor.

So our apparent excursus to view the 'cattle problem' brings us back once again to the inequities of Indian villages and the terrible poverty of many millions of their inhabitants; a poverty rooted in the caste system and the vertical patron–client organization of many rural societies and perpetuated by the social, economic and political power of the dominant groups. We have seen that this power has often been increased rather than diminished by the failures and distortions of the land reform programmes, and by the 'green revolution' in certain areas at least; and by the associated persistence, if not strengthening of the money-lending activities of the same groups and their associates. Moreover, the local political power of these groups has generally increased as State-level politicians, with their regional followings, have grown in power and as State politics have more and more influenced political events at the centre (compare pp. 95–6). Again, we have seen that in the mid-1960s Indian agricultural policy took a new turn, and became more technocratic and spatially concentrated, less concerned with distribution and more with production (not of course that production can be neglected: if there is no cake there are no slices). At the same time, as a stimulus to agricultural production, some would say at the instance of powerful rural interests, the terms of rural-urban trade moved in favour of agriculture, to the benefit of those who had surpluses to sell but to the disadvantage of those agricultural labourers who were paid in cash, and very exiguous cash at that.[64] The existence of these people (and they *are* people, not figures in an economist's tabulation) casts a shadow on India's hard-earned and sometimes vaunted buffer stocks, which would vanish overnight if everyone could eat a square meal.

Now all this is not to say that there are not dedicated Indians in many walks of life, particularly but not exclusively those touched with the Gandhian spirit, who genuinely seek the uplift of India's poor. Some of them press hard on government through voluntary bodies. Some of them are in the Ministries and the Planning Commission of New Delhi, and leave a good impression on office-bound diplomats and officials of the World Bank (with its 'new strategy' of rural development, aiming to seek out needy 'target groups' and supply basic needs). But the problem is to make the goodwill, the noble sentiments, the aid, the intentions of the great and good of New Delhi, effective at village level, where the target groups live and where the need is. One does not need to be a Marxist, or even a Marxian, to come to the conclusion that this penetration will not take place without either extraordinarily strong political will at the centre, or drastic social and political change lower down, or both.

India: mining and manufacturing

Agriculture and agrarian conditions are so vital to so many people in India, as in other South Asian countries, that I make no apology for according a relatively brief treatment to other aspects of the economy, beginning with mining and manufacturing and related sectors. We saw earlier in this chapter that these sectors already had some importance at independence (see p. 154); and their industrialization was central to government strategy (see pp. 170–2 and p. 174). Table 6.4 shows that, for a number of selected items, India can take credit for notable increases in production since 1950–1, the initial year of the first Five Year Plan.

There is no doubt, then, that Indian industrialization has been going apace, not least in those industries which, as the discussion earlier in the chapter has made clear (see pp. 170–1) lie in the public sector; though some industries, particularly cotton weaving in 'modern' mills, have done less well. The increase in the production of cotton cloth from handlooms and by small-scale industry is remarkable: the 6350 million metres total production in 1979–80 is made up of 2900 from handlooms and 3450 from small-scale industry. It will be noted that products useful to agriculture, such as fertilizers and tractors (of more doubtful utility, given the need for rural employment) show great increases; as do bicycles, of great importance to dwellers in town and country alike. It should also be noted that a number of items not tabulated, such as railway locomotives, electric pumpsets, and industrial machinery generally, are also now produced in quantity in India; while there has been a massive growth in capacity for generating electricity — from 2300 MW in 1950 to 31,000 MW in 1980: this has enabled current to be brought to 250,000 villages (compared with 3000 in 1950) and to energize nearly four million pumps. Power shortages have, however, as the sixth plan admits, 'become almost endemic in various parts of the country'.[65]

Some part of the industrial success has been assisted by foreign aid: Britain, West Germany and the USSR all helped, for example, with new steel works.

But all is not well with Indian industry.[66] Industrial production increased by an average of about 8 per cent per annum up to 1964, but then flattened off (though with fluctuations from year to year) and actually declined by 1.4 per cent in 1979–80. Many reasons have been adduced to account for this faltering. The plan itself urges that in the

Table 6.4 India: production of selected products of mining and industry, 1950–1 to 1979–80

Item	Units (metric)	1950–1	1979–80 (actual or anticipated)
Coal	million tons	32.8	104
Iron ore	million tons	3.6	39
Petroleum, crude	million tons	0.4	11.8
Petroleum products	million tons	0.3	26
Steel ingots	million tons	1.5	10
Cement	million tons	2.7	17.7
Fertilizer, nitrogenous	thousand tons N	11	2226
Fertilizer, phosphatic	thousand tons P_2O_5	11	757
Tractors	thousand	nil	62.5
Bicycles	thousand	99	3780
Cotton cloth, mill-made	million metres	3728	4085
Cotton cloth, handloom and smaller scale	million metres	1008	6350
Jute textiles	million tons	889	1336

Sources: Official sources, including sixth Five Year Plan

early years of import substitution industry had a 'captive market' (ensconced behind tariff walls, one should add, especially after 1957) and that later industrial growth had to rely on the pace of general economic development which, as we have seen (pp. 174–5) tended itself to falter after about 1965, partly because of the effects of disastrous drought.[67] The plan goes on to blame lack of investment, shortage of inputs like coal and power, and 'to an extent inefficient management'. Pramit Chaudhuri has investigated the charge that Indian industry is essentially high cost and inefficient, with much underutilized capacity. L.K. Jha stresses problems of management in a broader sense, to include the assumptions, models and methods of the planners and fiscal and taxation policy (with some reference to the 'black economy' which is, in India, often supposed to assume mammoth proportions and, by definition, to avoid the government's resource-gathering net).[68] But he does also mention the lack of effective demand, on which other observers place great emphasis. For the capital goods sectors of Indian industry (nearly all publicly owned) are, to a very considerable extent, providing goods for other public sector industries (for example, the steel industry for the railways), so that shortfalls in production are closely related both to planned targets and to inefficiencies on the demand side which prevent consumer industries from taking up what is targetted. But behind all this looms, once again, the poverty of the countryside and of the urban masses. Indian industry, especially in the private, consumer goods sectors, is producing very largely for the urban middle and upper classes. It is to these people that are sold the superficially impressive array of goods, from cosmetics to chocolate biscuits, displayed in the shops of New Delhi. One has only to go a few miles down the road to a small country town like Gurgaon to find the bazaar selling 'traditional' goods like foodstuffs, salt and handloom textiles, but few of the products of modern industry except for soap and, perhaps, such things as bicycles, electric torches and galvanized buckets. The prosperity brought to some areas and classes by recent agrarian changes, such as those associated with the 'green revolution' in Punjab, have wrought some modification in this picture; but the all-too-prevalent poverty of the village, which I have been at pains to stress and to stress again, cannot but affect aggregate demand for industrial products, directly and indirectly, notwithstanding India's considerable successes in the export market (of which more shortly). For whose benefit, in fact, *is* India's industrialization?

The same question is raised if one looks at employment in 'modern' industry. The relevant data are not easy to interpret. However, it would appear that factory employment, which stood at about 2½ million at independence, had risen to 6.2 million by 1977–8 (though it fell to 6.1 million in the following year).[69] But employment rose less rapidly than output: by 6 per cent between 1960 and 1965 (when output rose by 9 per cent) and by 5.4 per cent between 1965 and 1970 (output 18.4 per cent). And real wages have remained relatively static. For all the emphasis, then, on industry in the plans, a relatively small number of people (compared, that is, with the 120 million or so in agriculture) have gained by finding employment in factories at a period when landlessness has been increasing, and rural employment subject to the strains mentioned in the previous section, and when urban unemployment has been mounting. This is not surprising given the capital intensive nature of much factory industry and the inappropriateness of a great deal of imported technology; and shows that efforts to increase employment (not absent in recent plans, to be fair) must be redoubled.

'Modern' small-scale industry (defined in terms of plants employing less than 50 persons if power is used, less than 100 if it is not) employed some 4 million people in 1973–4 and 6½ million in 1979–80, but this included part-time as well as full-time workers. The same applies to the 13.3 million employed in 'traditional industries' in the latter year (these included handlooms, *khadi*, sericulture and other 'village industries').[70] It is thus, given the nature of the data, hard to be sure about the present total level of industrial employment in India, or accurately to compare employment in factories as compared with other industrial employment. What is clear, however, is that 'traditional' industry lives on (though often at a low level of productivity of such capital, government and otherwise, as is invested in it); and that industrial employment *in toto*, for all the strides that have been made, is far from being in sight of solving the national problems of unemployment and underemployment.

It is also clear that, in spite of measures like industrial licensing and the establishment of trading estates, 'modern industry' at any rate is still heavily concentrated in areas that had significant manufacturing at independence: Calcutta, Hooghlyside and south-eastern Bihar; Bombay–Ahmedabad and Bombay–Pune(Poona)–Nagpur; and Madras, Coimbatore and adjacent areas. There has, however, been noteworthy industrial growth in Punjab–Haryana–Delhi (which together now have some 6 per cent of factory employment). It is in these areas that foreign capital and technology, those controversial entrants into the Indian scene, are for the most part concentrated.

India: 'multi-level' planning: regional, 'target area', 'target group' and growth pole approaches

Clearly, then, industrialization in India has not or has not yet produced the 'balanced regional development' declared as early as 1948 to be an objective of Indian planning and, as we have seen, given a chapter to itself (albeit a somewhat ambivalent one) in the Third Plan (see pp. 172–3). Equally clearly, the 'green revolution' has tended to increase regional disparities. What, then, of planning and action designed to reduce these disparities?[71] It has already been stressed (p. 172) that Indian planning is overwhelmingly sectoral. Indeed, one has only to glance at the list of chapters in each plan for the point to strike home. We have also seen that a certain decentralization of planning and action followed the growth in the power of the States vis-à-vis the Centre; though this was a far cry from objectively planned 'balanced regional development', each State competing with others for resources from the Centre. Further, State planning machinery was long rudimentary and insufficiently related to a clearly defined strategy; though in some States (e.g. Tamil Nadu) this criticism has lost some or much of its force. States have varied widely, too, in action to reduce intra-State disparities, for example in administering concessional finance for development in their industrially backward areas. A review by the Programme Evaluation Organization of the Planning Commission in 1982 showed that a number of States (Bihar, Haryana, Himachal Pradesh, Orissa, Punjab and West Bengal) had taken the politically easier course of visualizing the all-round development of *all* districts.[72] Others did have policies of discriminating in favour of backward areas. Maharashtra, for example, was keen to disperse industry from Greater Bombay, while Andhra Pradesh was one of the first States to contemplate intra-State regional planning. The States have also engaged in the preparation of district and even block plans, which in theory at any rate could provide a means of redressing spatial imbalances.[73] But district planning has been far from successful in this and other ways. Block level planning is still with us in the sixth plan, with a declared emphasis on social justice and employment creation. It remains to be seen whether this programme, like so many others, will remain no more than pious hope and rhetoric in the face of the formidable social resistances of the dominant groups. One is bound to feel sceptical.

What of action by the Centre as distinct from the States? There have always been central schemes and projects with potential effects on the distribution of prosperity. Thus the three new steelworks of the early post-independence era were all located in green field (or green jungle) sites in the north-east Deccan, whence it was hoped that development would diffuse to surrounding areas. But, unlike the earlier Jamshed-pur plant, they have so far had but little diffusion effect. Again, the Centre has instituted transport subsidies for Jammu and Kashmir and for the north-eastern States to reduce the friction of distance; and its schemes for the resettlement of landless labourers took development of a sort into some remote wasteland areas.[74] From the fifth plan onwards there have been centrally-assisted 'target area' schemes for certain hill areas, for tribal areas and for the sensitive northeast, though on a small financial scale *in toto*.[75] 'Target group' schemes, like those for tribals and Harijans, are spatial in impact to the extent that the groups concerned are concentrated in backward regions or in selected districts: clearly this applies more to tribals than to Harijans — or to the 'target group' schemes for small and marginal farmers and for landless labourers already reviewed (pp. 192–3).

More important, however, though operating at the coarser State level, is the fact that since the fourth plan the Centre has disposed of its general, block grants to States on a formula that takes account not only of population and of outlays for special purposes such as major irrigation schemes but also low per capita incomes and 'special problems'.

A final area in which planning has made some attempt to alter regional distributions is that of urbanization. Thus there has been planning based on the major 'metropolitan cities' like Delhi–New Delhi, Calcutta and Bombay, with populations of over a million, gross overcrowding, and great poverty. Metropolitan plans like that for Bombay have involved a measure of decentralization.[76] At the other extreme from these and other 'million cities' lie India's vast number of villages; and in between lie smaller towns, ranging from small market towns to regional centres, though never in the nicely ordered hierarchy that characterizes Britain or western Europe. The hierarchical pattern is most completely approached in Punjab, Haryana and Tamil Nadu.[77] There has been some discussion in India on the desirability of somehow supplying a more complete hierarchy of 'central places' between metropolitan city and village, on the dubious assumption that such central places would energize the countryside by the diffusion of innovations, the provision of employment, and the marketing of agricultural produce. This has merged into the notion of 'growth poles', urban centres that should be foci for further desiderata like rural industrialization and the development of backward areas.[78] But the scope for government action, even if one is convinced of the general idea of building up central places as growth poles, is strictly limited: here a public sector industry or industrial estate, there a hospital or school, or a licensed market to build a small town into a larger; and Barbara Harriss has urged convincingly that the effects on the surrounding region will be limited and that regions get the central places that they deserve: that is, solutions lie in rural development. But it has been recently reported that Tamil Nadu, with reference to incentives for the development of backward areas already touched on, still favours 'the growth centre approach for providing infrastructure'.[79]

India's foreign trade

Since independence there have been very substantial changes in the volume, composition and direction of India's foreign trade, reflecting *inter alia* the economic development that has been the subject of this chapter; government policy; and exogenous factors over which India has no control.[80]

Taking total volume of foreign trade first, exports remained relatively stagnant, with some fluctuations from year to year, during the 1950s and early 1960s: at some 1100 to 1400 million US dollars at current prices. A number of authors have criticized the government for neglect of export potential during this period, for reasons that include an underestimation of the possibilities of increasing traditional exports like tea and jute; a development strategy that, as we have seen, put the emphasis on capital-intensive heavy industry instead of labour-intensive production that might well have found a comparative advantage in the export market; bureaucratic controls; and undue reliance on aid to finance heavy industrialization, rather than by pursuing an export drive. However, there was more emphasis on exports from the third plan onwards; and from 1966–7, following devaluation, exports rose to 2408 million dollars in 1972 and have grown by about 6 per cent per annum in the last decade. The sixth plan envisages a 9 per cent growth rate, which is probably overoptimistic.[81]

Imports, on the other hand, rose markedly in most years from 1953–4 or so, owing largely to the needs of industrialization. The growing gap between exports and imports led to a continuing shortage of foreign exchange. But from 1965–6 to 1970–1 imports declined, largely because of the stagnation in the economy to which I have drawn attention and because of a measure of successful import substitution. Since 1970–1 there has again been an upward tendency, to begin with because of the sharp hoist in oil prices. The sixth plan projects a rate of increase of imports of 9.5 per cent, in spite of forecasts of an end to food imports, oil again looming large; and is optimistic about the foreign exchange position, projecting an adequate inflow from tourism, remittances (a large item now from Indians overseas, especially in the Middle East) and investment income to cover the gap between exports and imports.

Over the years since independence there have been considerable changes in the composition of foreign trade. So far as exports are concerned, changes have been most marked since the middle 1960s. There has been a decline in such longstanding exports as tea, jute manufactures and cotton cloth, and a rise in such products of agriculture and animal husbandry as leather, leather manufactures, oil cake, and cashew kernels. But there have been sharper rises in exports of iron ore and of manufactures like iron and steel, engineering goods and chemicals: in 1970–71 these were worth respectively 156.4, 105.6, 155.3 and 39.2 million dollars. The sixth plan projects further increases in these and other manufactures such as garments, plastics and handicraft items (which it notes to be labour-intensive); though much will clearly depend on competitiveness (which it does not note).

Turning to trends in the composition of imports, these have included foodgrains in years of bad harvests; the sixth plan hopes that these imports are now at an end, but envisages continued imports of vegetable oils (a commentary on the state of oilseed production, to which I have referred: see p. 177). Imports of consumer goods have declined with industrialization; so have imports of capital goods (partly, of course, because of relative industrial stagnation since

1965). But imports of what are classed as intermediate goods have held up. The reason will become clear when one adds that these include fertilizers and petroleum products.

As for the direction of trade, the outstanding feature is the decline in India's trading relationship with the United Kingdom and the complementary building up of links with many other parts of the world.[82] In 1972–3 the United Kingdom received only 9 per cent of India's exports, compared with 28 per cent in 1955–6. Over the same period exports to Soviet bloc countries increased from less than 1 per cent to 24 per cent. By 1973–4, too, 25 per cent of India's exports were going to western Europe, and about 15 per cent each were going to North America, Japan, and other Asian countries. India may then be said to have escaped from the colonial relationship and to have a balanced, worldwide trading pattern. Much the same is true of imports. In 1974–5 only 4.8 per cent were coming from the UK, some 14 per cent from other west European countries, 16 per cent from the USA, 10.1 per cent from Japan, and 24 per cent (mainly oil) from other Asian countries.

The governments and peoples of India have, then, many solid achievements to their credit as a result of their labours since independence. Food grain production has increased at a rate generally faster than population growth, itself very rapid. India is able to manufacture a wide range of capital, intermediate and consumer goods all of which, if they were known at all before independence, had to be imported. The rail and road networks have been improved. Exports have been diversified and destinations widened. Altogether, the consequences of economic changes in the last 35 years are evident; as are the developments in school and university education and the emergence of scholars and scientists of international reputation, all supported materially by what has been achieved in the economy.

The preceding pages have, however, suggested that economic changes might have been greater and more beneficial if policies and their implementation had been different: if agriculture had from the beginning received as much attention as industry; if as much research had been devoted to rice and the millets as to wheat (though one recognizes the environmental difficulties); if the absolute or relative decline in the production of pulses had been halted; if industrial policy had been oriented to labour intensiveness and the production of goods needed to raise living standards; if there had been the political will and the means to tax agricultural incomes and tackle and tap the 'black economy'; if ... the list is endless.

'More beneficial'? The most crucial question of all those that might be asked of Indian economic development and its substantial record of achievement is 'Who benefits?' We have seen that, whatever gains have accrued to industrialists and to urban upper and middle classes, and to farmers over a wider spectrum than is admitted by all writers on agrarian change, many of the urban poor and of the much larger numbers of the rural poor have gained little if anything, and some are worse off. The numbers of the landless and of the rural poor generally have increased, in some places, it would appear, faster than population. The Mahatma's Harijans are still most severely disadvantaged.

At a deeper, yet more controversial level Frankel sees in India, as we have noted, the paradox, the contradiction between Nehru's two main aims: accommodative politics and radical social change (see pp. 175–6).[83] On the one hand, the Congress party, in maintaining its role as the broad-church party that would hold together a wide range of classes and interests, was bound to try and accommodate rural landed interests, who grew in power as time went on. Meanwhile the Government of India and its Planning Commission were formulating a number of policies that if fully implemented, would have eroded the economic, social and political power of the dominant castes, to say nothing of the big industrialists. Here lies the contradiction. So far, except (for the time being, perhaps) in Kerala and West Bengal, the power of the dominant landed interests is generally undiminished, if not augmented. The Nehru vision of a 'gradual revolution' to achieve his twin aims has indeed faded.

If, in now turning to the other countries of South Asia, beginning with Pakistan, I proceed partly, or even largely by comparison with India, I hope that my friends in these other countries, or readers primarily interested in one or more of them, will not be hurt, or offended or disappointed. Certainly I do not wish to imply that India is in any way the norm against which the achievements and problems of other South Asian countries must be measured. It is merely that time's winged chariot hurries near, and that space is scarce.

Pakistan: introduction

(The sections on Pakistan will, except where specific reference is made to East Pakistan (now Bangladesh) or where the context requires otherwise, refer only to Pakistan within its present boundaries, i.e. not including Bangladesh.)

In the early sections of this chapter we surveyed briefly the economy of the Indian Empire as it passed into independence. From that survey one may readily deduce that Pakistan at independence was even more of an agricultural country and a landlord's country than India, with very little modern factory industry. Its GNP per capita was lower than India's. Although it inherited most of the great irrigated areas of the Punjab and all of those in Sind, it had but little mineral wealth and large areas of arid territory in both hill and plain areas. Pakistan was also handicapped by having to set up an administration above the provincial level from scratch and, some would argue, by the flight of almost all of the Hindu commercial class, especially but not only Sindhis from Karachi. They were replaced by various Muslim merchant groups from Bombay and elsewhere. Finally, we have seen that Pakistan has had a disturbed political history since independence and partition (see pp. 100–6). This has in many ways hindered or distorted economic development in the country; and has meant that a high proportion of the budget and of GNP has gone on military purposes.

Pakistan: economic strategies

Not surprisingly, given the initial handicaps and the turbulent history, government economic planning in Pakistan took some time to get off the ground, and was then subject to marked changes of direction and emphasis.[84] The first Five Year Plan did not emerge until 1955; and was then largely frustrated by political instability. Economic strategies in Pakistan, as laid bare in this and subsequent plans and by other pronouncements and actions, have had a number of general characteristics which set them apart from those pursued in India. In Pakistan, it is true, government was (as in India) responsible for communications, irrigation, power and land reclamation. But otherwise, at least before the Bhutto era (1971–7), government was much less pervasive in economic affairs than in India. There were no great areas reserved for the public sector, as heavy industry was in

India; and a much greater role, and much more latitude, were accorded to the private sector, whether in agriculture or in industry. In fact the Pakistan Industrial Development Corporation (PIDC), an apparent exception to this policy, established industries that were handed over to private firms as they became viable.

Development in Pakistan has also been more export-oriented than in India.

Successive governments of Pakistan, moreover, generally placed much greater reliance than those of India on foreign, especially American, expertise (Harvard economists were prominent at one stage) and on foreign aid; and this served, as might be expected, to reinforce capitalist tendencies. This reliance owed something to desperate need at the time of independence, but was also related to Pakistan's involvement in defensive pacts and other manifestations of close relations with the United States, relations whose somewhat chequered history has been outlined in Chapter 5 (see pp. 140–5).

The Bhutto period, however, proclaimed 'Islamic socialism' (without being clear what that meant) and talked of nationalizing the 'commanding heights of the economy' and of showing greater favour to the public sector generally. It attempted more radical land reforms and attacked the concentration of industrial ownership in ways to be explored shortly. But after the overthrow of Bhutto in 1977 the earlier strategy was, generally speaking, restored, though with stronger Islamic overtones (for example, measures to abolish interest and usury; and closer economic relations with the Middle East). Recently (1982) the military government has announced that it is giving a new impetus to private sector investment, and relaxing bureaucratic controls.

Pakistan: agriculture

Like India, Pakistan has recorded some notable increases in food grain production since independence (all figures in metric tons). The production of wheat, by far and away the principal food grain, has increased (according to official figures) from 4.14 million tons in 1948 to 9.15 million tons in 1976–7. Until the mid-1960s there had been little general upward trend, and a great deal of fluctuation; overall, production was losing the race with population. But after 1965, with the introduction of HYVs, there was a rapid growth in production (111 per cent increase 1966 to 1976–7 — remarkable, and ahead of population, but not so great as in India). Increase in area played some part in this increase (Pakistan has its colonization areas, notably in the Thal, between the Indus and the Jhelum); but the main factor was an increase in yield, which nearly doubled from 1965 to 1976–7. Rice is a less important crop than in India, of course; but, given irrigation and Pakistan's *kharif* sunshine, one that is less subject to the environmental problems that have hampered India's 'green revolution' in rice. Rice production has in fact climbed fairly steadily from 0.75 million tons in 1948 to 2.63 million tons in 1976–7, though with some slackening in later years. Yields have, however, only increased notably since the HYVs came in: they increased by over 50 per cent between 1966 and 1976–7. The millets, *bajra* and *jowar* are in Pakistan fodder rather than food crops. Maize is, however, basic to the rural economy of the northern hill country, and is increasing in importance. Pulses, as in India, are a main traditional source of protein, but are agronomically a somewhat neglected crop. Of the oilseeds, cotton seed is the most prominent.

Cotton is, of course, the main commercial crop of Pakistan, and is largely concentrated in the canal-irrigated areas. Production grew from about 200,000 tons at independence to over 700,000 tons in the early 1970s, but has subsequently declined (to 569,000 tons in 1977–8). Area and yield have fallen too, partly because sugar cane gives higher returns to many cultivators.

It is generally true that, except for the era of Bhutto 'populism' (see pp. 103–4), government policy towards agriculture in Pakistan has been more production-oriented and less concerned with general rural development and the uplift of the villages and of their poor than in India (or, rather, in India before the Nehru vision faded). Pakistan, after all, had no Gandhi and no Nehru; and earlier American influence. As we have seen, agricultural production in Pakistan virtually stagnated until the mid-1960s, so that whatever government action there was has little to its credit. There was, in fact, once the country had settled down an effort in agricultural research and extension, and a Village Agricultural and Industrial Development Programme (Village AID) which invites comparison with India's Community Development.[85] For there were to be village level workers, stimulation of self-help projects, and liaison with specialists in health, sanitation and so on; all with much American assistance. But the main thrust was in terms of agricultural productivity. There was also a Rural Works Programme. Neither can claim great success, even in production terms (as is evident from the agricultural stagnation already stressed). B.L.C. Johnson says 'the scheme seems to have foundered on two rocks: ... the quality of the village workers who tended to be college graduates with little real experience of village life ... (and) the scheme trod on too many administrative toes by urging self-reliance, and perhaps excessive boldness in the under-privileged of the semi-feudal society'. This has an all-too-familiar ring. In the mid-1960s, however, following measures subsidizing tubewells and fertilizer, successful efforts were made to popularize the new HYVs which, as in northern India, owed much also to the sinking and mechanization of tubewells, private or public. With the inaugura-tion of the brief Bhutto era in 1971, there came a People's Works Programme akin to the old Rural Works Programme, and an Integrated Rural Development Programme (IRDP) recalling the old Village AID, and seeking to bring information, credit, inputs, and marketing to farmers.[86] Significantly, given the production-orientation of Pakistani efforts, this was launched by the Ministry of Food and Agriculture; and, for all Bhutto's populism and rhetoric (cf. pp. 103–4), was economic rather than social in its thrust. IRDP in fact was only implemented in a few pilot schemes. A further product of the Bhutto period was the Ministry of Production's plan for 'agrovilles', small market towns to be established all over the country to energize development on the lines of the Thana Development Centres associated with the Comilla experiment in East Pakistan (by then Bangladesh) (see pp. 219–20): shades, too, of the conflation of rural growth centres, central places and growth poles in Indian official and academic thinking. According to Shahid Javed Burki, 'the agrovilles plan was given up after the launching of one project — Shadab near Lahore'.

It is one of the superficially rather surprising things about government attitudes to agriculture in Pakistan that, given the general bias towards private enterprise, more use was not made of price incentives. In fact, however, in the words of Gilbert T. Brown of the World Bank, 'Export duties and bans and the government monopoly of raw cotton and rice exports have kept domestic prices for many agricultural commodities far below world market levels'.[87] Associated with its monopoly of rice exporting is the high relative price that is paid the farmer for *basmati*, the scented rice popular in Middle Eastern markets; this is one reason for the lower adoption rates, compared with India, of higher yielding but less exportable varieties (other reasons, which extend to wheat too are, of course, low farm prices generally and the poorer provision for credit and other rural services, rooted in the situation outlined in the preceding paragraph). Agriculture in the Pakistan Punjab *looks* more modern than that in India because of the prevalence of tractors, imported free of duty (though there are tractors enough in Indian Punjab too): but tractors do not generally raise yields per acre; they merely displace labour. However, since about 1973 the government has tended to raise prices. In October 1981, recognizing that declining yields in the rice economy, a principal prop to Pakistan's exports, owed much to lack of incentives it raised procurement prices — but still preserving a differential for *basmati*.[88] More recently still, in April 1982 Dr Mahbubul Haq, new Deputy Chairman of the Planning Commission, cited a breakthrough in agricultural production as a first priority but seems not to have been very specific about methods.[89]

One area, of course, in which successive governments of Pakistan can claim to have been active is that of irrigation and drainage. The great canals inherited from the Raj have been maintained, thanks in part to the new construction made under the Indus Waters Treaty (see pp. 69–70). The Thal area between the Indus and the Jhelum has been irrigated by a new canal system taking off from the Indus at Kalabagh. Two additional dams were constructed lower down the Indus to help solve the considerable problems of Sind. Government has also addressed itself to the grave problems of interrelated waterlogging, salinity and alkalinity (see p. 184) in canal-irrigated areas of Punjab and Sind. In 1974–5 some 1.8 million hectares were severely affected by waterlogging in April, when the problem is at a minimum, 1.5–2 times that area in September–October.[90] Salinity in the same year severely affected over 3 million hectares. SCARP (Salinity Control and Reclamation Projects) involve public tubewells to lower the water-table (and to irrigate if the water is suitable) and drainage works.

Pakistan: agrarian structure

I have several times emphasized that Pakistan is a landlord's country with a highly unequal land ownership pattern (some tribal areas are an exception). To repeat the figures already cited in Chapter 2 (see p. 13) in 1959 it was estimated that 3.3 million people (65 per cent of all landowners) held only 15 per cent of the cultivated area in holdings of under 2 hectares (5 acres) while a mere 6000 people (0.1 per cent of landowners) held 15 per cent of the cultivated land in holdings of over 208 hectares (500 acres). Since in parts of Punjab there was considerable peasant proprietorship, it follows that these national aggregate figures conceal even greater inequalities elsewhere. A few years later, in 1962, it was estimated that there were 1.6 million marginal owner-cultivators (with less than 5 hectares), 750,000 tenants with at least 3 hectares, no fewer than 1.8 million tenants-at-will, and 550,000 landless labourers.[91] At independence *zamindari* tenure was strong in Punjab outside areas of peasant proprietorship and of 'government' tenures in the Canal Colonies; and, while Sind was nominally a *raiyatwari* area, *jagirdari* had evolved and most cultivators were sharecropping tenants (*haris*) involved in a pyramid of dependency. In the years before 1958, Sind, Punjab and North-west Frontier Provinces all promulgated land reforms, but these were half-hearted in conception and implementation. This is not surprising given the dominance of landlord interests in politics. Ayub Khan, shortly after he came to power (see p. 101), enacted land reforms that abolished intermediaries: placed a ceiling at 208 hectares of irrigated land or twice that level for unirrigated; and gave tenants (including the *haris*) freedom from ejection except for non-payment of rent, failure to cultivate or to cultivate properly, or subletting. But there were a list of exemptions from the ceiling legislation, including orchards, and livestock farms; and some built-in loopholes (e.g. land could be gifted to heirs, including female relatives.) Not surprisingly, Ayub's measure was ineffective, given the land-holding interests of the ruling military and bureaucratic groups. But some bigger landowners did lose land, which was redistributed to no more than 200,000 families. Less than 5 per cent of the cultivated area was affected.

Soon there came the 'green revolution'. Given the only mildly reformed agrarian structure and the general agricultural policies of government, oriented to production rather than to equity, it is not surprising that initial adoption of the new varieties of wheat and rice and extensive use of fertilizer (whose consumption rose from 125,000 tons in 1965 to 419,000 tons in 1972) was mainly limited to the bigger farmers who already had, or soon sank tubewells and who had the capital, credit and influence to acquire fertilizers.[92] Tenants and small proprietors were absolutely, or at any rate relatively worse off; though some of them were adopters by the early 1970s.

Meanwhile, Bhutto had come to power and initiated his own programme of land reform in 1972. This reduced the ceiling to 60 irrigated or 120 unirrigated hectares (or 40 hectares for public servants) with no compensation and no exemptions; but a bonus equivalent to 10 hectares of irrigated land for those who had bought tractors or sunk tubewells before 1971. Farmers with less than 5 hectares irrigated or 10 acres unirrigated were exempt from land revenue. Tenancy was to be subject to the same conditions as in Ayub's measures, except that land revenue became a responsibility of the landlord. But landlords had warning of what was to be enacted, and there was much evasion by prior disposal. However, it is reported that, up to Bhutto's fall from power in 1977, 1.4 million hectares had been resumed by government under the ceiling provision, and something under half of this distributed free. But by 1977, when he was preparing for elections, Bhutto had become more dependent on landed interests who, Burki claims had, as a result of the reforms, no longer retained power through 'traditional feudal links' but through mutual interests with the peasantry.[93] Be that as it may, the military government that succeeded Bhutto has priorities other than land reform and social change.

As for agricultural credit in Pakistan, commercial banks, the official Agricultural Development Bank, and co-operative societies all function; but seem to be slanted towards bigger farmers, and to be less effective in Pakistan Punjab than in India.

Before we leave agrarian conditions in Pakistan, it is worth noting that, as in nearby States of India, there has been an officially-sponsored programme of consolidation of holdings, and for similar reasons. By 1974–5 nearly 7 million hectares had been covered.[94]

Pakistan: mining and manufacturing

Pakistan, we have seen, started its independent existence with very little by way of factory industry. Such mineral wealth and power potential as it was then known to possess also remained relatively unexploited. True, coal was mined in the Salt Range of Punjab, in Baluchistan and elsewhere to produce some 250,000 tons annually; oil came in small quantities from the Attock and other fields (about half-a-million barrels in 1948); and there was some mining of chromite. But effective capacity for power generation was only about 40,000 kW, largely from somewhat dilapidated thermal stations.[95]

Annual coal production is now over a million tons (much of it, however, of poorish quality); oil production is running at over 4 million barrels per annum and there are several refineries; natural gas, discovered in 1955 at Sui in Sind, is being produced at over 5 million cubic metres annually and, thanks to pipelines to major urban and industrial centres, is a major source of energy; copper ore, as well as chromite, is being mined; and some 2500 MW of power is being produced from hydroelectric schemes in the hills.[96] Here, then, is a substantial record of achievement in terms of production.

Cottage industries continue to provide employment and to produce fabrics, carpets and other goods. But the really spectacular growth has been in factory industry. Thus, in 1976–7 Pakistan was producing over 400 million metres of cotton cloth; 3 million tons of cement; 270,000 tons of steel products (a steel-making plant constructed with Russian assistance was to be inaugurated in 1983); 212,000 bicycles; and 824,000 tons of fertilizers. There was a concentration of factory industry in Karachi on the one hand, and in eastern Punjab on the other.

How had this quite impressive industrial performance come about? Up to the time of Ayub Khan's coup in 1958, the industrial scene was dominated by refugee merchant groups who had settled mainly in Karachi and nearby areas of Sind. There was, indeed, very rapid industrial and urban growth; and efforts were mainly bent to import substitution, behind a barrier of protection and with much foreign aid. Ayub is seen by Burki as the leader of a new middle class who attempted to reduce the power not only of the landed aristocracy but also of these merchant industrialists.[97] Fiscal measures encouraged export orientation; and a new group of industrialists did indeed break the monopoly of the Karachi merchants. But the new industrial power was concentrated in a very few families, twenty-two of them according to an opinion that became popular in the late 1960s.[98] During the brief Bhutto period of 'Islamic socialism' there was an attack on the twenty-two families, a burst of nationalization, and some initiatives in the public sector. But before Bhutto fell in 1977 private capital was already being allowed to reassert its position; and continues to do so.

'Regional planning' in Pakistan

Planning in Pakistan has been, as in India, overwhelmingly sectoral in character; and, given the free rein allowed to private enterprise, it is not surprising that the growth areas for both agriculture and industry have been predominantly those already relatively prosperous and urbanized: the irrigated areas of Punjab and Sind, the Karachi region and eastern Punjab for industry. Exceptions are to be found in newly irrigated regions like Thal (see p. 208). The reader will, it is true, find references to 'regional planning' in some of the works to which his attention has been directed.[99] But these relate to the disparities in terms both of economic indices and of government attention between the two 'regions' of Pakistan, West and East, as they existed before the secession of Bangladesh in 1971; and to measures necessary to moderate or to remove these disparities. The fact that they were not sufficiently mitigated, still less removed is, of course, one of the reasons for the dissatisfaction that underlay the secession movement (see pp. 70–3).

The foreign trade of Pakistan

Quantitative comparison of the foreign trade of Pakistan in the years from independence to the secession of Bangladesh with that in subsequent years is complicated by the fact that in the earlier period trade between West and East Pakistan is treated as internal and so excluded from official statistics, whereas in the latter period trade between Pakistan and Bangladesh is treated as foreign trade. For present purposes it is perhaps sufficient to be merely qualitative. At independence and for some time afterwards the exports of Pakistan reflected the unindustrialized nature of its economy, and consisted almost entirely of raw cotton and wool, cotton seed, and hides and skins.[100] Raw cotton alone made up 84 per cent of exports in 1949–50. Imports in these early years consisted of cotton yarn and cloth (the former for the handlooms), intermediate goods such as machinery and metal products, and other manufactures.

Between 1971–2 total exports grew, though quantification is complicated by the effects of inflation and of devaluation. What is clear is that raw cotton, which made up 29 per cent of exports in 1971–2, was responsible for under 3 per cent in 1976–7: a reflection of the alarming decline in production to which reference has already been made. Cotton cloth and yarn made up 29 per cent of exports in 1971–2, clearly showing the effect of industrialization since independence; and 25 per cent in 1976–7. Rice exports, 8 per cent of the total in the former year, had risen to 22 per cent in the latter, a consequence of the production primarily for export of *basmati*, with results for the 'green revolution' already noted. Exports of carpets, wool, and hides and skins have continued at modest levels, while a beginning has been made with the export of such specialist manufactures as sports goods and surgical instruments. By 1976–7, however, 41 per cent of Pakistan's exports were still made up of raw materials, semiprocessed goods providing 17 per cent and fully manufactured goods 42 per cent.

Imports into Pakistan since 1971–2 are dominated by machinery and vehicles (around 30 per cent) and other manufactured goods (16–17 per cent), though the composition of the latter has changed as industrialization has got under way. Chemicals and fertilizers grew from 8 per cent in 1971–2 to nearly 12 per cent in 1976–7, and mineral fuels (mainly petroleum products) from 7 to 18 per cent.

Like India, Pakistan has suffered from an imbalance between exports and imports and so from a deficit in its balance of trade. This was especially alarming in the mid-1970s. Pakistan has had to have recourse to foreign borrowing and other forms of aid. Latterly, remittances from Pakistanis abroad (especially in the Middle East) have been helpful.

As in the case of India, the United Kingdom as a market for exports and a source for imports has declined in importance over the years, to 7 per cent of total exports and 8 per cent of total imports in 1976–7. Pakistan in fact now trades worldwide, though its trade with India is pitifully low for sad but obvious reasons. A notable feature of recent years has been an increase in exports to and imports from the Middle East, 31 per cent and 18 per cent of the respective totals in 1976–7 (imports, of course, consist largely of oil.)

The economic development of Pakistan since independence clearly provides interesting contrasts with that of India over the same period, if only because of its greater reliance on private enterprise and on foreign advice and aid. Starting with many handicaps and with very little factory industry, the growth in its GNP was, once it had settled down after the trauma of partition, spectacular, and pleasing to those of its many advisers who saw development in just those terms. But that growth owed more to industry than to agriculture, which for some years failed to increase production of food grains at a rate sufficient to compensate for the growth of population; and the 'green revolution', in production terms, has been less spectacular in Pakistan's well-irrigated Punjab than acrosss the border in India. In terms of distribution, whether spatially or class-wise, there is little achievement to record, and Pakistan remains a very unequal society and, indeed, still largely a landlord's country, notwithstanding the mentions of equity in the plans and the rhetoric of the short-lived Bhutto period.[101] Clearly there is no emerging contradiction in Pakistan between radical social and economic aims and political accommodation of the kind that Frankel sees in India; but there may prove to be a contradiction between Islamicization and modernization in Pakistan's economic development.

Bangladesh: economic strategies

Since the present Bangladesh was, from 1947 to 1971, East Pakistan it is unnecessary to repeat what has just been said about economic strategies in Pakistan during that period. Especially in the first years after secession, Bangladeshis and their friends were apt to complain, with a good deal of justification, that these strategies, with government policy generally, bore unequally on the two wings of Pakistan: claiming, for example, that the foreign exchange earnings of jute exports, raw and manufactured, from the East were used by the central government for the benefit of the West, as was most foreign aid; that raw jute was anyway consistently underpriced; that government revenues collected in the East were, in large measure, spent in the West; and that industrial development, when it began in the East under government-encouraged private enterprise, was mainly in the hands of West Pakistanis, especially Punjabis, and was in any case much less than in the west; in fine, that a poverty-stricken, overpopulated province was neglected and exploited by West Pakistan, and treated as a dependent colonial territory.[102] This picture needs, however, a little modification. We have seen that there were those who saw interregional disparities within Pakistan as primarily a matter of disparities between the two wings. And government did develop hydroelectric power and natural gas resources; while the PIDC induced some industrialization, particularly in terms of jute and cotton textiles.[103] A steel rolling mill and an oil refinery were also, belatedly, set up at Chittagong, which grew into a major port and city. Agriculture, too, received some official support, though, as we shall see, food grain production failed overall to keep pace with population increase.

Bangladesh started its independent career in 1971 with many handicaps: over and above its crushing poverty and population pressure, and the inadequacies of development under Pakistan, great disruption and damage had been caused during the struggle for 'liberation'; though these were to some extent mitigated by the rallying-round of friends in the international community.[104] A high level of aid and of advice from innumerable visiting experts has continued ever since.

The strategies and mechanisms of government planning during the early years of independence bear at least a superficial resemblance to Indian practice. Thus a Planning Commission was set up, and a Five Year Plan formulated to start in 1973, on the assumption that there would be a mixed economy — said at the time, however, to be a stage in the transition to socialism. The Commission was, however, more technocratic than India's, relying almost exclusively on talented Bangladeshi economists; and there was less interplay with politicians and bureaucrats. The plan placed strong emphasis on agriculture (not surprising in a country 90 per cent of whose population is rural) and on employment. Some socialist policies, notably hasty nationalization of industries, were implemented even before the plan was finalized. The implementation of the plan itself soon ran into difficulty, not least because of declining morale in the public service and growing confusion and corruption (see p. 106). Planned targets were for the most part not achieved and production fell in a number of sectors. Since the coups of 1975, socialism has gone by the board. There have, for example, been attempts to attract foreign capital, particularly in an export processing zone planned for Chittagong; while as I write (1982) the newest military ruler has announced measures of denationalization (already initiated by his predecessor), though he has also said that agrarian reforms were proposed, including 'a due share of crops to the landless'.[105] Moreover, the Planning Commission has survived, and worked on a long-delayed second plan to cover the period 1980 to 1985, with objectives that include the assurance of 'basic needs', the expansion of employment, and more equitable income distribution; and strategic emphasis on comprehensive rural development with local participation, and on agriculture (with self-sufficiency in foodstuffs by 1985), but not neglecting industry.[106] It remains to be seen whether achievement will match the brave words of the planners, who, as in India, seem increasingly isolated from what is really happening in the countryside.

Bangladesh: agriculture

Food grain production in Bangladesh, both before and after 'liberation', has generally speaking shown less remarkable increases than in either India or Pakistan; and has shown considerable fluctuations from year to year, with famine conditions in 1974.[107] The generalized trendline for the period 1950–80 in fact shows a growth rate of only 2.2–2.3 per cent, and has since 1961 been less than the rate of increase of population, which, as we have seen (p. 162) was respectively 2.7 per cent and 3.3 per cent for the periods 1961–74 and 1974–81. However, aggregate production has grown from around 8 million tons in the late 1950s to some 13 million tons in 1980. Not surprisingly massive food imports, much in the form of aid, have been necessary in many years. Downward fluctuations in food grain production, apart from those during and just after 'liberation', mainly reflect the incidence of cyclones, droughts and abnormal floods, to all of which this unfortunate country is all too prone. Upward fluctuations, like those of 1977–8, are hailed with ill-founded optimism as good auguries for food self-sufficiency by 1985. Meanwhile, most Bangladeshis remain underfed: indeed, increasingly so.

Rice is, of course, by far and away the principal food crop. In Bangladesh it is grown in three overlapping seasons. *Aus* paddy is sown with the pre-monsoon rains in March or April and harvested during the monsoon in July or August. *Aman* paddy, which may be broadcast in March/April or sown in July/August for transplanting, grows till November or December. *Aus* and *aman* varieties may, on some land, be sown mixed, as an insurance against one of the crops failing; while *aman* varieties include the broadcast, low-yielding deep water rices able to grow in flood-water up to 20 feet deep; but also, in the case of transplanted *aman*, the traditional varieties producing the finest rice. *Boro* is the dry season crop, grown between November and May either in low land with natural moisture or, increasingly, under irrigation. There is considerable variation from place to place, even from field to field, in the possibility of growing one or more of these paddy crops; and also variation from year to year in depth and timing of floods to complicate the farmer's decision-making even further.

Transplanting is spreading to the traditionally broadcast *aus* and even to deep water rices.

Much of the admittedly inadequate increase in rice production has come from increased sown or planted area (more by multiple cropping than by land reclamation): least in *aman*, the main crop, but significantly in *aus* and since 1965 or so in *boro* because of the increased use of low-lift pumps, mainly diesel-powered, in association with HYVs and, of course, artificial fertilizer. *Boro* yields per acre have roughly doubled since 1965. This is, in fact, the most important aspect of the production side of Bangladesh's 'green revolution', and one with physical scope for the future. But there has been some adoption of different HYVs and other improved varieties in *aus* and transplanted *aman*. But to improve the yields of the deep water rices is a difficult and intractable problem, in the absence of flood control, itself a problem to which the same adjectives are applicable on any but the strictly local scale.[108]

Wheat acreage has grown from almost nothing to over a million acres in 1980, with the possibility of irrigation and later the introduction of HYVs. Other food crops include various pulses and oilseeds (generally dry-season crops); and sugar cane. The principal commercial crops are jute, which has generally covered some 2 million acres, competes with *aus* paddy in certain topographical situations, and loses to *aus* when this is grown by transplanting; and tea.

Given the semi-aquatic environment of Bangladesh, it is not surprising that fish form a prominent part of the diet, and provide protein (as do pulses, oilseeds and vegetables); but recent price rises have taken it out of reach of the poor.

What of government efforts to stimulate agricultural production? During the Pakistan period the remarks already made (pp. 208–9) are broadly applicable. As in West Pakistan, the strategy was predominantly production-oriented; and, in those terms, not very successful: though the provision of pump, tubewell and other irrigation (now covering nearly two million acres) did provide the infrastructure for the adoption of HYVs of rice and wheat in *boro*. And agricultural research was continued. Moreover, in the early 1960s a notable and generally successful experiment in rural development, which attracted considerable attention internationally, was begun in Comilla District. This involved co-operatives for credit and marketing; irrigation; training; rural works programmes; and an attempt at popular participation through the establishment of 'development councils' at *thana* (subdistrict) level. The Comilla recipe was taken up, in part, by the IRDP already mentioned in connexion with Pakistan, and applied to other districts of East, as of West Pakistan.

Independent Bangladesh has continued to spread the Comilla recipe. Some 267 *thanas* out of 475 are said to have been covered by 1980, some of them with the help of various aid agencies, and with mixed success. It would, however, appear that this rural development programme, with its more participatory, less bureaucratic approach can take some of the credit for the adoption of HYVs for a marked increase in co-operative credit, and for some of the spread of pump and tubewell irrigation. So can government policy to subsidize irrigation pumps and fertilizers (whose use doubled, to about 900,000 tons, between 1975–6 and 1979–80). And behind all this effort stand government research organizations like the Bangladesh Rice Research Institute.

Nevertheless, it will be clear that even in production terms Bangladesh agriculture has many shortcomings. Self-sufficiency in foodstuffs at adequate nutritional levels is still far away, though some physical potential exists. There are probably a number of reasons for this: inadequate funds, for all the lipservice to the primacy of agriculture in the plans and other pronouncements; lack of administrative and technical experience; a multiplicity (as in India) of overlapping agencies; insufficient appreciation of the environmental differences between seasons, and between areas in what, for all its deltaic character, is a highly varied country in terms of micro-relief and soils; and, of course, exogenous factors like natural disasters and hoists in oil and fertilizer prices. It is also clear that there is little special effort to spread innovations, and what it takes to innovate, to the small farmer. This leads us on to considerations of equity.

Bangladesh: agrarian structure

The agrarian structure of East Pakistan at independence was highly unequal. It was also a land of *zamindari* tenure;[109] but many of the *zamindars* were Hindus who fled to India at partition. This facilitated land reforms enacted in 1950 and 1957 which abolished intermediaries and, as with comparable enactments in India (see pp. 185–6) provided that the occupier of land should pay revenue direct to the state. A ceiling was placed at 33 acres on land held for self-cultivation by ex-*zamindars*. There was further legislation under Ayub, placing a general ceiling at 100 acres. As may be imagined, these measures made little difference to tenants and less to share-croppers.

Land reform was a prominent plank in the platform of the Awami League during the struggle for independence from Pakistan, but actual measures were relatively feeble. True, in 1972 the general ceiling was lowered to 33 acres (but few holdings exceeded this area); and land revenue was abolished on holdings below about 9 acres. There were also proposals for co-operative cultivation. But little further was done under Mujib, and little has been done since; though there continue to be discussions in academic, planning and visiting-expert circles on such matters as the desirable ceiling, the amount of land that might be distributed, the production (as well as the equity) results of effective and relatively low ceilings, and the minimum holding for adequate subsistence. Meanwhile, there remain gross inequalities in agricultural land holding, as is shown by Table 6.5.

Table 6.5 Size-distribution of total owned land in rural Bangladesh, 1978

Acres	Percentage of total households
Zero	14.69
0.01–1.00	44.68
1.01–5.00	32.14
5.01–10.00	5.82
10.01–15.00	1.51
Over 15.00	1.16

Source: derived from Jannuzi and Peach, op. cit. (note 109), p. 107.

From data such as these the conclusion has been drawn that Bangladesh is a land of minifundists; and it is indeed the case that the table shows (with what accuracy one does not know) that 91.51 per cent of rural households own holdings between zero and 5 acres. But the relatively small proportion of larger landowners, with holdings that are still miniscule by, say, British standards, are powerful men in their villages. It is clear, too, that the average size of both owned and operational holdings (the two are different because of much renting-in and -out) is diminishing under relentless population pressure, insufficiently relieved by migration to towns or out of the country;

and that the number of landless, and of owners of holdings that cannot, even with multiple cropping, provide a livelihood, is growing all the time. The plight of these, the very poor, is indeed pitiful, and little helped in the past by programmes such as IRDP (though co-operatives of landless are now being organized). And those who migrate to Dhaka and other towns are usually only marginally better off as they struggle to find a niche in the 'informal economy' of petty hawkers, rickshaw-pedallers, casual labourers and the like.

Bangladesh: mining and manufacturing

Bangladesh, as a country most of which is delta, has little mineral wealth, and hardly any of it was exploited in 1947. Coal is known to exist under the delta, but mining would be difficult and expensive. Deep limestone mining has, however, begun. Since the early 1950s, natural gas has been discovered in a number of places, and from one of them there is a pipeline to Dacca. Natural gas now provides about 40 per cent of the energy consumed, and hydroelectricity almost as much; all of this is a post-1947 achievement.

Cottage industries were not unimportant in 1947, and there has been much talk of giving them high priority because of their labour-intensiveness. But progress in both cottage and small-scale industries so far has been disappointing, though not negligible. Government rhetoric is not translated into action. Textiles (Dhaka muslin was once famous), leather goods and *bidis* (small cigars) are some of the chief products.

We have seen that modern factory industry was almost non-existent in 1947, apart from a few jute and cotton mills in and around Dhaka; but then something was achieved, albeit largely by Punjabi entrepreneurs and, so far as Chittagong's steel mills and refinery are concerned, belatedly. Since 'liberation' there has been much disturbance. Not till almost the mid-1970s did jute manufactures and cotton yarn production attain their pre-'liberation' levels, at some 540,000 tons and 42 million kg respectively; but cotton cloth was ahead at 75 million yards. A useful industrial development was the establishment of three fertilizer (urea) factories using natural gas as feedstock; and of a number of paper mills. But modern factory industries only account for about 5 per cent of GDP; and Nurul Islam has highlighted the inefficiency, excess capacity and unprofitability of many of them.[110] Clearly the road to industrialization in Bangladesh, whether in the cottage, small scale or factory sector is no primrose path.

The foreign trade of Bangladesh

For reasons already discussed at the outset of our short discussion of the foreign trade of Pakistan, comparison between the imports and exports of Bangladesh from 1947 to 1971 with those of the subsequent period are not easy to make. We have also cited the view that trade was in various ways distorted in favour of West Pakistan.

In 1979 the imports of Bangladesh totalled 1537 million US dollars and its exports only 662 million US dollars.[111] While imports and exports respectively grew by 7.0 and 6.5 per cent between 1960 and 1970, the corresponding figures for the period 1970–9 are 0.6 per cent and minus 4.1 per cent. These figures speak eloquently of the difficulties of the new-born country in its international trading relations. Twenty-one per cent of the imports by value in 1978 were of food; 25 per cent of fuels; 18 per cent of machinery and transport equipment; and 32 per cent of other manufactures; while the composition of exports in the same year was 36 per cent primary commodities (mainly jute and tea); 50 per cent textiles and clothing (in some lights a remarkable figure); and 12 per cent other manufactures. As in the case of Pakistan (and, indeed, India) some help has been given by remittances, especially from Bangladeshis in the Middle East in closing the gap between imports and exports that remains after aid has been taken into account.

Immediately after 'liberation' in 1971 Bangladesh had high hopes that India would replace [West] Pakistan as a market, especially for tea and jute. But these hopes have not been completely fulfilled, not least because India can produce all the commodities that Bangladesh can export. More recently, with the restoration of better relations with Pakistan, trade (especially in tea) has begun to flow more freely in that direction once more.

What can one say in summary of the economic development of Bangladesh? Clearly one is here dealing, sympathetically one hopes, with a chronic case of underdevelopment compounded of an agrarian economy with but little industry so far; of enormously heavy pressure of population still rising very rapidly, at 3 per cent per annum, so that it is hard enough for production to keep pace with population growth, let alone to improve living standards of the tens of millions of very poor people in villages and towns; of severe lack of capital and of government revenue for developmental investment and also, it would appear so far, of entrepreneurial and administrative talent; of gross and growing inequalities in wealth and income; and of hydra-headed corruption and recurrent political crises and coups. Yet behind this sombre picture lies a resourceful peasantry whom one cannot fail to admire if one gets out into the villages, where great ingenuity is using every scrap of land as many times annually as it will stand: a peasantry which, perhaps largely in spite of, rather than because of, the governments and officials who come and go and talk endlessly, has survived and laid hold, when they can, of the new varieties and technology and introduced their own innovations — for example, by transplanting traditionally broadcast crops; albeit at the cost of an increasingly skewed distribution of land and income.

Sri Lanka: economic strategies

We have seen (pp. 156–7) that Sri Lanka had at independence what was essentially a colonial export economy. It grew and exported tea, rubber and coconut products, largely to the United Kingdom, and imported foodstuffs, especially rice, to supplement home production. Largely as a result of the productivity of its export sector, it had a GNP per capita approximately twice that of India and Pakistan when they reached independence. It had few factory industries, and imported most of its manufactures, again largely from the United Kingdom.

Already before independence, however, steps had been taken to modify the economy, especially after the country attained internal self-government, with adult suffrage, in 1931.[112] The new ministers were interested, for example, in peasant colonization in the Dry Zone, of which more shortly, and in modest industrialization. The First World War and the depression of the 1930s had shown the dangers of reliance on food imports, dangers that were felt even more acutely in the Second World War. The depression had underlined the need for diversification more generally; and wartime shortages gave a fillip to industrialization. Meanwhile population was growing fast, as was landlessness in the Wet Zone and hills.

Independence on 4 February 1948 brought no trauma, as it did in India and Pakistan. Indeed, the change was for a time barely no-ticeable, for the same UNP group remained in power (see pp. 97–8);

and there was no commitment to socialism, no Gandhianism, to supply an ideology of change. But, as we have seen, the general election of 1956 *was* mildly traumatic, for it brought an alternative party, the SLFP, to power; while successive general elections have, broadly speaking, seen alternately in power these two main parties and their allies. To some extent, alternations in government have brought oscillations in economic policy: more conservative under the UNP, more socialistic under the SLFP.

But before exploring some of the principal oscillations, it is necessary to stress that there have also been important continuities, most of them falling into the category of welfare policies and justifying the claim that Sri Lanka is some sort of welfare state. Thus, as we shall see, all governments have maintained a policy of Dry Zone agricultural colonization, mostly supported by the restoration or construction of irrigation works, and like the complementary 'village expansion' schemes, aimed largely at the relief of landlessness, which may be seen as a populist purpose. Governments of both complexions have also maintained policies of improving yields on land already cultivated by such means as plant-breeding, agricultural extension and fertilizer subsidies, though with differences in detail and in vigour. Both kinds of government have operated guaranteed price schemes, which, with input subsidies and the non-collection of irrigation dues, have constituted a distributive measure for producers; and subsidized rice rations, at various levels of quantity and subsidy — clearly a distributive measure for consumers, and also populist in character. And all governments have maintained what is, for a Third World country, a high level of expenditure on health and education; so that Sri Lanka rates high in terms of the 'Physical Quality of Life Index' (PQLI), based as it is on life expectancy; the inverse of infant mortality; and literacy.[113] The PQLI for Sri Lanka is in fact higher than that for Washington, DC. But so many of these infancy-surviving, long-lived, literate Sri Lankans are unemployed, perhaps two-thirds of those in the 15–29 age-group; so all is not well, as we shall see.

Why these continuities in 'welfare' policies? It is possible to invoke populism related to a long history of adult franchise, with a literate and politicized electorate; and the tendency for parties out of power to seek to outbid parties in power as elections approach.

It might also be said that most governments, whatever their colour, have submitted the plantation sector to relative if not absolute neglect, for reasons that are a mixture of rather crude dependency theory under which the plantations, whatever the nationality of their ownership, are seen as 'imperialist enclaves'; lack of political punch on the part of estate owners; and even less punch on the part of the disenfranchised estate labourers of Indian origin (see p. 99).

But over and above these continuities there *have* been oscillations in economic policy: first, in general attitudes to planning. From independence to 1956, there was really no strategic planning. The first UNP government did set up a Planning Secretariat, but the Six-Year Programme of Investment, 1954–5 to 1959–60 was really no more than a set of departmental estimates, redolent of colonial times. But Bandaranaike, on coming to power with his SLFP in 1956, set up a planning machine obviously based on the Indian model; and its Ten Year Plan emerged in 1959.[114] This did present a coherent strategy: namely, to avoid headlong industrialization, especially in terms of heavy industry, given the country's lack of natural resources and the smallness of its internal market; but rather to achieve suitable industrialization progressively by importing capital goods, to be paid for by increasing traditional exports, and exporting the products of diversified agriculture and import substituting industries. The 1959 plan is generally seen as a dead letter, for it was soon overtaken by foreign exchange crises related largely to difficulty in expanding exports; though parts of its strategy can be discerned as a thin thread running through later years. But changes in sectoral policy, especially in relation to industry, have also played their part.

Industrial policy was a relatively minor part of early UNP thinking, though in the early 1950s such public sector plants as a hydroelectricity station and a cement plant were opened and others were in gestation when the SLFP came to power in 1956. But the SLFP government initiated a number of new public sector industries in rapid succession and also (and related to the foreign exchange crisis) restricted imports and encouraged private sector consumer goods industries, though with a somewhat ambiguous attitude to foreign capital. There were no very marked changes of industrial policy during UNP rule from 1965 to 1970; but since that party came back to power again in 1977 there has been a very pronounced oscillation away from whatever may be seen as socialistic in SLFP policy. For a Free Trade Zone was established north of Colombo and strong efforts made to attract foreign capital on the frankly capitalist model of Singapore.

Land reform is another field in which, on the face of it at any rate, the SLFP has been much more enthusiastic than the UNP. True, under the latter a Paddy Lands Act was enacted in 1952, but it was limited to the ineffective regulation of tenancy in two districts. The SLFP's act of the same name passed in 1958 was much more thoroughgoing, at least on paper, involving security of tenure and maximum rent for tenants island-wide, and elected Cultivation Committees to manage cultivation. More spectacular and far-reaching was the SLFP government's ceiling legislation of 1972, which affected mainly commercial crops grown by local companies and individuals: surplus land really was collected. An amendment of 1975 effectively nationalized foreign-owned estates. These land reforms were not reversed by the UNP government of 1977, though it did initiate changes in the operation, and in the management of lands held by the state; and it did abolish Cultivation Committees.

Sri Lanka: agriculture

It is conventional, but misleading, to treat the agriculture of Sri Lanka as falling in two distinct sectors, a peasant sector devoted to rice and other locally-consumed food crops, and an export sector producing for overseas markets: misleading if only because, in the Wet Zone and hills anyway, many 'peasants' grow crops on small holdings in addition to their rice. We shall proceed crop-wise.

In the production of rice Sri Lanka has achieved noteworthy increases both in production and in yield, though both fluctuate from year to year for climatic reasons: from some 300 thousand tons per annum at and after independence to some 900 thousand to a million tons in the late 1970s. This raised the contribution of local production to national supplies over the same period from 35–40 per cent to 50–60 per cent; and there has been euphoric talk of self-sufficiency and even exports. Since about 1965, in fact, production has been gaining on population increase. It was in about the same year that national yields began to increase quite steeply, as a result first of locally-bred long-strawed hybrids but later as short-strawed HYVs, crosses between IRRI varieties and local strains. But what distinguishes Sri Lanka from other South Asian countries is the great part played by increased area under paddy, largely as a result of the colonization schemes in the Dry Zone to which reference has already been made. Since independence, in fact, the paddy area harvested has increased by well over 100 per cent. But, as a number of enquiries has shown, colonization is generally an expensive process, primarily but not exclusively because of the costly irrigation works needed if rice is to be grown.[115] Quite apart from government subsidies already mentioned, the cost of such paddy cultivation to the economy is high: so will be the cost of rice exports if euphoria ever becomes fulfilled in achievement. Yet massive irrigation works like those of the Mahaveli Ganga scheme continue to be constructed.

Turning to the principal export crops the production story is less satisfactory. Tea production did increase from just under 300 million pounds annually at independence to over 500 thousand pounds in 1965, without any substantial increase in area. But since then there has been a more or less steady decline to some 414 million pounds in 1982. In the case of rubber, annual production rose slowly from around 150 million pounds at independence to about 200–230 million pounds in the 1950s and early 1960s, after which there was a sharp increase to over 350 million pounds in 1970; since then production has declined to some 330 million pounds. Coconut production is more difficult to quantify since it takes place not only on a few estates but also on a multitude of small holdings and from a few trees in homesteads; and is consumed by growers to an unknown extent. Available data suggest that production was more or less static, fluctuating between 2500 and 2800 million nuts per annum from 1960 to 1970, and then declining, with fluctuations, to 2000–2200 million nuts. The reasons for the recent decline in production in the export sector are a matter of some controversy, and include taxation, adverse weather and prices, and neglect by owners in anticipation of land reform or otherwise; but G. H. Peiris, an authority on the Sri Lanka land reforms, concludes 'the possibility that the institutional transformation is also responsible ... cannot be ruled out' and cites the alienation of former estates to peasants in small units; the disturbance, perhaps only temporary, in converting estates into co-operatives; the history of non-profitability in the State Plantations Corporation, which has taken over many estates; and corruption and general inefficiency.[116] Now, while successive governments have supported export agriculture by subsidizing replanting schemes; and while there are research institutes for each of the three principal crops; nevertheless there is the record of relative neglect of the export sector to which I have already drawn attention. Diversification of crops has also been insufficiently pressed: for instance, by encouraging the cultivation of oil palm, as has been done so successfully in Malaysia. It remains to be seen whether some of these troubles will be overcome by the UNP government, with its different ideological slant, and policy of improving incentives to producers of both paddy and export crops.

Sea fisheries, it should be mentioned, are of considerable importance in Sri Lanka.

Sri Lanka: agrarian structure

Data on land-holdings in the peasant sector do not enable us to determine the size-distribution of paddy land alone. It seems clear, however, that outside the colonization schemes average holdings, though varying from area to area, are growing smaller under the pressure of population (and no doubt in the older colonization schemes too, in spite of conditions of tenure that forbid fragmentation).[117] For *all* 'smallholdings', irrespective of crop, in 1973, 'some 42 per cent of operators (not owners) farmed between one-eighth and one acre' while 'just under 3 per cent of the operators farmed some 22 per cent of the total', suggesting considerable inequality in the use of land.[118] What is clear is that land reform legislation has so far made little difference to inequality in the peasant sector, particularly where paddyland is concerned (for the ceiling at 25 acres avoids almost all paddy holdings); while case studies suggest that Cultivation Committees did little to undermine the power of the 'big men', who, with tractorization and other changes incident to the 'green revolution', tend to grow in influence: 'a new feudalism of technology' is the telling phrase used by C. N. Jayaweera.[119]

Turning to the estate sector, I have already remarked that surplus land really was collected; and we have seen that foreign-owned estates really were nationalized; and that a variety of structures were employed (alienation to peasants; operation of estates by co-operatives and by a state corporation) in farming the sequestered land. What were the equity effects of all this? Richards and Gooneratne conclude: 'The major comment on land reform is that despite its extent the rural social and economic structure was hardly changed' because the ceiling for export crops left 'the latter village-based landlords untouched'; because popular participation was discouraged in favour of indirect participation through, and direct control by, political representatives; and because village groups had no say in the disposal of estate land and may have suffered where, for example, new managements forbade grazing by cattle that had been countenanced by former management.[120] It may well be that it was the politicians and their clients who did best out of 'land reform'. And the Indian estate labourer, usually forgotten in these discussions, certainly benefited not at all.

Sri Lanka: mining and manufacturing

Sri Lanka has little mineral wealth beyond graphite, gemstones and mineral sands, though it does possess limestone for cement-making, and potential for hydroelectric power in the highlands. Since independence, plant with a capacity of 331 MW has been installed to harness about one-fifth of that potential; and the Mahaveli Ganga scheme will add substantially to this.

Since 1948, as a result of policies already discussed, manufacturing industry has grown in importance, and now accounts for some 20 per cent of GNP (4.7 per cent in 1948).[121] Industries include petroleum refining; ceramics; steel rolling and wire; plywood; textiles, chemicals; and a range of consumer goods industries which, as in other countries of South Asia, cater mainly for the urban upper and middle classes. Production in 1978 (in almost all cases to be compared with zero at independence) included 575,000 tons of cement, 37,000 tons of mineral sands, 33,000 tons of steel products, 153,000 tons of salt and 18,000 metres of cloth — all of these from industries controlled by state corporations. These are, of course, small quantities compared with production from the larger South Asian countries; but Sri Lanka is a small country, and the figures quoted do not include the results of the recent efforts to attract foreign capital. These efforts are credited already with a considerable reduction in the unemployment which is one of Sri Lanka's main problems, but were set back by destruction during the 1983 communal riots.

Craft industries survive and, indeed, benefit from the growing tourist trade, attracted by Sri Lanka's beaches and marvellous scenery and, in the case of the more discerning, by its antiquities.

It is a characteristic, of course, of an underdeveloped country that it has a large primate city, a triton among the minnows; and Colombo is no exception. Nevertheless, economic activity in Sri Lanka is not so concentrated in the capital as in some Third World countries, for reasons that include the existence of unused or underused land in the Dry Zone, long repellent to settlement because of malaria but in recent decades the scene not only of agricultural colonization but also of spontaneous settlement and of development (some of it on the part of state industrial corporations); and the tendency of tourism in very recent years to spawn hotels in many scattered coastal and inland locations.[122] Most private sector consumer goods industries have, however, located in or near Colombo; and it may well be that the Free Trade Zone and other developments under the UNP government will lead to increased polarization of industry on the capital city.

The foreign trade of Sri Lanka

Sri Lanka at independence had, we have emphasized, a colonial export economy. In 1950, 96 per cent of exports were made up of tea, rubber and coconuts products (contrary to impressions of 'spicy breezes', spices only contributed about 1½ per cent).[123] By 1978, the three principal agricultural exports were still forming 73 per cent of total exports, in spite of the decline in production that has been noted, and in spite of measures of economic development since independence. Industrial products were, however, contributing 14 per cent and gemstones 4 per cent, so there was some change.

Over 30 per cent of imports in 1950 consisted of food grains, mainly rice; this, as a result of increased home production, had fallen to 19 per cent by 1978 (rice 4.7 per cent). Over the same timespan, petroleum products had increased from 2.3 to 17.2 per cent; chemicals from 1.6 to 8.9 per cent; and machinery from 3.1 to 12.4 per cent but textiles, yarn and clothing had fallen from 14.3 to 8.4 per cent. It may be judged then, that the results of industrialization so far have been to increase imports of intermediate goods without much impact on imports of consumer goods.

But a major characteristic of Sri Lanka's economy since independence has been the emergence of a yawning gap between exports earnings and the cost of imports. This was particularly the case between 1966 and 1975: in subsequent years there was some improvement, some contribution being made by remittances and aid.

As might be expected, the United Kingdom has fallen from its position as the dominant trading partner of Sri Lanka, taking 25 per cent of exports and supplying 20 per cent of imports in 1950. In 1978, Sri Lanka's exports to Pakistan, the USA, the UK and China were all of the same order of magnitude (at 7–9 per cent of total exports) and there was a long list of countries taking from 2 to 6 per cent. Sources of imports were also highly diversified, Saudi Arabia and Iran, as oil suppliers, being prominent.

Here, then, is a country with an economy and a recent history of economic development different in a number of important respects from those of other South Asian countries. Because of welfare policies more or less consistently pursued, it has much to its credit in education, health services, infant mortality and life expectancy; and, some might add, in lowering its birth rate (see pp. 162–5). But inequalities, much poverty and frighteningly high unemployment persist in spite of the efforts of the present government. Moreover, and while one does not wish to re-enthrone GNP, there is the fact that GNP per capita, nearly twice India's at independence, is now of the same order of magnitude as India's. Clearly, whatever may be true of welfare or distributive measures, growth has been relatively low. The question arises, therefore, whether the welfare measures we have reviewed are responsible, in whole or in part, for the absorption of resources available to the government that might otherwise have gone to growth-oriented development. Richards and Gooneratne conclude, fairly I believe, that 'it is problematical to single out welfare policies as leading to slow growth'.[124] Clearly, Sri Lanka has difficulties arising from lack of mineral resources, small size and colonial heritage that do not in the same way affect India and Pakistan. But it is also possible to point to such shortcomings as the relative neglect and ossification of the export sector and misplaced and expensive policies, some of which we have underlined.

The economic development of Nepal

Not surprisingly, Nepal is one of the poorest and most backward countries of the Third World, low in the rank order of such countries no matter what index is chosen. Adherents of the dependency school of underdevelopment see it, in fact, as the periphery of a periphery, a dependency of India which is in turn a dependency of the world capitalist system; while within the country the valley around Kathmandu acts as the core within a periphery of a periphery to even more peripheral and remote rural areas.[125] Readers of pp. 130–4 may, however, wonder whether Nepal *is* such a dependency of India, given the history of relations between the two countries and the way in which Nepal, since the Second World War, has skilfully walked a tightrope and secured economic aid from all and sundry. Be that as it may, it is certainly true that Nepal has one of the characteristics of the least-developed countries, the lack of accurate statistical data about it, particularly if one is looking for time series.

Some 94 per cent of Nepal's labour force are said to be engaged in agriculture, growing rice in the plains of the Tarai at the foot of the hills and crops such as maize, wheat and various millets in terraces in the hills. According to official figures (for what they are worth) paddy production is increasing only slowly, from 2.20 million tons in 1964–5 to 2.35 million tons in 1971–2.[126] Over the same period maize production declined from 854,000 to 759,000 tons while millet production increased slightly and wheat (126,000 to 223,000 tons) showed a more marked increase, reflecting the rather pale green revolution in Nepal, though fertilizer consumption seems to have increased since the late 1960s (while remaining at low levels); in the hills most production is for subsistence and does not enter the market; but some farmers in the Tarai are able to produce a surplus for sale, helped by the roads that aid donors press on the willing recipient.

Since 1960 the government has set up various organizations, from research stations and credit institutions to extension agencies; but they do not seem to have made much impact. The government has also taken in hand the planning and organization of resettlement in the Tarai, to which there is a good deal of immigration, both from the hills and from India.

For in the hills massive pressure of population on land has built up, and has been doing so in many areas for some time.[127] Sedentary agriculture has replaced shifting cultivation and pastoralism, and has in turn extended on to steeper and steeper slopes, so that in spite of terracing there is much soil erosion. Some authors in Nepal therefore see its agrarian economy in a crisis that may soon become a catastrophe.[128] The Tarai, and remittances sent home by emigrants, including Gurkhas who serve in the Indian and British armies, act as temporary, but only temporary safety valves.

So far little relief has been afforded by industrialization. In fact, retrogression in cottage industries has been documented, retrogression because of manufactures flooding in from India. As for modern industry, there are many rice, oil and sugar mills, especially in the Tarai. Sugar production is said to have trebled to 7559 tons in 1971–2; and tanned leather production to have increased from 30.8

thousand kg in 1964–5 to 170.8 thousand kg in 1971–2. But these illustrative outputs are still clearly very small.

This is in spite of the fact that Nepal has a formal planning machine and has produced a series of Five Year Plans, all very much on the Indian model (even unto words about regional balance) but without Indian resources, economic talent, and entrepreneurship. All this, too, is in spite of massive aid from various quarters (see p. 134) which observers who are by no means cynics see as largely, if not mainly providing jobs for an ever-increasing bureaucracy, and thus helping to prevent trouble from educated and urban groups who might otherwise seek to unseat the none too stable monarchy.

What, then, of equity? There are great disparities of wealth and income in this poor country. True, some of the grossest inequalities were tackled in 1960, when 'vast land grants made during the last century to nobles, successful generals, and other favoured state functionaries were abrogated' and other limited land reforms instituted.[129] But there are still landowners and wealthier peasants who employ the labour of others, or use share-croppers; though it is true that most cultivators are owner–cultivators. There *have* since 1977 been schemes specifically to help small farmers by encouraging co-operation and providing credit; but it is too early to say how the schemes will fare.[130]

Given then, the ecological unbalance in the hills, the generally undeveloped and unequal state of the economy, and the limited gains made by aid and government agencies so far, Nepal gives but little ground for optimism; though a recent report on basic needs in Nepal does conclude that the crisis is now 'so visible and so acute' that there are officials thinking of new approaches 'compatible with the "basic needs" approach'.[131] 'There should be no false optimism, given the nature of the political economy of the country, but neither should there be despair and pessimism regarding the possibilities of change in Nepal in the interests of the deprived.'

Notes and references

1 Spate, O. H. K. (1954) *India and Pakistan*, 1st edn, London, contains good accounts of the economy in general, and of agriculture in particular, as they were at about the time of independence.
2 See Potter, D. C. (1964) *Government in Rural India*, London.

3 Bhagwati, J. N. and Desai, P. (1970) *India: Planning for Industrialization*, London, Chapter 3.

4 Ibid., pp. 19–24, 48, 50.

5 Ginsburg, N. (1961) *Atlas of Economic Development*, Chicago.

6 See Spate, O. H. K. (1954) op. cit.; and his (1947) 'The partition of the Punjab and of Bengal', *Geographical Journal*, 110, 201–22 and (1948) 'The partition of India and the prospects of Pakistan', *Geographical Review*, 38, 5–29.

7 See Farmer, B. H. (1974) *Agricultural Colonization in India since Independence*, London, passim, especially 56, 87–8 and 107–9.

8 Compare Snodgrass, D. R. (1966) *Ceylon: an Export Economy in Transition* Homewood, Ill., and Ponnambalam, S. (1981) *Dependent Capitalism in Crisis: The Sri Lanka Economy, 1948–1980*, London. See also Wickremeratne, L. A. (1977) 'The Economy in 1948', in De Silva, K. M. (ed.) *Sri Lanka: A Survey*, London, 131–43.

9 See Farmer, B. H. (1957) *Pioneer Peasant Colonization in Ceylon*, London.

10 See for example Frankel, F. (1978) *India's Political Economy, 1947–1977: the Gradual Revolution*, Princeton, NJ; but see the review by Brass, P. R. (1981) 'Class, ethnic group and party in Indian politics', *World Politics*, 33, 449–67 at 466–7.

11 See Cassen, R. H. (1978) *India: Population, Economy, Society*, London, 5–6; and compare Macfarlane, A. (1976) *Resources and Population: A Study of the Gurungs of Nepal*, Cambridge; and Miranda, A. (1982) *The Demography of Bangladesh*, Bergen.

12 Planning Commission, Government of India, (1961) *Third Five Year Plan*, New Delhi, 22.

13 Robinson, E. A. G. (1974) 'The economic development of Malthusia', *Modern Asian Studies*, 8, 521–34.

14 Crude birth and death rates from The World Bank (1981) *World Development Report 1981*, New York, Table 18; Cassen, R. H. (1978) op. cit.; and Balakrishnan, N. and Gunasekara, H. M. (1977) 'A review of demographic trends', in De Silva, K. M. (ed.) op. cit. (crude birth and death rates are those actually recorded, unadjusted for the age composition of the population).

15 Fernando, D. F. S. (1972) 'Recent fertility decline in Ceylon', *Population Studies* 26, 445–53 and (1975) 'Changing nuptiality patterns in Sri Lanka', ibid., 29, 179–90.

16 For projections for India on various assumptions see Cassen, R. H. (1978) op. cit., 127–43.

17 The World Bank (1981) op. cit., Table 17 read with pp. 188–9.

18 Cassen, R. H. (1978) op. cit., Chapter 3. See also Blaikie, P. M. (1975) *Family Planning in India: Diffusion and Policy*, London.

19 See, for example, Ponnambalam, S. (1980) *Dependent Capitalism in Crisis: The Sri Lankan Economy 1948–1980*, London, 61.

20 Mamdani, M. (1972) *The Myth of Population Control: Family, Caste and Class in an Indian Village*, New York. See also Bondestam, L. and Bergstrom, L. (1980) *Poverty and Population Control*, London; and Cassen, R. H. (1978) op. cit., p. 67.

21 See, for example, Mathur, R. M. (1959) 'Food resources and population growth', in *Proceedings of the International Geography Seminar, Aligarh Muslim University, 1956*, Aligarh, 228–41.

22 Of the multitude of general works on economic development in India since independence the following may usefully be cited here: Hanson, A. H. (1966) *The Process of Planning: A Study of India's Five Year Plans*, London; Streeten, P. and Lipton, M. (eds) (1968) *The Crisis of Indian Planning: Economic Planning in the 1960s*, London; Bhagwati, J. N. and Desai, P. (1970) *India: Planning for Industrialization*, London; Mellor, J. (1976) *The New Economics of Growth: A Strategy for India and the Developing World*, Ithaca and London; Chaudhuri, P. (1978) *The Indian Economy*, London; Frankel, F. (1978) op. cit.; Jha, L. K. (1981) *Economic Strategy for the Eighties*, New Delhi; and Bagchi, A. K. (1982) *The Political Economy of Under-development*, Cambridge, 227–36.

23 See Frankel, F. (1978) op. cit., p. 67; Bhagwati, J. N. and Desai, P. (1970) op. cit., p. 140; and Farmer, B. H. (1974) op. cit., pp. 30, 96–8 and 202–3.

24 Bhagwati, J. N. and Desai, P. (1970) op. cit., pp. 140–1.

25 Farmer, B. H. (1974) op. cit., especially pp. 56–9, 87–8, 102 and 108.

26 See Bhagwati, J. N. and Desai, P. (1970) op. cit., Chapter 13 for a critical review of licensing policy.

27 (1960) *The Third Five Year Plan*, New Delhi, Chapter 9 is entitled 'Balanced regional development'.

28 See, among many examples that might be cited, Streeten, P. and Lipton, M. (eds) (1968) op. cit. and Myrdal, G. (1968) *Asian Drama*, Harmondsworth, Vol. I, Chapter 7; and Mellor, J. (1976) op. cit.; Chaudhuri, P. (1978) op. cit.; Frankel, F. (1978) op. cit.; and Toye, J. (1981) *Public Expenditure and Indian Development Policy, 1960–70*, Cambridge.

29 For aid inflows (and foreign exchange reserves), 1950–1 to 1970–1 see Toye, J. (1981) op. cit., p. 44.

30 USAID administrator in New Delhi quoted in Frankel, F. (1978) op. cit., p. 286.

31 Streeten, P. and Lipton, M. (eds) (1968) op. cit., pp. 10–11.

32 Frankel, F. (1978) op. cit.

33 Ibid., p. 102.

34 See Potter, D. C. (1964) op. cit.

35 In Farmer, B. H. (ed.) (1977) *Green Revolution? Technology and Change in Rice-growing Areas of Tamil Nadu and Sri Lanka*, London, 136 and Chapter 11.

36 Frankel, F. (1978) op. cit., pp. 274–92.
37 See Shanmugasundaram, V. (ed.) (1972) *Agricultural Development of India: A Study of Intensive Agricultural District Programme*, Madras, and Desai, D. K. (1972) 'Intensive agricultural district programme', in Chaudhuri, P. (ed.), *Readings in Indian Agricultural Development*, London.
38 See also Toye, J. (1981) op. cit., pp. 46–7.
39 Of the vast amount of literature on the 'green revolution', some of it controversial, the following may usefully be cited here: Frankel, F. R. (1971) *India's Green Revolution: Economic Gains and Political Costs*, Princeton, NJ; Harriss, B. (1972) 'Innovative adoption in Indian agriculture — the high yielding varieties programme', *Modern Asian Studies*, 6, 71–98; Byres, T. J. (1972) 'The dialectics of India's green revolution', *South Asian Review*, 5, 99–116; Etienne, G. (1973) 'India's new agriculture: a survey of the evidence', ibid., 6, 197–213 and (1982) *India's Changing Rural Scene*, Delhi; Shand, R. T. (ed.) (1973) *Technical Change in Indian Agriculture*, Canberra; Randhawa, M. S. *et al.* (1974) *Green Revolution: a Case Study of Punjab*, Delhi; Sen, B. (1974) *The Green Revolution in India: a Perspective*, New Delhi; Dasgupta, B. (1977) *Agrarian Change and the New Technology in India*, Geneva; Farmer, B. H. (1977) op. cit.; Mencher, J. P. (1978) *Agriculture and Social Structure in Tamil Nadu*, New Delhi; Farmer, B. H. (1979) 'The "green revolution" in South Asian ricefields: environment and production', *Journal of Development Studies*, 15, 304–19; Harriss, J. (1982) *Capitalism and Peasant Farming: Agrarian Structure and Ideology in Northern Tamil Nadu*, Bombay; and Farmer, B. H. (1983) 'The "green revolution" in India', *Geographical Journal* (forthcoming).
40 For irrigation in India see Spate, O. H. K. and Learmonth, A. T. A. (1967) *India and Pakistan*, 3rd edn, London, pp. 230–3 and Johnson, B. L. C. (1979) *India*, London, Chapter 4. For agriculture without irrigation see Hill, P. (1982) *Dry Grain Farming Families*, Cambridge.
41 Farmer, B. H. (1974) op. cit., p. 41 and Clay, E. J. (1982) 'Technical innovation and public policy; agricultural development in the Kosi Region, Bihar, India', *Agricultural Administration*, 9, 189–210.
42 See, for example, Madduma Bandara, C. M. (1977) 'Hydrological consequences of agrarian change', in Farmer, B. H. op. cit., Chapter 21.
43 See, for example, Murthy, Y. K. (1976) 'Utilization of irrigation facilities', in Indian Society of Agricultural Economics, *Role of Irrigation in the Development of India's Agriculture*, Bombay, 16–30.
44 See Johnson, B. L. C. (1979) op. cit., p. 78 and (for examples), Farmer, B. H. (1974) op. cit., pp. 163–4.
45 Clay E. J. (1982) op. cit., 197–200. For the inadequacies of soil surveys in India, see Farmer, B. H. (1945) (1974) op. cit., pp. 144–6.

46 Tarlok Singh (1945) *Poverty and Social Change: A Study in Economic Reorganisation of Indian Rural Society*, London; (1969) 2nd edn with a reappraisal, Bombay. See also Farmer, B. H. (1974) op. cit., pp. 92–8.

47 See Frankel, F. (1978) op. cit., pp. 68–70 and Warriner, D. (1969), *Land Reform in Principle and Practice*, Oxford, 150–6.

48 See Farmer, B. H., (1974) op. cit., pp. 252–6.

49 Quoted by Warriner, D. (1969) op. cit., p. 136. There is a vast literature on land reform in India. See, in particular, Warriner, D. (1969) op. cit., Chapter 6; Dandekar, V. M. and Rath, N. (1971) *Poverty in India*, Bombay; Lehmann, D. (ed.) (1974) *Land Reform and Land Reformism*, London, Chapters 5–9; Frankel, F. (1978) op. cit., passim; Bagchi, D. (1981) 'India', in Mushtaqur Rahman (ed.), *Agrarian Egalitarianism: Land Tenures and Land Reforms in South Asia*, Dubuque, Iowa; and Herring, R. J. (1983) *Land to the Tiller: the Political Economy of Agrarian Reform in South Asia*, New Haven and London.

50 Warriner, D. (1969) op. cit., p. 142.

51 Harriss, J. (1982) *Capitalism and Peasant Farming: Agrarian Structure and Ideology in Northern Tamil Nadu*, Bombay, 115–8.

52 Warriner, D. (1969) op. cit., p. 171; see also Bagchi, D. (1981) op. cit.

53 Planning Commission, Government of India (1981) *Sixth Five Year Plan*, New Delhi, 114–15, see also Bagchi, D. (1981) op. cit., p. 102; and Jones, S. *et al.* (ed.) (1982) *Rural Poverty and Agrarian Reform*, New Delhi, Introduction and Chapter 4.

54 See Bagchi, D. (1981) op. cit., p. 115 and Farmer, B. H. (1974) op. cit., pp. 252–60.

55 See Farmer, B. H. (1974) op. cit., especially Chapter 6.

56 See Farmer, B. H. (1960) 'On not controlling subdivision in paddy-lands', *Transactions, Institute of British Geographers*, 28, 225–35.

57 Here I am in substantial agreement with Chambers, R. (1978) 'Towards rural futures', *Discussion Paper, Institute of Development Studies*, Brighton, 3: 'The green revolution turns not red but brown'.

58 See Farmer, B. H. (1977) op. cit., especially Chapter 8; and Etienne (1982) op. cit.

59 See, for example, Frankel, F. (1978) op. cit., pp. 336–9 and the review in the *Sixth Plan*, pp. 109–10, and Harriss, B. (1981) *Transitional India and Rural Development*, New Delhi.

60 See Farmer, B. H. (1977) op. cit., p. 114 and Harriss, J. (1982) op. cit., pp. 185–98.

61 See Dasgupta, B. ((1977) op. cit., pp. 293–313.

62 See Raj, K. N. (1969) *Investment in Livestock in Agrarian Economies*, Delhi (originally in (1969) *Indian Economic Review*, 4); and (1967) 'The cow: a symposium', *Seminar* 9, 10–55.

63 Crotty, R. (1982) 'EEC surplus contributes to India's hunger', *Geographical Magazine*, 54, 338–40.

64 See Byres, T. J., 'Land reform, industrialisation and the marketed surplus in India', in Lehmann, D. (ed.) (1974) op. cit., pp. 249–52.

65 *Sixth Plan*, p. 233.

66 For Indian industry see especially Bhagwati, J. N. and Desai, P. (1970) op. cit.; Chaudhuri, P. (1978) *The Indian Economy: Poverty and Development*, London, especially pp. 147–76; and, particularly for spatial aspects, Johnson, B. L. C. (1979) op. cit.

67 *Sixth Plan*, p. 259.

68 See Jha, L. K. (1980) op. cit., and Chaudhuri, P. (1978) op. cit., p. 154; and, for fiscal policy, Toye, J. (1981) op. cit.

69 Bhagwati, J. N. and Desai, P. (1970) op. cit., p. 31; *Sixth Plan*, p. 218; and Chaudhuri, P. (1978) op. cit., p. 152.

70 *Sixth Plan*, p. 187 (*Khadi* is homespun cloth popularized by Mahatma Gandhi).

71 See in particular Misra, R. P., Sundaram, K. V. and Prakasa Rao, V. L. K. (1974) *Regional Development Planning in India*, Delhi; Sundaram, K. V. (1977) *Urban and Regional Planning in India*, New Delhi; and Sundaram, K. V. (1983) *Geography of Underdevelopment (The Spatial Dynamics of Underdevelopment)* New Delhi, Chapters 1,9.

72 As reported in (1982) *The Hindu: International Edition*, 5 June. See also Wanmali, S. (1983) *Service Centres in Rural India: Policy, Theory and Practice*, New Delhi, for regional development in Andhra Pradesh.

73 See Sundaram, K. V. (1983) op. cit., (forthcoming), pp. 210–11.

74 Farmer, B. H. (1974) op. cit., pp. 100–1 and 111–17.

75 See *Sixth Plan*, Chapters 25, 26.

76 See Sundaram, K. V. (1977) op. cit., pp. 6–12.

77 See Chapman, G. and Wanmali, S. (1981) 'Urban–Rural relationships in India: a macro-scale approach using population potentials', *Geoforum*, 12, 19–43.

78 See Harriss, B. (1976) 'The Indian ideology of growth centres', *Area*, 8, 263–9 and references there cited.

79 In (1982) *The Hindu: International Edition*, 5 June.

80 On India's trade see, for example, Mellor, J. (1976) op. cit., Chapter 8; Chaudhuri, P. (1978) op. cit. pp. 70–5; and Johnson, B. L. C. (1979) op. cit. pp. 39–43.

81 *Sixth Plan*, Chapter 6.

82 See Lipton, M. (1975) *The Erosion of a Relationship: India and Britain since 1960*, London.

83 Frankel, F. (1978) op. cit.

84 Although Pakistan has not attracted as much economic analysis and writing as India, there is nevertheless a considerable literature, partly because of the involvement of American economists. This includes: Andrus, J. R. and Mohammed, A. F. (1958) *The Economy of Pakistan*, Oxford and (1966) *Trade, Finance and Development in Pakistan* Karachi; Mahbub Ul Haq, (1963) *The Strategy of Economic Planning: A Case Study*

of Pakistan, Karachi; Lewis, S. R. (1969) *Economic Policy and Industrial Growth in Pakistan*, London, and (1970) *Pakistan: Industrialization and Trade Policies*, London; Falcon, W. P. and Papanek, G. F. (ed.) *Development Policy: The Pakistan Experience*, Cambridge, Mass.; MacEwan, A. (1971) *Development Alternatives in Pakistan*, Cambridge, Mass.; Brecher, I. and Abbas, S. A (1972) *Foreign Aid and Industrial Development in Pakistan*, Cambridge; Griffin, K. B. and Khan, A. R. (eds) (1972) *Growth and Inequality in Pakistan*, London; Moin Baqai and Brecher, I. (eds) (1973) *Development Planning and Policy in Pakistan 1950–1970*, Karachi; Korson, H. (ed.) *Contemporary Problems of Pakistan*, Leiden, especially pp. 81–98; Rashid Amjad (1974) *Industrial Concentration and Economic Power in Pakistan*, Lahore, and (1982) *Private Industrial Investment in Pakistan, 1960–70*, Cambridge; Ziring, L. *et al.* (eds) (1977) *Pakistan: The Long View*, Durham, NC, especially Chapters 6–8; Johnson, B. L. C. (1979) *Pakistan*, London, a geography; and Burki, S. J. (1980) *Pakistan under Bhutto, 1971–1977*, New York.

85 See Andrus, J. R. and Mohammed, A. F. (1958) op. cit., pp. 42–4 and Johnson, B. L. C. (1979) op. cit., pp. 155–6.

86 See Brown, G. T. (1977) 'Pakistan's economic development after 1971', in Ziring, L. *et al.* (eds), op. cit., especially p. 189, and Burki, S. J. (1980) op. cit., pp. 139–41.

87 Brown, G. T. (1977) op. cit., p. 203.

88 (1981) *Dawn Overseas Weekly*, 16–22 October.

89 Ibid., 2–8 April.

90 Johnson, B. L. C. (1979) op. cit., p. 83.

91 See King, R. (1977) *Land Reform: A World Survey*, London, 303–8; Johnson, B. L. C. (1979) op. cit., pp. 102–5; Sanderatne, N. (1974) 'Landowners and land reform in Pakistan', *South Asian Review*, 7, 123–36; and Herring, R. J. (1983) op. cit.

92 There is a considerable, and not uncontroversial literature on the equity effects of the 'green revolution' in Pakistan. See, for example, Alavi, H. A. (1970) 'Elite farmer strategy and regional disparities in the agricultural development of West Pakistan', in Stevens, R. D., Alavi, H. A. and Bertocci, P. (eds), *Rural Development in Pakistan*, Honolulu; Etienne, G. (1972) 'Croissance agricole et disparités regionales au Pakistan', in *Etudes de Géographie Tropicale offertes à Pierre Gourou*, Paris; Dilawar Ali Khan and Chaudhari Haider Ali (1973) 'Income impact of the green revolution', *Pakistan Economic and Social Review*, 11, 67–82; Rashid Amjad and Sen, A. (1977) *Limitations of a Technological Interpretation of Agricultural Performance: A Comparison of East Punjab (India) and West Punjab (Pakistan), South Asia Papers, South Asia Institute*, Lahore; and Herring, R. (1980) 'Zulfikar Ali Bhutto and "eradication of feudalism" in Pakistan', *Economic and Political Weekly*, 15, 599–64.

93 Burki, S. J. (1980) op. cit., p. 193.

94 Johnson, B. L. C. (1979) op. cit., p. 155.

95 Andrus, J. R. and Mohammed, A. F. (1958) op. cit., Chapter 11.

96 Johnson, B. L. C. (1979) op. cit., Chapter 11.

97 See Burki, S. J. (1980) op. cit., Chapters 6, 7.

98 See Rashid Amjad, (1974) op. cit. For the industrialization of Pakistan see also Lewis, S. R. (1969 and 1970) op. cit.; Brecher, I. and Abbas, S. A. (1972) op. cit.; and Rashid Amjad, (1983) op. cit., forthcoming.

99 See, for example, Mahbub Ul Haq, (1963) op. cit., Chapter 4; Stern, J. J. (1971) 'Growth, development, and regional equity in Pakistan', in Falcon, W. P. and Papanek, G. F. (eds) (1971) op. cit., Chapter 2; and Bose, S. R. (1972) 'East–west contrast in Pakistan's agricultural development', in Griffin, K. B. and Khan, A. R. (eds), op. cit., Chapter 2.

100 See especially Johnson, B. L. C. (1979) op. cit., pp. 36–41.

101 See, for example, Bergan, A. (1972) 'Personal income distribution and personal savings in Pakistan', in Griffin, K. B. and Khan, A. R. (eds), op. cit., Chapter 8.

102 See, for example, Khan, A. R. (1972) *The Economy of Bangladesh*, London; and Johnson, B. L. C. (1975) *Bangladesh*, London, (2nd edn 1982).

103 See Qazi Kholiquzzaman Ahmad, (1978) 'The manufacturing sector of Bangladesh — an overview', *Bangladesh Development Studies*, 6, 385–416.

104 For post-'liberation' economic development in Bangladesh see in particular Faaland, J. and Parkinson, J. R. (1976) *Bangladesh: the Test Case for Development*, London; Haroun Er Rashid, (1981) *An Economic Geography of Bangladesh*, Dacca; Nurul Islam, (1977) *Development Planning in Bangladesh*, London, and (1978) *Development Strategy of Bangladesh*, Oxford; and Stepanek, J. F. (1979) *Bangladesh — Equitable Growth?*, New York.

105 Reported in (1982) *Bangladesh Today*, London, 16–30 June.

106 See (1981) *Bangladesh Today*, 15–28 February, 1–14 March and 15–31 March.

107 Johnson, B. L. C. (1975 and 1982) op. cit. bears the stamp of an authority on Bangladesh agriculture who knows his subject intimately from field experience. See also Stepanek, J. F. (1979) op. cit. and Rafiqul Huda Chaudhury (ed.) (1980) 'Food policy and development strategy', *The Bangladesh Development Studies*, 8. I am indebted to Steve Jones for permission to use data and ideas cited by him in the course of lectures given in the Centre of South Asian Studies, University of Cambridge in 1981. See also Mahabub Hossain and Jones, S. (1983) 'Production, poverty and the co-operative ideal: contradictions in Bangladesh rural development policy', in Lea, D. and Chaudhuri, D. P.

(eds) (1983) *Rural Development and the State: Contradictions and Dilemmas in Developing Countries*, London, Chapter 6; and Amartya Sen (1981) *Poverty and Famine*, Oxford, Chapter 9.

108 See Farmer, B. H. (1979) op. cit.

109 See, *inter alia*, Zaman, M. A. (1975) 'Bangladesh: the case for further land reform', *South Asian Review*, 8, 97–115; Clay, E. J. (1976) 'Institutional change and agricultural wages in Bangladesh', *The Bangladesh Development Studies*, 4, 423–40; Clay, E. J. and Sekandar Khan, M. (1977) *Agricultural Employment and Under-Employment in Bangladesh: The Next Decade*, Dacca; King, R. (1977) op. cit., pp. 308–10; Nurul Islam, (1978) op. cit., pp. 30–40; Iqbal Ahmed (1978) 'Unemployment and underemployment in Bangladesh agriculture', *World Development*, 6, 1281–96, and Jannuzi, F. T. and Peach, J. T. (1980) *The Agrarian Structure of Bangladesh: An Impediment to Development*, Boulder, Col.

110 See Nurul Islam (1978) op. cit., Chapter 3, especially pp. 55–62.

111 World Bank (1981) *World Development Report 1981*, New York, p. 152.

112 See Snodgrass, D. R. (1966) *Ceylon: An Export Economy in Transition*, Homewood, Ill., especially Chapter 4; also Farmer, B. H. (1957) *Pioneer Peasant Colonization in Ceylon*, London, especially Chapters 5–7. For the economic development of Sri Lanka see also Karunatilake, H. N. S. (1971) *Economic Development in Ceylon*, New York; International Labour Organisation (1971) *Matching Employment Opportunities and Expectations*, Geneva; Samarasinghe, S. W. R. de A. (ed.) (1977) *Agriculture in the Peasant Sector of Sri Lanka*, Peradeniya; De Silva, K. M. (ed.) (1977) *Sri Lanka: Land, People and Economy*, London; Ponnambalam, S. (1980) *Dependent Capitalism in Crisis: The Sri Lankan Economy, 1948–1980*, London; and De Silva, K. M. (1981) *A History of Sri Lanka*, London, passim.

113 For the PQLI see Morris, M. D. (1979) *Measuring the Condition of the World's Poor: The Physical Quality of Life Index*, New York.

114 See Farmer, B. H. (1961) 'The Ceylon Ten-Year Plan, 1959–1968', *Pacific Viewpoint*, 2, 123–36.

115 See Farmer, B. H. (1957) op. cit., Chapter 16 and Government of Ceylon (1970) *Report of the Gal Oya Project Evaluation Committee*, Sessional Paper No. 1 of 1970, Colombo.

116 See Peiris, G. H. (1975) 'The current land reforms and peasant agriculture in Sri Lanka', *South Asia*, 5, 78–89; and (1978) 'Land reform and agrarian change in Sri Lanka', *Modern Asian Studies*, 12, 611–28. See also King, R. (1977) op. cit., pp. 310–13; and Herring, R. J. (1983) op. cit.

117 Farmer, B. H. (1957) op. cit., pp. 289–91 and (1960) op. cit.

118 See Richards, P. and Gooneratne, W. (1980) *Basic Needs, Poverty and Government Policies in Sri Lanka*, Geneva, 78–81.

119 Farmer, B. H. (ed.) (1977) op. cit., especially pp. 370–7 and Chapter 12.

120 Richards, P. and Gooneratne, W. (1980) op. cit., pp. 98–9.
121 Johnson, B. L. C. and Scrivenor, M. Le M. (1981) op. cit., Chapter 6.
122 See Samarasinghe, V. (1977) 'Some spatial aspects of agricultural development in Sri Lanka', in Samarasinghe, S. W. R. de A. (ed.) (1977) op. cit., Chapter 1.
123 There is a useful treatment of foreign trade in Johnson, B. L. C. and Scrivenor, M. Le M. op. cit., pp. 30–35.
124 Richards, P. and Gooneratne, W. (1980) op. cit., pp. 163–76.
125 See Blaikie, P. M., Cameron, J. and Seddon, D. (1980) *Nepal in Crisis: Growth and Stagnation at the Periphery*, Delhi. See also Bhooshan, B. S. (1979) *The Development Experience of Nepal*, New Delhi.
126 Blaikie, P. M. *et al.* (1980) op. cit., p. 50.
127 See Macfarlane, A. (1976) *Resources and Population: A Study of the Gurungs of Nepal*, Cambridge.
128 See Blaikie, P. M. *et al.* (1980) op. cit.
129 Ibid., p. 47. See also Regmi, M. C. (1976) *Landownership in Nepal*, Berkeley.
130 Blaikie, P. M., Cameron, J. and Seddon, D. (1979) *The Struggle for Basic Needs in Nepal*, Paris, p. 88.
131 Ibid., p. 97.

ENVOI

Such, then, is one man's view of the complex and rapidly-changing South Asian scene; though that one man would be the first to recognize with gratitude how much he has learnt, not only from other authors and research workers, but also from South Asian people at all levels from senior government officers to cultivators in their fields and 'tribals' in their forests. It is, further, one man's view that is, he hopes, broad enough to take in the scene as perceived by observers with widely differing backgrounds, theoretical and ideological; for there is much that is controversial about South Asia.

It is no part of the purpose of this book to try to look over the horizon and forecast the future. Let it just be said that there are grounds for both despair and hope as one contemplates what that future might be; despair, because all the chapters of this book have given grounds for pessimism, or at any rate caution in predicting a bright future. To a western liberal at any rate, there can only be sadness at the present and likely future plight of the Harijans in many parts of India, or of the tenants of Sind, or of the landless labourers of Bangladesh, or of the Indian estate labourers in Sri Lanka; sadness, too, at the political instability and periods of autocracy that in Pakistan and Bangladesh have blighted the bright hopes held out for democracy at independence; at the manipulation of the system by vested interests of various kinds in India and at the violence associated with unrest in a number of parts of the same country; and at the possibility that Sri Lanka's parliamentary democracy may disappear under one-party dominance. One does not have to be a Marxist to wonder whether change sufficient to help the really disadvantaged and to put an end to the rule of corrupt politicians and the dominance of influential castes and classes can come about without revolution: yet there are few signs of a revolutionary situation except, perhaps, in Kerala and West Bengal; and a revolution, however well-intentioned, would not fail to do great damage. Again, the international scene gives little ground for hope that the South Asian subcontinent and the ocean around it will be left to settle its affairs in peace and without outside interference.

On the other hand, and especially if one compares the countries of South Asia, different *inter se* though they are, with most other parts of the Third World, then there are grounds for hope rooted in achievement since independence. This is particularly, though not exclusively, the case with the economic development discussed in chapter 6 of this book, making all due allowance for problems and inefficiencies and backward areas, for phenomena like the slackening of Indian industrialization, for the adverse effects of exogenous factors, and for the manifest failure of benefits to trickle down to the disadvantaged. For, as we have seen, increases in production in a number of sectors have indeed been notable, more notable than in most other parts of the Third World; and must be seen against the background of the first signs, in some South Asian countries or parts of countries at any rate, of a slackening in the rate of population increase. And South Asia assuredly does not lack men and women of great ability and of high principles, some of whom, I hope, will read this book which, for all its criticism, is intended to be sympathetic to the people of the subcontinent as they face truly formidable problems, and appreciates such bright spots as the relative freedom of the Indian press, and the irrepressibility of the intelligentsia in all of the countries of South Asia.

INDEX